PROHIBITION

PROHIBITION

THE LIE OF THE LAND

Sean Dennis Cashman

THE FREE PRESS
A Division of Macmillan Publishing Co., Inc.
NEW YORK

Collier Macmillan Publishers
LONDON

Copyright © 1981 by THE FREE PRESS
A Division of Macmillan Publishing Co., Inc.

THE FREE PRESS
A Division of Macmillan Publishing Co., Inc.
866 Third Avenue, New York, N.Y. 10022

Collier Macmillan Canada, Ltd.

Library of Congress Catalog Card Number: 80–1853

Printed in the United States of America

printing number
1 2 3 4 5 6 7 8 9 10

Library of Congress Cataloging in Publication Data

Cashman, Sean Dennis.
  Prohibition, the lie of the land.

  Bibliography: p.
  Includes index.
  1. Prohibition—United States—History. I. Title.
HV5089.C3   363.4′1′0973   80–1853
ISBN 0-02-905730-2

For JOHN WALSH
Fellow of Jesus College, Oxford

CONTENTS

Appendixes

PREFACE

On December 27, 1900, a middle-aged woman went into a hotel bar in Wichita, Kansas, and broke it up. Using the cobblestones she was carrying, she smashed the picture of a nude, the mirror behind the counter, and the bottles of liquor on it. The bar was in the Carey Hotel; the woman was Carry Nation of Kentucky.

Kansas was supposed to be a dry state where liquor could not be sold, and therefore the saloon was illicit. Carry Nation nonetheless was attacked by bartender, saloonkeeper, and the women conducting their own business there. She carried out other raids in Topeka, Medicine Lodge, and Kiowa, usually with an ax. Motivated by prurience and sexual nausea, she was part fraud, part fanatic, but not a complete fool. Her activities attracted press copy and massive publicity for the prohibition movement at the turn of the century. She later formed a National Hatchet Brigade for attacks on saloons and capitalized on her notoriety by touring the country as a vaudeville act. Subsequently she appeared in *The Drunkard*, the play adapted from T. S. Arthur's *Ten Nights in a Barroom* which also served as a vehicle for the very different talents of W.C. Fields. Her attacks on saloons had nothing in common with the political acumen of leaders of the Anti-Saloon League. But "breaking the bars" constituted an appropriate metaphor for what the League was accomplishing.

Prohibitionists led by the Anti-Saloon League wanted to eliminate the saloon. They had already succeeded in the rural West, were beginning to convince the South, and stood poised to capture the cities of the North. Then with daring and skill they campaigned for national prohibition of alcohol itself. With the notorious Eighteenth Amendment and Volstead Act, which took effect in 1920, they achieved their aim.

Thus began an extraordinary episode of modern history, prohibition in America—the lie of the land. Henceforth prohibition was to be indissolubly associated with the license and chaos of the "Roaring Twenties."

Temperance had proved a good servant to individuals; prohibition was a bad master for a nation. Fanatical prohibitionists led by Wayne Wheeler and Bishop Cannon could not resist showing four presidents and eight Congresses their power. But they were imprisoned by the defects of their own device. Their carefully devised restriction of public taste left them more tongue-tied than anyone else. Bootleggers, gangsters, and racketeers had license to get into the act. Al Capone, Johnny Torrio, Lucky Luciano, Larry Fay, Big Bill McCoy, and Texas Guinan, among others, could not begin to supply public demand for liquor.

"Jimmy," a bootlegger, "confessed" to Paul Gallico, "I couldn't exist if it weren't for the fact that I have the cooperation of the local police, the State constabulary, the municipal police, and 85 percent of the citizens . . . . Tell the average person that you've got a load of liquor in your car, and he'll hide you, lie for you, and help you. It's a moral help as well as a physical one." For bootleggers and their protectors, gangsters, personified the duplicity of public and politicians. They were rewarded with untold riches. Yet a society that needed their services refused them recognition and then made them scapegoats for its ills: religious bigotry and xenophobia, lawlessness and violence, reckless speculation and governmental corruption. When Al Capone complained, "They talk about me not being on the legitimate. Why, lady, nobody's on the legit," he was near the truth. It seemed there was a danger of prohibition's turning the United States into a wasteland fit only for cynics, parasites, and profiteers. Over half a million people were convicted in federal courts for violating prohibition. Worse, thousands died—from poisonous liquor, in gang wars, and while resisting arrest.

In the Depression of the 1930s prohibition was an irrelevance and, after thirteen years and ten months, it was repealed.

But it remains a subject of considerable historical interest and importance for a number of reasons. By any standards the abnormal age of "normalcy" was a crucial one for America. As Daniel Snowman explains, "Society was right in the middle of a number of very important transitions: no longer rural, but not yet dominated by either industry or the white-collar professions; no longer overwhelmingly either Anglo-Saxon or Protestant, but not yet resigned to the idea of becoming a genuinely pluralistic society." In this mixture of old and new, prohibition, intended to purge society, turned out to be an explosive device that came close to undermining it. It has, moreover, remained a point of reference for all governments subsequently contemplating bans on commodities such as cigarettes and marijuana. Its failure is cited as proof that such bans are bound to backfire. The cultural legacy survives in cocktail recipes, gangster movies, underworld slang, and myths about the Mafia.

Furthermore, both in its own time and later, prohibition, with its mix of chaos and violence, sexual license and financial greed, has been widely used as a metaphor for the problems and preoccupations of modern society. When Bertolt Brecht and Kurt Weill collaborated on a parable of modern times, *The Rise and Fall of the City of Mahagonny* (musical, 1927; opera, 1930), they set it explicitly in the world of Chicago gangsters. In 1944 Weill explained: "For every age and part of the world there is a place about which fantasies are written. In Mozart's time it was Turkey. For Shakespeare it was Italy. For us in Germany, it was always America. We had read about Jack London and knew absolutely all about your Chicago gangsters, and that was the end. So of course when we did a fantasy it was about America." Weill was paying a tribute to the fascination the age of prohibition has continued to exert on all sorts of people—especially those who have never visited the United States and whose knowledge of America is based on its most commercial forms of art. The crime thrillers of Raymond Chandler, Dashiell Hammett, and James A. Cain, and the gangster films of Edward G. Robinson and James Cagney, are known all over the world. Without prohibition none would have come into existence—at least not in anything like the same form.

PROHIBITION

So, yet another book on prohibition? One is certainly needed, for two reasons that might at first appear contradictory. One is that although many books have been written on the subject and there are, in addition, many on the 1920s that discuss prohibition, none is truly comprehensive, covering the whole range of its social, political, and cultural aspects. Charles Merz's famous interpretation, *The Dry Decade*, published in 1931 before the demise of the experiment, set a standard of political analysis that has not been surpassed. It is a source of inspiration, a model of substance and style. Others, subsequent to prohibition, have given more emphasis to various cultural, social, and criminal aspects and added to our knowledge. In one sense we are better informed now on the subject than ever before. For instance, though there was always a good deal of conjecture, very little was actually known about syndicate crime until the early 1960s. And not until then were all historians able to distinguish between the schools of interpretation that saw prohibition as either an experiment or a reform. Now we can take stock of a wider variety of ideas, analyses, and interpretations of prohibition.

But the second reason for writing another book now is that, in another sense, we are much worse informed than before. More than half a century after the events much of the original evidence is disintegrating with age. Moreover, precinct centers and district attorneys' offices do not have the capacity to retain or the staff to cherish criminal records of the 1920s as well as keep track of an increasing volume of new information. Thus the story of prohibition, like the detective yarns it encouraged, has to be pieced together from such concrete information as is still available and before some of it disappears altogether. Even the widely known folklore loses its interest as the eyewitnesses themselves pass from the scene.

The files of the Chicago Crime Commission at 79 West Monroe Street, Chicago, Illinois, fill an invaluable gap between original and secondary sources. The commission was founded in 1919 by a group of businessmen interested in the scientific study of crime based on statistics. Its holdings consist of newspaper clippings, transcripts of trials, reports of successive commissioners, and a small library. The material covers not only crime in Chicago but in society across America.

In sum, this book attempts an analysis of the reasons why the United States adopted national prohibition and a description of the consequences to society in the 1920s. It reviews the reasons for repeal in the 1930s and considers the lasting legacies of the "noble experiment." It tries to measure the serious problems of prohibition and capture something of the frivolous side of the age.

In addition to the sources mentioned already it is based on various primary materials: the files of the government's Wickersham Commission and its report; the *Congressional Record*; contemporary accounts in New York and Chicago papers; debates in national journals; reports by professional associations; and various memoirs. Secondary sources read in Chicago, Washington, New York, and at Yale include contemporary, partisan histories of the prohibition and antiprohibition movements, more recent social, political, and cultural histories, and biographies.

SEAN DENNIS CASHMAN

ACKNOWLEDGMENTS

Mr. Stephen A. Schiller, executive director of the Chicago Crime Commission, gave permission for me to undertake research at the Commission, and I was given invaluable help there by Mr. Myke Novotnik, who suggested and found material for me to look at. Mr. Walter Carpenter, Mr. James Harwood, and Ms. Mary Ellen Troutman made arrangements for me to study material in the Washington National Records Center at Suitland, Maryland. The resources of Sterling Memorial Library, Yale University, were also made available to me by courtesy of a helpful and informed staff. Ms. Mary Ison of the Library of Congress guided my selection of illustrations in the collection there, and the available photographs of the Customs Service and the Bureau of Alcohol, Tobacco, and Firearms were given by permission of Mr. Bill Mason, Mrs. Karen Durkalski, Mrs. Christine Ligoske, and Mr. Howard Criswell.

I began this book in the summer of 1979 during a study leave from my duties in the Department of American Studies at Manchester University, England. I thank my colleagues and especially Professor Peter Marshall for making this leave possible.

Mr. Colin H. Jones, of The Free Press, gave helpful advice and encouragement during the writing of the book. Mrs. Rosemary Cleworth typed the manuscript.

—ONE—

AMPHIBIOUS AMERICA

A QUESTION MOST FREQUENTLY ASKED of historians of the United States is: "Why was prohibition passed?" And it does not crop up only in conversations in bars. The premise of the question is, of course, incredulity at something as extraordinary as the notorious Eighteenth Amendment. Approved by Congress in 1917, it forbade "the manufacture, sale or transportation of intoxicating liquors" and provided Congress and state legislatures with authority to enact enforcement measures. By January 1919, forty-six of the forty-eight states had ratified the amendment, and only Connecticut and Rhode Island later withheld their assent. Whereas we can—without any detailed knowledge—appreciate the sincere motives of temperance societies in blaming liquor in general and the saloon in particular for the social evils of alcoholism and even poverty, we find it difficult to accept that their arguments could convince Congress to ban beer, wines, and spirits. Temperance in small doses in some areas is one thing; prohibition as a remedy across a nation is something else.

Our incredulity arises in part because the law contradicted an ancient human desire and in part because we know the consequences. The decade we call the Roaring Twenties—the Jazz Age, the Age of Ballyhoo—owes its social character as much to boot-legging, speakeasies, gangsters—and cocktails—as it does to flappers, model-T cars, Wall Street speculators, the novels of the lost generation, and jazz. We know the arguments used by the drys to claim that prohibition was a benefit: that drinking among poor people was reduced; that employers noted a decline in absenteeism and inefficiency; and that people spent more money on food, clothing, and home furnishings. But we also know the counterclaims of the wets: that drinking became more fashionable than ever and led to a decline in social behavior; that the immoderate law could not be enforced; that prohibition brought about greater corruption in city government and an increase in gangsterism and racketeering. And it is this argument that is the most persuasive indictment of prohibition. It might almost be said that it led to a breakdown of law and order with the connivance of those in authority. The remedy was worse than the disease. Intolerance led to indulgence.

But the faults of prohibition were, in the main, understood after the event, not before. Only two leading politicians were both perceptive and eloquent in opposition to prohibition while the Eighteenth Amendment was being discussed. One was Henry Cabot Lodge of Massachusetts, who declared in the Senate debate itself: "Where large masses of the people would consider it even meritorious—at least quite venial—to evade and break the law, the law would inevitably be broken constantly and in a large and effective way." The other was William Howard Taft, president from 1909 to 1913. His objections were: it would involve the federal government in an issue best settled locally and thence lead to an extension of the federal government; it would be unpopular in the large cities; it would provide new opportunities for corruption and crime. These criticisms were made public in the 1919 *Yearbook of the United States Brewers' Association*; as generalizations about what would go wrong, they have not been surpassed.

———◆———

Dramatic as the incidence of prohibition appears, it was not sudden. It was the culmination of a century of agitation. And it was the case that what had been achieved by the outbreak of the First World War set the pattern and established the precedent for the twenties.

In the United States the prohibition movement accompanied and complemented the temperance movement. From the mid-nineteenth century the temperance movement, which had been inspired by religious ideals, was sustained by the spread of scientific information on the physiological effects of alcohol. In 1866 the English physician Sir Benjamin Ward-Richardson exploded the myth that alcohol kept the body warm. Thereafter alcohol was considered not a source of energy but, rather, a cause of disease. In 1892 the German professor Emil Kraepelin gave the lie to the belief that alcohol was a stimulant. The findings of other scientists that alcohol depressed the heart, making regular drinkers prone to serious illnesses, convinced thousands of educated people that even moderate drinking damaged the body. The prohibition movement developed from their social and political conviction that the liquor trade was damaging the body politic.

Mark Twain described the period after the Civil War as a Gilded Age, a triple pun, as it turned out, on its gold, its guilds (or monopolies), and its guilt. Its gilt was the amber color of whiskey, for the liquor trade was central to its corruption.

The liquor industry comprised the manufacture of beer, wine, and spirits by brewers, vintners, and distillers, and its sale by wholesalers and retailers. It was associated with big business and had huge financial resources. Moreover, it was corrupt and predatory. Its interests lay with machine politics and commercial vice. It used its influence to block political reform in general and to subvert honest government in towns and cities. Thus it was to become a prime target for various reform movements, including progressivism.

The relationship between the liquor trade and the federal government was historical. In the Internal Revenue Act of July 1, 1862, the government acquired revenue from the retail sale of alcohol by charging retailers and manufacturers a license fee. Initially the license fee was twenty dollars a year for retailers and, for manufacturers, a dollar per barrel of malt liquor and twenty cents per gallon of distilled liquor. By 1914 more than a third of the federal government's revenue came from the liquor trade.

The existence of the Internal Revenue System was a constant incentive to the liquor trade to bring political pressure on administrations and Congress alike. To that end the United States Brewer's Association was organized in 1862. It held a Beer Congress on October 3, 1863, with the specific intention of getting the tax on beer, already down to sixty cents, reduced further to fifty cents. The industry made no bones about its political objectives. At the New York congress of 1868 President Clausen of the association said this

3

aim was "To secure candidates for the Legislature, who would, without regard to political party, promote and protect the brewing interest."

By the late 1880s the brewers represented in the association manufactured 78 percent of the country's beer. The temporary introduction of prohibition by constitutional amendment in Rhode Island in 1886 was a strategic blow to the northeastern industrial wet bloc. The liquor interests then formed a National Protective Association in 1887, paid for by annual levies on distillers and wholesalers of between twenty-five and one thousand dollars in proportion to annual income. The money was spent on publicity on behalf of the trade in any state where a campaign for constitutional prohibition was taking place.

The United States Brewers' Association was the first liquor lobby to pursue a policy of putting pressure on Congress and administration after the Civil War, but it was not the only one. In league with it were the United States Manufacturers' and Merchants' Association, the National Wholesale Liquor Dealers' Association, the National Association of Wine and Spirit Representatives, and the National Retail Liquor Dealers' Association. One of the most notorious scandals was exposed in 1874: the St. Louis Whiskey Ring. With the collusion of Treasury officials it had defrauded the Internal Revenue Service of millions of dollars of taxes on distilled whiskey. President Ulysses S. Grant supposedly said, "Let no guilty man escape," but he himself ensured that his secretary, Babcock, did so. It was not the only scandal, and others were permitted by a lax Congress.

Not only were the liquor trade's relations with government nefarious, but its corporate forms were also open to censure as monopolies. Like other industries, brewing and distilling became increasingly concentrated at the end of the nineteenth century and the beginning of the twentieth. Between 1899 and 1914 the number of breweries decreased from 1,509 to 1,250. By 1914, 100 breweries were producing half of the nation's beer. And between 1899 and 1914 the number of distilleries decreased from 967 to 434. Capital investment increased nearly ten times as fast as the population and nearly four times as fast as the national wealth.

Although the liquor trade was the aim of prohibition, it was the saloon that became its first target. In 1909 there was one saloon for every three hundred people. There were more saloons in the United States than there were schools, libraries, hospitals, theaters, or parks, and more certainly than churches.

4

By the turn of the century many saloons were controlled by the brewers as adjuncts to the alcohol monopolies. Intense competition among the brewers drove them to control the retail sale of their beer. And high license fees imposed on the saloons by progressives who wanted to drive disreputable places out of business resulted in alliances between saloonkeepers and brewers. Individual owners could not always raise the $500 or $1,500 for a license and borrowed from the brewers directly or by mortgaging the bar. In return for the loan they undertook to sell only the brewer's particular brand of beer. One prohibitionist, D. Leigh Colvin, estimated that by 1900 the percentage of bars controlled by brewers in midwestern cities was as high as 65 percent in St. Louis, 70 percent in Kansas City, 75 percent in Toledo, and 90 percent in Indianapolis, Minneapolis, and St. Paul. The *Chicago Tribune* of February 9, 1906, excoriated the consolidation of liquor empires: "Forty-two breweries situated in this and neighboring cities take out 72 percent of the saloon licenses issued in Chicago. It appears that they are gradually monopolizing the saloon-keeping business and are driving the 'small, respectable, struggling saloonkeeper' . . . out of it." Once he became the brewers' front the small saloonkeeper was obliged to flout the liquor laws and take part in vice and criminal activities to stay open. The Sunday-closing regulations were widely ignored, and in New York in 1908 more than 5,000 of the 5,820 saloons in the boroughs of Manhattan and the Bronx stayed open on Sundays despite the law. Some bar owners cooperated with prostitutes, gamblers, and petty criminals such as pickpockets in order to increase their sales by "improving" their facilities. Thus one prohibitionist, Dr. Herrick Johnson, commented ruefully: "Low license asks for your son; high license for your daughter."

It is, moreover, not mere coincidence that the prohibition movement and the Industrial Revolution originated, developed, and culminated in the same periods. In the late nineteenth and early twentieth centuries accidents arising from drunkenness at work were more dangerous than before. Mistakes with mechanical drill, loader, and conveyor belt had more damaging consequences than those with pickax, shovel, and wheelbarrow operated by hand. Abstinence was an absolute prerequisite of employment for many an industrial boss obliged to protect his workers and, more important, his machines and production. Henry C. Frick, Du Pont Powder, and American Sheet and Tin Plate were among these manufacturers. Some companies discriminated against drinkers in matters of promotion and dismissal. Others denied benefit payments to workers whose sickness or injury was in any way caused by their drinking. In 1899 the American Railway Association proposed the adoption of Rule G, which stated: "The use of intoxicants by employees while on duty is prohibited. Their habitual use, or the frequenting of places where they are sold, is sufficient cause for dismissal." By 1904 about a million employees had to observe this rule.

Between 1911 and 1920, forty-one states adopted workingmen's compensation laws that further stimulated the temperance movement in industry. By making employers compensate workers for industrial accidents the law obligated them to campaign for safety through sobriety. In 1914 the National Safety Council adopted a resolution condemning alcohol as a cause of industrial accidents.

———————◆◆———————

In its early days the prohibition movement was not a crucial component in federal politics. The political inspiration for prohibition in the progressive period came as before from outside the principal parties. The metaphor of the writer William Hazlitt on the Whigs and Tories of the House of Commons in early-nineteenth-century England was equally apt for the Republicans and Democrats in early-twentieth-century America. The two parties were like competing stagecoaches splashing each other with mud but going by the same road to the same place. The Republicans and Democrats were agencies to capture power. Thus they searched for, or were confronted by, popular issues. They were not organizations committed to any philosophy beyond the most orthodox generalities of their interest groups. They did not interpret their task to include making controversial issues accessible to popular debate. Thus, until 1916, neither party committed itself to woman suffrage and, until 1920, neither committed itself to national prohibition. Major problems were brought to the fore by splinter groups and nonpartisan organizations. Solutions were debated by the major parties only after their popularity had been tested. The election of 1896 was unusual in that Democrats and Republicans had truly different platforms. By taking the platform of the Populist party and calling for a currency based on silver as well as gold the Democrats pre-empted them.

At other elections the parties blurred their differences. Yet they relied on the stimulus of nonaligned groups to suggest reforms. Measures for farm relief, immigration restriction, conservation, hours and conditions of work were based on ideas of a wide variety of organizations: the American Federation of Labor, the chambers of commerce, the League of Women Voters, the Farmers' Non Partisan League, and the Anti-Saloon League. Both the main parties looked on these groups as political blocs containing people, sensitive to certain issues, whose votes could be culled.

Like other pressure groups, the Anti-Saloon League, founded first at Oberlin, Ohio, in 1893, was content to work to its end, statewide prohibition, through the existing political structure. By comparison the Prohibition party, founded in 1869, campaigned to less effect because its pursuit of third-party status was a prerequisite, an end not a means. The comparative shrewdness of the leaders of the Anti-Saloon League, Ernest H. Cherrington, the principal secretary, and Edwin C. Dinwiddie, the first of its congressional lobbyists, was a byword of political expediency. The league's very title was ingenious, inviting to people who detested the saloon and the social evils it maintained but were not prohibitionists. The league was soundly based. It already had church patronage from Congregationalists and Baptists before it became a national organization in Washington in 1895. Churches had previously been chary of charging into political parties but now they were converted to a cause supposedly susceptible to immediate reform. By 1908 the number of churches cooperating with the league was forty thousand and only four states had no state league organizations. Moreover, there was no lack of funds. The general counsel, Wayne B. Wheeler, told a Senate Campaign Fund Investigating Committee in July 1926 that the prohibitionists had spent $35 million since 1893 to create and sustain public support in their cause.

Before the league only Kansas, Maine, and North Dakota were dry states. At the outbreak of the First World War the situation was very different. Between 1907 and the fall of 1914, eleven more states had adopted prohibition: Arizona, Colorado, Georgia, Mississippi, North Carolina, Oklahoma, Oregon, Tennessee, Virginia, West Virginia, and Washington. Many pockets within other states had done so by local option. Thus 74 percent of the total territory of the United States in which 47 percent of the population lived was dry. The exception to this general trend was provided by industrial centers, mill towns, and large cities. There were more bars in Chicago than in all the South. In the period before American intervention in the war, the number of states with total prohibition almost doubled to include: in 1915, Alabama, Arkansas, Idaho, Iowa, South Carolina; in 1916, Michigan, Montana, Nebraska, South Dakota; in early 1917, Indiana, New Hampshire, Utah.

However astonishing this situation was in various sections of the country, it does not signify that prohibition had reached such epidemic proportions that it already had national support. Twenty-seven states had adopted prohibition but fifteen were west of the Mississippi, eight south of the Potomac, and two (Maine and New Hampshire) were in the rural Northeast. In the South it was believed that alcohol intensified racial problems. A tenth of the total population was made up of Negroes, most of them living in degrading and unrelieved poverty and squalor. Most were in the South and in two states, Mississippi and South Carolina, they predominated. The South was mainly rural and the poorest section of the whole country in a period when town and city were overtaking the countryside in numbers of population. According to popular myth, drink incited the Negroes to violence in this situation with horrendous consequences. Moreover, the South had no significant settlement of recent immigrants instilled with enthusiasm for beer, wine, and spirits.

Of the thirteen industrial states only Indiana and Michigan had passed statewide prohibition. In Indiana this had been done by the state legislature without a popular vote. In some ways the vote in Michigan was the most crucial of all because the result was a defection of a northern industrial state previously regarded as the political property of the wets. As Larry Englemann, the historian of prohibition in Michigan, suggests, "The wet wall had been breached." Irrespective of the disproportionate share of representation of the rural areas in the state legislature, it had been achieved by an overwhelming popular majority in a referendum of 1916. Detroit, the only large and wet city, was deluged in dry votes from elsewhere. Yet the liquor interests might have seen the inevitable result of the prohibition movement in Michigan before the war. Even by 1911, forty of the state's eighty-three counties had gone dry by local option.

The general contagion spread more after Woodrow Wilson's declaration of war on Germany in 1917. The same year New Mexico went dry. In 1918, Florida, Nevada, Ohio, Texas, and Wyoming adopted prohibition and, in 1919, Kentucky did so. By 1920, 95 percent of the total territory of the United States and 68 percent of the population was dry by state law or local regulation.

However, any assumption that national prohibition was a logical, if dramatic, extension of state prohibition is based on a misunderstanding, for the states that had adopted prohibition had not done so on exactly the same terms. They were dry, but not barren or

8

bone dry. The prohibitionists made no secret of this. Wayne Wheeler compiled a book of *Federal and State Laws Relating to Intoxicating Liquor* for the Anti-Saloon League in 1918. It shows differences between the dry states. Some states allowed the importation of liquor with restrictions of time and amount: Alabama, Virginia, and the Carolinas. Others allowed the importation of liquor for personal use without such restrictions: Iowa, Maine, Michigan, New Hampshire, and North Dakota. Mississippi and Tennessee allowed the manufacture of homemade wine. West Virginia exempted both imported liquor and homemade wine from its prohibition law.

Thus in these states the law was not aimed at the abolition of alcohol but the shutting of the saloon and liquidation of the liquor trade. And it was different in principle from national prohibition because it depended on local support rather than federal coercion. It compromised the cause with local conditions: national prohibition was to cast out any possibility of compromise.

Only thirteen states were completely arid: Arizona, Arkansas, Colorado, Georgia, Idaho, Kansas, Montana, Nebraska, Oklahoma, Oregon, South Dakota, Utah, and Washington. The total area of these states was only 36.9 percent, a little more than a third of the United States, and their total population was only 14.3 percent, or a seventh, of the country's population.

The evidence as to whether so much statewide prohibition was or was not accomplished by popular request is barely related to the disproportionate influence of the rural areas in the state legislatures. In only ten states was prohibition passed by the legislature without some form of popular vote: Alabama, Arkansas, Georgia, Indiana, Iowa, Mississippi, Nevada, New Hampshire, Tennessee, Utah. In all the others the electorate was directly consulted by an initiative or referendum or some other device. At a time of mass immigration on an unprecedented scale, recent immigrants did not have the chance to vote until they were citizens. By and large women did not have the vote at all, and neither did most blacks. By 1917, less than 4 percent of the adult population voted at all in referenda and only half a million votes separated the majority from the minority: 1,967,337 to 1,437,402. And the popular votes in the seven states that adopted prohibition by constitutional amendment between 1917 and 1919 illustrate the declining proportion of people in favor: 970,243 for and 837,461 against, a majority of only 132,782. The evidence hardly suggests a solid bloc in favor of prohibition even in the rural states.

The leaders of the Anti-Saloon League had no illusions about their general score. Moreover, they were concerned that, although more states were passing prohibition, people in general were drinking more. Between 1900 and 1910, the per capita consumption of liquor rose from 16.98 percent to 20.53 percent; by 1913 it was 22.80 percent. The league's leaders concluded that alcohol was, despite local prohibition, still being transported from wet to dry land. Thus they turned their attention to interstate legislation and to Congress. There they enlisted the support of Edwin Y. Webb of North Carolina, in the House, and William S. Kenyon of Iowa, in the Senate, for a bill to prevent the transport of alcohol to states forbidding its sale. The Webb-Kenyon Act did not abolish the total transportation of liquor from wet states to dry but only importation of liquor "in violation" of state laws. Advised by his attorney general, George Wickersham, that the bill violated the basic principles of commerce, President Taft vetoed it. It had already been passed by substantive majorities and was then passed over his veto by 63 votes to 21 in the Senate and 246 to 45 in the House to become law in February 1913.

The Anti-Saloon League now changed its emphasis. Instead of calling for prohibition within the states, it projected national prohibition by constitutional amendment at its Jubilee Convention to celebrate its twenty years at Columbus, Ohio, in November 1913. It announced the fact in the capital with a march of four thousand strong down Pennsylvania Avenue on December 10, 1913. However, the first attempt to pass national prohibition introduced by Richmond Pearson Hobson of Alabama in the House failed. It was passed by 197 votes to 190 but did not secure the necessary two thirds majority. Nevertheless, this was the beginning of the successful campaign for national prohibition, realized by the Eighteenth Amendment, ratified in 1919 to take effect in 1920. National prohibition still did not become a platform of either party. Yet when America entered the First World War, the likelihood of the Anti-Saloon League's attaining its end was high. And the very vacuum of professional political initiative on national prohibition in successive Congresses ironically helped ensure the victory of the dry cause. If professional politicians had intended to manipulate the league like a marionette, they discovered it was the puppet who was pulling the strings.

The drys, however, had got the measure of their opponents, whom they were willing to cajole, expose, or blackmail in support of their cause. Wayne B. Wheeler, the general counsel of the Anti-Saloon League, enjoined it to summon its skills against a wet candidate of either party and even to support a candidate who drank but would vote for prohibition against a teetotaler who opposed prohibition. F. C. Lockwood exculpated such hypocrisy with an appropriate dry metaphor in 1914: "The League has always thought it wise to take a half loaf where it could not get a whole one—a crumb, even, if there was no more to be had." The league's arguments were persuasive. Wheeler published lists of congressional candidates who supported the league and invited the opponents of prohibition to do the same. The league would then concentrate on a campaign to defeat the "wet list" unless the rival candidates repudiated their wet associations. Often they did. Votes for candidates who supported the league, especially among women's groups, church membership, and rural areas in the South and West, were so substantive they could not be disregarded. In the congressional election of 1914 the league sent fifty thousand speakers into congressional districts at a cost of $2.5 million.

With the passing of time, the wets' ability to weather storms of political protest promoted by the drys weakened. By 1916, members of the United States Brewers' Association openly admitted to the Senate Judiciary Committee that they had made a tactical error in refusing to reform the saloon earlier. Even they were now ready to remedy the situation and do so to provide "real temperance, which means sobriety and moderation; not prohibition, which has proved a fallacy and failure."

As a gesture to public relations the Brewers' Association had already founded a new organization, the National Association of Commerce and Labor, under Percy Andreae in 1913. But the brewers were up to their old tricks. The same Senate committee discovered in 1918 that the reform of the saloon meant in practice funding allies and associations to keep prohibition at bay, and feuding with businesses the brewers regarded as unfriendly. Thus they withheld trade from such companies as the Delaware, Lackawanna, and Western Railroad; Goodyear Rubber; Grasselli Chemical of Cleveland; Heinz Pickle; S.S. Kresge; Pennsylvania Railroad; Pittsburgh Coal; United States Steel; and the Santa Fe Railroad.

In Texas brewers flouted election laws to fight prohibition between 1900 and 1911. Eventually nine brewers, one of which was

Anheuser-Busch, were charged, did not contest the action, and were fined $289,000 with costs. In 1904 a grand jury in New York found that liquor dealers had raised money precisely to corrupt the state legislature. Before an election campaign in Texas in 1911 a leading brewer, Adolphus Busch, had written in a letter, "I will not mind to give $100,000 extra if necessary."

———————— ◆ ————————

In the crucial years from 1913 to 1919, Congress had little or no effective guidance from political leaders. No president was elected on the issue of prohibition, but the response of three principal contestants shows the leading contenders first reluctant then willing to press for prohibition in their pursuit of popular support.

Presidential election campaigns from 1896 to 1916 were dominated by three men, William Jennings Bryan, Theodore Roosevelt, and Woodrow Wilson, sometimes known as "the Titans." At least one of them ran in each campaign, and sometimes two. Although the campaign for a "return to normalcy," which Warren Harding won in 1920, ended the age of the Titans, it was nevertheless the foreign policy of one of them, Wilson, that dominated the election that year.

These men played a part in the growing campaign for national prohibition. But it is not an honorable one. They took their place at the head of the procession only when they realized where it was heading. Each began as a wet and ended as a dry. The change of heart was a matter of political expediency. It was also the result of disappointment rather than success. For Bryan it was an attempt to regain former prestige; for Roosevelt to maintain his prominence; for Wilson to retain power. None truly succeeded. As the English scholar Andrew Sinclair has shown, their progress is important as a complement to and illustration of a political trend.

William Jennings Bryan was a natural recruit to the dry cause but a slow convert. His parents were teetotal and he signed pledges of abstinence periodically as an exercise in public relations. But it was with the help of Omaha business and liquor interests that he first captured a seat in Congress as a Democrat for Nebraska in 1890. On the basis of his eloquence, he was nominated for president at the Democratic convention in Chicago in 1896 and his general platform was an appeal to agrarian values. The specific plank was bimetalism, a currency based on silver as well as gold. His prepossessing appearance and sonorous tones embodied and voiced country piety and prejudice. But simple rural values were simplistic when translated into political panaceas for complex urban problems. However, he was only too well aware of his party's obligations to brewers and cities for financial support to advocate prohibition. He used alcohol to rub himself with to remove sweat on the campaign train and often met his public reeking of gin.

He lost the election of 1896 and those of 1900 and 1908 by a wider margin each time. Blaming his poor poll in 1908 on the defection of the brewers, he began a campaign for county option on prohibition in Omaha. He argued that progressive reforms, the initiative and referendum, in Nebraska had been defeated by politicians in the pay of wet interests who feared that these devices would be used to have bars closed. In all probability Bryan himself feared that his prestige was flagging: he would not get the chance to run for the presidency again. Prohibition provided a platform for self-promotion.

At the Nebraska convention of 1910, he debated the issue, divided the party and helped defeat the wet candidate for governor. Later, as Woodrow Wilson's first secretary of state, Bryan was under pressure from prohibitionists to promote the cause and from the president to procrastinate. Defying Wilson, he campaigned for states' rights on prohibition in sixty speeches around the country in 1915. After his resignation from the cabinet over American policy to Germany, he felt free to become outspoken on prohibition. At a dinner in Washington in December 1916, he said his party also was free: "The Democratic Party, having won [the elections of 1916] without the aid of the wet cities, and having received the support of nearly all the prohibition states and the states where women vote, is released from any obligation to the liquor traffic." Speaking in support of the American war effort from 1917, he mixed metaphors of patriotism, peace, and prohibition for audiences in the West and South. He also accepted eleven thousand dollars from the Anti-Saloon League in 1919.

Theodore Roosevelt's attitude to prohibition was more ambiguous. Indifferent to social arguments for it, he was canny enough to appreciate their political impact. He knew the divisive effect the prohibition movement was beginning to have on national politics. In 1884, he opposed an unsuccessful resolution before the New York State Legislature for a referendum on state prohibition as an unpopular infringement of personal liberty. But as a police commissioner in the reform administration of Major William Strong in New York in 1895, he prosecuted violations of a law closing bars on Sundays. In an unpublished paper of 1897, he distinguished between the rights of the prohibitionists' argument and the wrongs of their pursuit of it: "Among poorer people especially there is probably no other evil which is such a curse as excessive drinking." Yet this evil could hardly be cured by "the intemperate friends of temperance." He deplored the division among progressive voters when a dry candidate ran in an otherwise conventional election between a reform and a machine candidate. The prohibitionists intended to play both ends against the middle but split the reform vote and thereby ensured victory for the traditional party machine. Roosevelt's essential premise was political expediency.

As president from 1901 to 1909, he maintained prohibition was a local and not a national issue. He evaded confirmation of either the dry or the wet side and avoided confrontation and he advised his successor, William Howard Taft, to do the same. Thus, in 1914, both sides claimed his support. In private he wrote to William Allen White, editor of a Kansas paper, the *Emporia Gazette:* "As for prohibition nationally it would merely mean free rum and utter lawlessness in our big cities."

Yet a year later, he began to swim with the tide to dry land. His patriotic and political instincts led him to accommodate prohibition for the sake of the war effort. He wrote to an associate, Raymond Robbins, "I do not want to go in advance of the people on this issue . . . but I believe they will ultimately come to the national suppression of the liquor traffic and I am heartily with them when they do so come to it."

If by background Woodrow Wilson might have been sympathetic to prohibition, his political instinct opposed it until the end of his career. His father and grandfather were Presbyterian ministers and moderate drinkers. While president of Princeton, he became progressive Democratic candidate for the governorship of New Jersey in 1910. Against the advice of Boss Smith, who believed the support of the liquor interests essential to the success of any candidate, he said that the prohibition issue "should be settled by local option." In doing so he avoided alignment with wets or drys, held the Democratic coalition together, and carried the state.

Later, like Roosevelt, but more by accident than design, he persuaded both wet and dry camps that he supported them when he ran for president in 1912. In New Jersey, where the Democrats were predominantly wet, he had already written to the Anti-Saloon League that he still favored local option. But in Texas, where the party was predominantly dry, he wrote that he favored statewide prohibition.

As president from 1913 to 1921, he required wet support. The Webb-Kenyon Act represented the extent to which he would accept prohibition. Even after America entered the First World War, he did not favor an extension of prohibition and deplored the prohibitionists' attempt to manipulate a national emergency to narrow ends. His subsequent conversion to the dry cause was indissoluble from his foreign policy. The First World War, and not the Titans, dominated events. Hitherto they had shown lassitude rather than leadership and now their ideas were overwhelmed by circumstances.

To win the war, the federal government placed the country's resources at its disposal and took unprecedented control of railroads, industries, shipping, fuel, and food. The prohibition movement gained momentum with the rationing of foodstuffs at the expense of brewing and distilling. For drys and wets argued that while the United States was assenting to voluntary rationing to provide Europe with grain, it was subversive of the war effort to liquidate crops and convert them into alcohol. Drys advised the administration to keep alcohol from army camps and shipyards. Josephus Daniels, the secretary of the navy, was a confirmed dry and, as early as April 5, 1914, had forbidden the use of alcohol in the navy. In June 1917 he extended the compass of prohibition and ended the practice of distributing contraceptives to sailors going on shore leave. Congress then designated dry and decent zones around military camps.

Prohibition was debated five times by Congress in 1917 before discussion of the Eighteenth Amendment. Each time the dry cause gained ground.

The first debate was in February on an amendment by Senator James A. Reed of Missouri and Congressman Charles Randall of California to a bill excluding alcoholic advertising through the mail. Randall was the only member of the Prohibition party in Congress; Reed was a wet, yet his proposal was to forbid the use as well as the sale and transportation of alcohol in dry states and went further than the contemporary proposals of the Anti-Saloon League. But the Reed bone-dry amendment was a so-called wet-joker, for it took the

15

onus and responsibility of enforcement granted to the individual states in the Webb-Kenyon Act of 1913 away from them and gave them to the federal government.

The District of Columbia Prohibition Act to ban the sale and traffic of alcohol in Washington was the second law. But the drys knew the tastes of Congress too well, and the act did not ban people from drinking alcohol. Congress also voted prohibition for the territory of Alaska and passed legislation to allow Puerto Rico a popular vote on prohibition for the island.

The last debate centered around another law, the Lever Food and Fuel Control Act, passed on August 10, 1917, which contained a prohibition clause on which the drys in Congress insisted. It carried a penalty of a five-thousand-dollar fine and two years imprisonment. Wilson was then persuaded by the food administrator, Herbert Hoover, to reduce the alcoholic content of beer to 2.75 percent by weight. He did so by proclamation on December 8, 1917. At the same time he limited the amount of food that could be used in brewing to 70 percent of what it had been in 1916.

Yet now a wrangle ensued between Wilson and the wets over prohibition in which the Anti-Saloon League remonstrated with him in a letter of April Fool's Day, 1918: "The people have been requested to have heatless days, meatless days, wheatless days and to eliminate waste . . . yet the breweries and saloons of the country continue to waste foodstuffs, fuel and manpower and to impair the efficiency of labor." Wilson, however, would not yield and neither would the league. The impasse was resolved by the league's amending the Agricultural Appropriations Bill of 1917 to ban the use of foods in beer, wine, and spirits. Wartime prohibition was passed in Congress to take effect on July 1, 1919, unless the forces had been demobilized. By then Wilson accepted the measure. He also forbade the use of food in making beer by proclamation on September 16, 1917, but refused to declare dry areas around strategic industrial plants.

The prohibitionists' cause was strengthened by the Supreme Court's decision in the case of *Crane* v. *Campbell* of 1917 that possessing alcohol for personal use was not a constitutional right.

————————◆◆————————

The final resort of the drys, the Eighteenth Amendment, was a cunning political ploy. It obliged Congress to pass national prohibition while, paradoxically, evading its own responsibility. Irving

Fisher, a Yale professor serving on the Council of National Defense, advised the Anti-Saloon League to take advantage of the unease of even wet congressmen at the failure of wartime prohibition in the fracas over the Food Control Bill. An amendment to the Constitution would seem a means of reconciling wet and dry points of view, "on the theory that it did not really enact prohibition, but merely submitted it to the states." Once it had been passed by Congress, a measure for wartime prohibition could be introduced to fill the gap between the adoption of the amendment and its taking effect.

The original form of the Eighteenth Amendment, brought forward by Senator Morris Sheppard of Texas on July 30, 1917, was shorter and simpler than that eventually passed. One section prohibited the manufacture, sale, and transportation of intoxicating liquor, the other gave Congress power of enforcement. The gist of the short speeches in favor was that prohibition would release large numbers of men for munitions and shipbuilding and for the army and would save the equivalent of eleven million loaves of bread a day. In other words the arguments were based on exigency. The substance of the debate devolved on three issues. Could prohibition be enforced? The drys argued that since prohibition was more popular than ever a law to ensure it would have as much support as laws against robbery and violence. What would compensate government for its loss of excise revenue with the closing down of the liquor trade? The drys argued that increased national prosperity and the comparatively new federal income tax of 1913 would be adequate compensation. Would prohibition increase the interference of the federal government in individual freedom? The drys argued that progressive reforms and wartime emergency had already augmented governmental power and people had adjusted to it. By giving the states concurrent powers of enforcement prohibition would decrease the trend toward centralization.

The debate was accompanied by the accommodations between the two sides arranged by Senator Warren G. Harding of Ohio. In the process the wets believed they were buying time. Thirty-six of the forty-eight states had to ratify the measure before it became part of the Constitution, and the wets counted on controlling thirteen state legislatures. Thus the wets argued for an (unprecedented) time limit of six years for ratification. The drys compromised at seven in exchange for another wet proposal, that the liquor trade should have a year to wind up its affairs. In accepting this the drys were unintentionally confirming a temporary legitimacy on the beer, wine, and spirit industry.

PROHIBITION

The Eighteenth Amendment banned the "manufacture, sale, or transportation of intoxicating liquors" in the United States and empowered Congress and the states "to enforce this article by appropriate legislation." It did not prohibit buying and drinking alcohol. It did not explicitly proscribe possession of alcohol nor its domestic manufacture. It was the trade and not the article itself that was beyond the pale. Those who could afford to stock up in advance or continue to buy later on were not breaking the law by doing so.

The vague wording of the amendment indicates that the prohibitionists were careful not to push their luck too far. The Anti-Saloon League's principal aim had been to get a principle accepted. Enforcement was not a subsidiary but a secondary matter. It could be discussed later with less aggravation if enabling legislation were debated on the need to support an established law and not on the merit of the law itself. One change to the amendment devised in the four months between its passage by the Senate in August and its reception in the House in December reversed the principle of the Reed bone-dry law. It gave the states, and not the federal government, power of enforcement. This was to involve the states and relieve the central government from the expense and organization of enforcement officers.

In the Senate the amendment was passed by 65 votes to 20 and in the House by 282 to 128. Compared with the first attempt at national prohibition the drys had gained 85 votes in the House. Of these, 39 were Republican votes from midwestern congressmen promoted by the Anti-Saloon League to oust wet Democrats in the 1914 and 1916 elections. This does not mean the Democrats had become a party of the wets. Any difference between the parties was based on geography. Northern Democrats owed their allegiance to wet cities and were opposed by dry Republicans at elections. Southern Democrats owed their allegiance to the dry countryside. But because the South was dominated by the Democrats the Republican candidates there were free to pick and choose sides between wet and dry. The Democrats, however, were now identified in part with a dry and in part with a wet region and were divided on the issue of prohibition with ruinous political consequences.

Easy generalizations to explain why prohibition was passed at a critical juncture of events persist to this day—even though some contradict others and many are misinterpretations of the evidence. According to one, national prohibition was a consequence of woman suffrage. According to a second, it was foisted on the country without due warning by a precipitate Congress. According to a third, it was a triumph of countryside over town. And according to a fourth, it was an emergency measure to conserve food reserves in the war. Together these generalizations constitute four fallacies of: female franchise; a fast one pulled on Uncle Sam's folks; fundamentalism and the farm over free thought and the factory; food and fuel for the First World War.

The first and second deserve scant attention. Woman suffrage did not bring about national prohibition. Prohibition was passed before the Nineteenth Amendment, which gave women the vote, except in Ohio, where women did vote on the ratification of the Eighteenth. Even in the matter of statewide prohibition women had the vote in only seven states that adopted prohibition before American intervention in the war: Arizona, Colorado, Idaho, Montana, Oregon, Utah, and Washington. The misconception that the prohibitionists pulled a fast one on the public over national prohibition arises out of the brevity of debates in Congress on the Eighteenth Amendment. The Senate debate lasted for thirteen hours on three days, July 30 to August 1, 1917; the debate in the House lasted only seven hours on a single day, December 17, 1917. This evidence, however, supports the view that by then rhetoric was superfluous. The real debate had taken place between autumn 1913, and spring 1917. The die was already cast.

Nevertheless the other generalizations, that the support for prohibition was rural and that such a thing could only be accomplished in the exigencies of war, do illuminate the whole subject.

The most striking character of the votes on national prohibition remains the dichotomy between town and country. Rural America was politically ascendant on the eve of the period when more people were to live in the town than the country. (A town was interpreted in the 1920 census as a place of twenty-five hundred inhabitants or more.) In the United States Senate and in the state senates the rural areas were overrepresented at the expense of the towns. In New York State one voter in Putnam County had as much representation as four voters in Rochester, five in Syracuse, and seven in some districts of New York City. In Michigan electors in Antrim, Alpena, Livingston, and Midland counties had as much representation even in the state house as two-and-a-half electors in Detroit. The drys would not agree to national prohibition being decided by state referenda for fear of defeat by the popular, urban, and wet votes.

Whereas the amendment only just passed the House, in the Senate it passed by a majority of three to one. Only twenty senators opposed it: nine from the eastern seaboard states with huge urban populations; seven from the South still advocating states' rights; four from states with considerable liquor interests. A similar disparity between town and country is shown in the voting figures for ratification in the state senates and lower houses. Of the forty-six states that ratified the amendment the total senates' vote was 1,310 to 237, whereas the total lower houses' vote was 3,782 to 1,035. The drys had advised Congress to support the amendment because it gave the states the final right to decide. When the matter came to the state legislatures, where only a simple majority was sufficient to secure ratification, the drys declared that the states were obliged to ratify an amendment passed by a two-thirds majority of Congress. Even if the drys could not rely on support from the lower houses where wet towns had an accurate, proportionate influence they could count on the senates and then try and cow the lower houses.

The Anti-Saloon League and its allies were past masters at lobbying state legislatures and swinging crucial votes, for it was in the state capitals they had first sharpened their wits. The wets, who had insisted on a time limit for ratification by the states, were mistaken if they thought that thirteen wet states could hold out even after wartime hysteria had evaporated. The case for ratification was presented to state legislatures by men who claimed support of millions of voters, the case against was presented by men speaking less persuasively from their own beliefs.

The significance of the war in the passage of the Eighteenth Amendment can hardly be overstated. Again and again the prohibitionists used a basic appeal to emotion purveyed in the Senate debate by William Kenyon of Iowa: "If liquor is a bad thing for the boys in the trenches, why is it a good thing for those at home? When they are willing to die for us, should we not be willing to go dry for them?" And indeed the war obscured the issue to the benefit of the prohibitionists. From June to December 1917, while Congress was discussing prohibition, the press prevailed on the public with news of Ypres, Trentino, Flanders, and Verdun. Second place in press copy went to the arrival of American troops in France, the British march into Palestine, and the fall of Kerensky's government in Russia to the Bolsheviks. People sustained intense interest in the war above all else. And they did not want to identify themselves with any view advertised as subversive of the war effort. Thus in 1917 the *New York Times* published only eight items of news about the amendment at all and only one letter of protest. Other papers were equally indifferent.

Until the war people living in cities—or, more correctly, the elite that led them—received news, opinion, and stimuli from a wide variety of sources. By comparison those in the country did not. Their reception of new ideas was restricted, their own views based on prejudice rather than reason. But the war made the city like the country. Domestic support for American involvement in the "war to make the world safe for democracy" was based on a paradox. To set Europe free the United States had to be restricted. Freedom of speech and political dissent were suppressed by various forms of censorship. Government propaganda analyzed the issues for the people as it thought fit. Whatever the merits of the American political system tolerance was not one of them in these years. As a wartime visitor from Britain observed: "It does not seem to me that you have a surplus of democracy here—certainly not enough to warrant exporting any of it." People in towns and cities were as likely to accept stereotypes of good and evil as those in the countryside. In this new climate doubt, debate and ambiguity were wrong.

----◆----

The debate about prohibition was of crucial concern to one ethnic group—the German-Americans. Their interest was ruthlessly exploited by both dry and wet sides in different ways. And it was the circumstance of the war that, once again, created a situation in which the drys were bound to win.

Before and during American involvement in the war German-Americans found their natural loyalty to their adopted country severely tested by their affection for their former home. Worse, even the great majority who accepted the situation and their part in it were nevertheless subject to a coercive form of nationalism. Those with German-sounding names were obliged to change them, and German-language papers had to provide the Justice Department with translations so that the government could censor them. From the sublime to the ridiculous, all things German were exorcised. Beethoven was banned in Boston since German music was thought subversive, and pretzels were barred in saloons in Cincinnati. Sauerkraut became "liberty cabbage."

Brewers and German-Americans linked forces with results fatal for both. By 1914 the National German-American Alliance, organized initially in 1901 by Dr. Charles John Hexamer to spread German culture, had more than two million members. In the states where it was strongest—New York and Pennsylvania in the East, and Ohio, Wisconsin, Indiana, Illinois and Iowa in the Midwest—the drys were unable to secure statewide prohibition before the war. For beer gardens were a focal point of German culture, and it seemed to German-Americans that prohibition was essentially a persecution of their ethnic heritage. From 1913 onward, financially supported by liquor interests, the alliance began to lobby Congress and administration in competition with the prohibitionists. At the start of the First World War the alliance shifted the focus of its activities to try and make the United States truly neutral. But while it did so it invited the Anti-Saloon League to equate patriotism with preparedness against Germany and thence with prohibition.

All the wartime efforts of the German-American Alliance to counter adverse publicity were turned against it by its enemies. Its ill-judged indictments of England were construed as disloyalty to America. In November 1917 Wayne Wheeler told the *New York Times:* "The liquor traffic aids those forces in this country whose loyalty is called into question at this hour. The liquor traffic is the strong financial supporter of the German-American Alliance. The purpose of this Alliance is to secure German solidarity for the promotion of German ideals and German Kultur and oppose any restriction or prohibition of the liquor traffic." The Anti-Saloon League was prepared to crush the ethnic culture when the German-Americans became involved with its opponents. The opportunity arose when a major case of political corruption by the brewers came to light.

In Philadelphia on March 4, 1916, a federal grand jury returned 101 indictments against brewers for their political activities, 100 against 72 breweries and 1 against the United States Brewers' Association. When the cases came to trial witnesses for the brewers explained how its records were burned every month. The New York office of the association was searched and the files still there were seized. To avoid public exposure the defendants pleaded guilty and paid fines of almost 160,000 dollars. However, Wayne Wheeler was not to be cheated of his prey. He knew the general contents of the files and wanted them made public. Chance provided an opportunity that could be exploited. A Gustave Ohlinger of Toledo wrote to him that the German-American Alliance, which had previously been in financial difficulties, was now solvent. Wheeler had already persuaded Senator William H. King of Utah to draft a bill to repeal the alliance's charter and paid Ohlinger to come and testify before King's committee on February 23, 1918. Wheeler did not want it known that he and the league had instigated the investigations. Nevertheless the committee had made him responsible for collecting evidence and finding witnesses. Wheeler was overjoyed at the impact of Ohlinger's appearance: "before he had testified twenty minutes the committee was on fire. They are now glad to accept the responsibility of the whole investigation." Wheeler successively estimated the newspaper copy it secured as worth twenty-five thousand, then fifty thousand, then a million dollars to the prohibition movement.

Wayne Wheeler was now able to enlist Theodore Roosevelt's opposition to the German-American Alliance and, because of Roosevelt's prestige, ensure support throughout the country. On April 11, 1918, the alliance voted to disband.

Wheeler's next move was to prepare a resolution calling for an investigation into the brewers' political activities, which he had introduced in Congress by Senator Wesley Jones of Washington. A subcommittee of the Senate Judiciary Committee was established and revealed widespread political corruption by the liquor trade.

Wheeler used his influence to get A. Mitchell Palmer appointed attorney general after Thomas W. Gregory resigned the post in 1919. Thereafter he always reminded Palmer of his debt. Thus it was Palmer who accused the defunct alliance and the brewers of having bought newspapers for half a million dollars to promulgate their point of view. He alleged that the brewers and distillers were pro-German and that the alliance impeded the assimilation of German immigrants into American society. German-language papers, which lost revenue from advertising and sales during the war, collapsed in 1917 and 1918. After the war anti-German hostility remained high within the general tide of xenophobia. German societies that had suspended themselves for the duration found they could not resume meetings in 1919. As Maldwyn Jones, the historian of American immigration, puts it, "To be accepted in America, immigrants had in future to conform wholly to a single set of values—those of the English speaking majority." For German Americans prohibition was a cruel parody of the Treaty of Versailles adding insult to injury.

————— ◆ ▬ —————

Enforcement of the Eighteenth Amendment, which was to take effect on January 16, 1920, was provided by the National Prohibition Enforcement Act devised by Wayne S. Wheeler but named after

Andrew Volstead of Minnesota, who presented it in the House. An "intoxicating liquor" was defined as one with a two-hundredth part of alcohol or one half of one percent. Farmers, however, were guaranteed their right to sweet cider.

The crucial proportion of 0.5 percent—the famous "one-half of one percent"—had no scientific basis. It did not, of course, represent the amount of alcohol it would take to make someone drunk. Like the government's relations with the liquor trade, it went back to the taxation levied in the Civil War. The government required some standard by which it could assess what exactly constituted alcohol in order to levy excise duty. Many malt beverages looked, smelled, and tasted like beer and spirits but contained only a small amount of alcohol. It was the commissioner of Internal Revenue and not chemists of the Treasury Department who decided that a slight amount of alcohol such as "one-half of one percent" would exempt a drink from tax. His casual phrase was intended as an illustration but in time hardened into a rule. It was eventually codified by a Treasury decision on April 26, 1905.

Volstead devised an enforcement unit, subsidiary to the Bureau of Internal Revenue, to which fell the task of trapping transgressors. It also had the job of regulating the legitimate use of alcohol in industry, medicine, and the sacrament. Even the most ardent drys were cautious of provoking public antagonism with too severe a measure. The seventy-three sections of the act were the result of compromises. Thus only three congressmen voted for a provision to make domestic possession of liquor illegal. The drys were attempting to get enforcement to the limit of people's endurance, not beyond it. It was passed in the House by 287 votes to 100 and in the Senate without a roll call on October 27, 1919, over Woodrow Wilson's veto.

Wilson's own reluctant conversion to the dry cause was indissoluble from his fight to get the Treaty of Versailles and League of Nations ratified by the Senate. When that failed he could hardly retract. From the Paris Peace Conference in 1919 he called on Congress to raise its wartime ban on beer and light wines until January 16, 1920, when the Eighteenth Amendment and the Volstead Act came into force. Congress did nothing. Wilson's campaign manager, Joseph E. Tumulty, advised him that if the ban were not raised the wets would turn against the Democrats. Faced with a truculent Congress, his only way of doing this would be by presidential proclamation. Tumulty urged this on him. The snag was that by this device

Wilson would advertise the Democrats as wet, provoke a reaction against them in the elections of 1920, and in turn precipitate a defeat for the Treaty of Versailles and his postwar plans. Therefore he resorted to a legal technicality: until the forces were demobilized wartime prohibition was essential. The dry complexion of the Democrats obviated further attempts at compromise on prohibition. In any case the principal issue of the elections of 1920 was Wilson's foreign policy.

The Anti-Saloon League was overconfident and now over-reached itself. At an international prohibition conference in Washington on June 3, 1919, it formed a World League Against Alcoholism. Nothing less than international prohibition would do to make democracy safe for the world by making it intelligent and sober. The league wanted temperance reform written into the Treaty of Versailles. But its plan to send seven representatives to the Paris Peace Conference was too much for Britain and France. At their request the State Department refused to issue the representatives passports and they could not travel.

The success of the prohibition movement at the turn of the century belongs to the Anti-Saloon League. By concentrating in the agrarian West and depressed South—the areas where industrial arguments in favor of prohibition were irrelevant—the league established an unassailable foundation. It is true that this basis was more impressive in terms of geographical size than numbers of population and in religious fervor rather than scientific argument, but it was secure. Thus it was prejudice of country over city, racism over reason, religion over rationale, that made prohibition a central issue in early twentieth-century politics. In other words, it was a victory of the beliefs of the nineteenth century over the needs of the twentieth. However it was the progressive movement, by raising issues of the trusts and the huddled masses, that created a political atmosphere in which the prohibition movement could thrive.

Harry Philips, a reporter of the *New York Evening Sun*, summed up American history in 1930 as "Columbus, Washington, Lincoln, Volstead, two flights up and ask for Gus." People did not want the liability of permanent abstinence. Justin Stewart, the biographer of Wayne Wheeler, likens prohibition to a New Year's resolution, passed in the complacency of moral enthusiasm, observed for a while, and then forgotten. It was to be dismissed by the seasoned drinker with the sort of casual indifference drivers showed to speed limits. Bootleggers, cocktails, gangsters, and speakeasies now had license to get into the act.

—TWO—

HOW THE
LAND LIES

The period between the world wars has exercised a curious fascination for people who lived through it and for people who know it only by reputation. American novels and poems, plays and films, art and music, produced in the twenties and thirties have survived in popular and critical esteem. And the political and social character of American history of those decades is sharply delineated. It contains a savage irony. It is like the pharaoh's dream before Joseph in Chapter 40 of Genesis. Joseph interpreted the seven lean cattle who devoured the seven fat cattle and the seven wasted ears of corn that ate the seven robust ears as seven years of famine following seven years of plenty. For the United States the frenetic years of affluence and pleasure after 1920 were abruptly terminated by the Wall Street crash of October 29, 1929. The years of prohibition were the years of high jinks in the Roaring Twenties. National prohibition did not dry up the stocks of booze. The law was openly flouted and new springs of alcohol were tapped. Some, the cocktail, the nightclub, survived it. The availability of alcohol attenuated the acts confiscating it. But then a real drought came for agriculture, and for business. The depression of the 1930s followed the tawdry affluence of the 1920s. Prohibition sputtered on until 1933, but its repeal was inevitable in the recession. Thus when the country was dry it was verdant; when it turned wet it was arid. In the twenties and thirties the opposites "dry" and "wet" were, ironically, the obverse of each other. They were complementary, not contradictory. The proof of the paradox can be seen in the ways the public, the police, and the politicians treated prohibition.

After the debates in Congress national prohibition was inevitable. Mississippi was the first state to ratify the Eighteenth Amendment, on January 18, 1918. Four more states did so the same month: Kentucky, North Dakota, South Carolina, Virginia. Ten others followed suit that year. And twenty states ratified the amendment between January 1 and 15, 1919. On January 16, 1919, Nebraska gave its approval and thus became the thirty-sixth state to do so. On January 29 the State Department proclaimed the Eighteenth Amendment ratified and set January 16, 1920, as the date when it would go into effect.

Before then people were twice served notice of the coming of national prohibition. From June 30, 1919, the country became dry under provisions for wartime prohibition although the armistice had been signed seven months earlier on November 11, 1918. Since the manufacture of alcohol was forbidden, people who could afford to bought up remaining stocks of alcohol. Institutions came off best: the Yale Club purchased enough bottles to last fourteen years, an accurate calculation of its needs. Then, on October 28, 1919, the Volstead Act was passed. This provoked a final spree over Christmas and New Year but one fraught with ominous precedents. Alcohol was sufficiently scarce for people to chance new recipes. More than a hundred people in New York drank whiskey distilled from wood alcohol and died. Sixteen bootleggers were charged in Massachusetts for selling it to them.

The executive and legislature had brought about national prohibition. The wets accused these branches of government of having failed them. They now turned to the judiciary in a forlorn hope that absolute prohibition could still be avoided. Throughout 1920 the Supreme Court dashed wet hopes in decision after decision. By five votes to four the Court upheld the Volstead Act and its limitation of the alcoholic content of beer to 0.5 percent, on January 5, 1920. On

January 12 it found against the New Jersey Retail Liquor Dealers' Association, which wanted to test the Eighteenth Amendment and the state's obligation to enforce it. Six months later the Court upheld the amendment and Volstead Act on June 7. In a series of decisions that day it found against Rhode Island, New Jersey, Wisconsin, the Kentucky Distilleries and Warehouse Company, and George C. Dempsey of Boston.

Daniel C. Roper, commissioner of Internal Revenue, told the *New York Sun* in January 1920: "The Prohibition Law will be violated—extensively at first, slightly later on; but it will, broadly speaking, be enforced and will result in a nation that knows not alcohol." Yet four years later J. Chapman reported in *Outlook*, on January 16, 1924, that prohibition was satisfying three tremendous popular passions: "the passion of the prohibitionists for law, the passion of the drinking classes for drink, and the passion of the largest and best-organized smuggling trade that has ever existed for money."

Within a year the problems of enforcement were obvious: the diversion of industrial alcohol; congestion in the courts; police lassitude; unwillingness of states to share enforcement with the federal government; governmental corruption; insufficient funds; political hypocrisy. The law led to seizures of property, violence, and even killings by those whose task was to supervise it and those whose intention was to subvert it. Federal statistics for the period from 1920 to 1929 estimate 190 people were killed as a direct consequence of the enforcement laws: 135 criminals and 55 prohibition officers.

———◆———

There were five means of obtaining alcohol: by smuggling; by turning industrial alcohol into drinkable liquor; by "moonshining" and home brewing; by medical prescription; by strengthening the alcoholic content of near beer or just continuing traditional brewing.

In early 1920 a new phrase came into the English language to describe smuggling of liquor into the United States: "rum running." Smuggling provided the surest way of getting liquor of high quality. It was also the safest way. The total frontier of the United States was 18,700 miles made up of approximately 12,000 miles of coast, 3,700 miles of land borders and 3,000 miles of lake and river front.

Alcohol was smuggled into the United States from Canada and Mexico and the West Indies and from ships outside the three miles of territorial waters around the United States, the so-called Rum Row. Statistics of what was sold within the United States by these routes are, of course, unavailable. But statistics of liquor exported from Europe to American countries that had a common border with the United States are known. Between 1918 and 1922 Canada increased its importation of liquor from Britain almost six times, Mexico eight times, and the West Indies almost five times. In the Bahamas the rise was from below 1,000 gallons of spirits to about 386,000 and in Bermuda from less than 1,000 to more than 40,000. The Department of Commerce issued low estimates of the value of liquor smuggled into the United States: $20 million in 1922; $30 million in 1923; $40 million in 1924.

Hundreds of thirsty people would travel every Friday night or Saturday morning by train from New York and New England to Montreal or Quebec in Canada, and then back by Monday, just to soak themselves silly. These weekend jaunts were commemorated in a song, "Goodbye, Broadway, Hello, Montreal."

Travelers returning from Canada who declared liquor at the border were not fined but their liquor was confiscated. If they concealed liquor but were discovered they were fined two dollars a bottle for beer and five dollars for wine and spirits as well as losing the liquor. To save a court case the breach of law was treated as a civil rather than a criminal matter. Travelers signed a formal "Assent to Forfeiture and Destruction" of their goods, which they surrendered, and paid a fine as an "Offer of Civil Settlement."

Men used belts as well as pockets to hide pint bottles. Women concealed bottles in their bloomers and corsets and false busts. Hay and lumber were the most common camouflage for illicit liquor being smuggled in bulk. Newsprint was also used and so were laths. Geraldine Farrar, the singer, had her own private railroad car and tried smuggling liquor hidden in the piano. Florenz Ziegfeld, the impresario, also had a private railroad car and did not bother to hide the liquor until he, too, was found out and relieved of three thousand dollars' worth of alcohol.

Professional smuggling from Canada was an easier business than smuggling from the open sea. It was close to large industrial cities such as Detroit, from which it was separated by short stretches of water. Liquor transported in large quantities was supposedly destined for Mexico or the Caribbean. On August 16, 1921, the Essex Export Company was the first of many large organizations granted a charter to hold "liquor for export sale, either in a bonded liquor warehouse or any other warehouse" with the express intention of selling it to the American market.

The Detroit River, eighteen miles long and one mile wide, was owned jointly by the United States and Canada. Breweries and distilleries in the Ontario border cities of Sandwich, Windsor, and Walkerville could provide the substance, wharves there and in LaSalle and Amherstburg could stock the supply, and several islands could afford the shelter for large smuggling operations. One journalist described the lie of the land as "a rum runners' paradise; it is as though a sympathetic creator had fashioned the district especially for such a purpose." At least 900,000 cases of liquor were transported within Canada to the border cities in the first seven months of 1920. Statistics suggest the per capita consumption rose from 9 gallons before the war to 102 gallons in the twenties. This was not, of course, the case. People living in the province of Ontario could not buy liquor there but they could import it from elsewhere. Residents of Ontario living close to the frontier with the United States began ordering huge quantities purportedly for their own consumption but actually to sell to smugglers or to smuggle across the border themselves.

The liquor business in Detroit, comprising the smuggling, manufacturing and distribution of alcohol, provided fifty thousand people with jobs. Its annual output was valued at $215 million, placing it ahead of the chemical industry and second only to automobile production. In 1928 the head of the prohibition river patrol in Detroit, Slocum Sleeper, said his men had confiscated $2 million worth of liquor and a fleet of more than fifty speed boats in twelve months.

Many smugglers came from farther afield than the Great Lakes. The terrain of northern New York was ideal for smugglers. There were plenty of towns large enough to afford shelter but too small to merit customs stations. The forestation afforded cover in flight. Since customs offices were closed at night and the border was largely unguarded, most smugglers made their journeys then. Caravans of as many as fourteen cars could pass unchallenged through the countryside around Lake Champlain. Leo Filion told the writer Alan S. Everest of a farmer living by Lake Champlain who even trained his horses as smugglers. He could load one with liquor in Canada and turn it loose to find its way home by itself without attracting anyone's attention.

Alcohol was also smuggled by rail. Cars were labeled in Canada as if they were destined for Mexico and then diverted and unloaded at night in the United States. One device used by smugglers was to pretend to ship legal products from Buffalo to Detroit via Canada. The cars were inspected and sealed in Buffalo by customs officers. Liquor was substituted for the stated cargo in Canada and then the cars, with counterfeit seals, were dispatched for Detroit, where they were not inspected a second time. Because of the capacity of railroad cars the amounts of liquor smuggled in this way were huge as the few seizures indicate. On November 19, 1927, for instance, three, supposedly carrying gears, were impounded at the North Detroit Station by prohibition agents who discovered they contained $200,000 worth of whiskey and wine ready to be sold for Thanksgiving.

The common method of smuggling was in automobiles with concealed compartments. There were two principal ways of preparing cars for carrying alcohol. One was the pan, a piece of steel twelve to eighteen inches deep shaped like a roasting pan which hung under the body suspended from the chassis. The pan could carry more than seven hundred bottles if they were carefully packed. The other was by removing the seats and building compartments in their place and concealing them with a slender steel shell shaped like a seat covered with a satin slip. Expensive sedans came back into fashion: each could accommodate between thirty-five and forty cases.

An individual operator could buy beer in Canada for $4.50 or $5.00 a case and sell it in Plattsburgh, New York, for $10.00. In New York City the same case would fetch as much as $25.00. A smuggler with a carload of twenty-five cases could thus make $600.00 a run from Canada to New York City, less the traveling costs. Rye whiskey bought in Canada for $4.00 a bottle fetched between $7.00 and $9.00 in Plattsburgh and $12.00 in New York, making a profit of $8.00. The profit on Scotch whiskey was greater, $12.00. Champagne could be bought in Canada for between $4.00 and $7.00 a bottle and could be sold in Chicago, Detroit, and New York City for $20.00.

A smuggler could make two trips a week in summer and one in winter if the roads were clear of snow. The expenses of organizations were greater and they charged more than individuals. Their additional costs included relay teams of drivers, storage spaces near the border and en route. Larry Fay built up (and lost) a nightclub business on his early profits of running a fleet of taxis from New

York to Montreal and back. On the return journey each had several cases of whiskey that could be sold for $80.00 apiece.

In Canada provincial assemblies controlled the retail sale of alcohol, but its manufacture, importing, and exporting was controlled by the Dominion from the capital, Ottawa. The Canadian government stood to gain financially from smuggling operations. It levied a tax of $9.00 per gallon on alcohol consumed in Canada but refunded this tax on liquor that had been exported, after presentation of a customs receipt from the country to which it was exported. Because smugglers could not furnish a receipt from United States customs officers the tax remained with the Dominion government as if the alcohol really had been consumed at home, a bonus of $30 million a year, one fifth of all Dominion and provincial revenues.

However, in 1929 the Canadian prime minister, McKenzie King, introduced a bill in the House of Commons in Ottawa prohibiting the release of liquor for export to any country that had made it illegal to import beer, wine, and spirits. He said the argument against Canadian involvement with smuggling was entirely moral and that the estimated loss of $9 million revenue a year could be borne more easily than the present situation when Canada's diplomatic relations with the United States were being jeopardized. People suspected that in exchange for a new law making it illegal for Canadians to export liquor King was being vouchsafed relaxed and open access for Canadian immigrants to the United States. The bill became law on June 1, 1930. Immediately the Canadian authorities demonstrated their intention to carry out its letter.

———————◆▸—————————

Apart from Canada, liquor smuggled into the United States came from overseas. There were several rum rows on the coast—off Boston, New Jersey, Chesapeake Bay, Oregon, and California—but the most notorious were those off the eastern shore of Long Island, and the Gulf of Mexico.

It was William ("Big Bill") McCoy who first provided "the real McCoy," good spirits. A former seaman, he became a smuggler operating from Nassau in the Bahamas until 1925 when he was arrested, tried, and convicted of violating the Volstead Act and sentenced to nine months in the federal penitentiary in Atlanta. But smuggling could not remain a matter of individuals against the state. It was becoming big business. Grace Lythgee, a widow from California, ran a wholesale liquor business for smugglers in Nassau and was one of many known as Queen of the Bootleggers. Rear Admiral Bullard of the Coast Guard told Congress in 1932, "smuggling is now carried on almost exclusively by large, highly organized international syndicates. . . . The operations are controlled entirely by radio in secret code." In fact there were at least a hundred radio stations along the Atlantic coast performing this function. Bullard reckoned there were ninety-one smuggling vessels on the Atlantic coast and the heaviest traffic was along Long Island and New Jersey. The bases were St. Pierre, Miquelon, the Bahamas, and other islands of the West Indies. In the Gulf of Mexico there were forty-seven vessels operating along the coast from Florida to Texas based on Belize, British Honduras. On the Pacific coast there were thirty-three ships based on other ships anchored off the west coast of Mexico.

In the matter of enforcing laws against smugglers Congress was generous to the Coast Guard. In 1924 it appropriated $13 million to recondition 20 old naval destroyers from the First World War. By 1928 the Coast Guard had 33 cruisers, 25 destroyers, and 243 offshore patrol boats and comprised 11,000 officers and enlisted men under the command of Admiral F. C. Bullard. He believed that given adequate funds smuggling could be stopped.

In case of pursuit smugglers had various ways of abandoning the valuable merchandise. The submarine was a low-lying craft without its own power that was towed behind a large boat but cut loose and sunk in the event of pursuit. Bags of liquor, each attached by a long rope to a box of salt, were sometimes dropped overboard. By the time the hue and cry was over, the salt had dissolved, the empty box had surfaced and acted as a buoy to guide smugglers back to their wares. Big Bill McCoy was credited with inventing the burlock, a half case of whiskey with a triangular shape containing three rows of one, two, and three bottles, wrapped in burlap. If it had to be jetisoned in a chase it would sink and not bob afloat to be picked up by the Coast Guard and used as evidence.

However, flight did not always avail smugglers. Occasionally sea battles were fought between the Coast Guard and smuggling ships. The most spectacular, between the rumrunner *Homestead*, registered in Ontario, and Coast Guard cutters *Red Wing* and *Seminole*, took place a hundred miles off Montauk Point and lasted thirty-six hours beginning on February 7, 1925.

In a vain attempt to stem the flow of liquor the Supreme Court and the administration made a series of decisions to step up the search rights of the Customs Service and close the loopholes in the law by which alcohol could be let into America. On May 15, 1922, by six votes to three, the Supreme Court ruled that alcohol could not be transported through the United States in bond nor transferred from one foreign ship to another in an American port. On April 30, 1923, it ruled that American ships could carry and sell liquor outside the three-mile limit but not bring it into port. The same restriction applied to foreign vessels. On June 13, 1923, the secretary of state, Charles Evans Hughes, suggested that the three-mile limit of sovereignty should be extended to twelve miles to make rum running more difficult. By 1924 even the British government was embarrassed by the enormous profits it gained from breaking the laws of its ally, the United States. On May 22, 1924, the two governments reached agreement for searches and seizures of ships "an hour's steaming distance" from the coast. By the end of the year similar agreements were made with Denmark, France, Germany, Holland, Italy, Norway, Sweden, and Panama.

The United States could prosecute smuggling in both criminal and civil actions. Since most of the vessels involved were foreign, their activities were a matter for civil prosecution with the intent of securing the forfeiture of the cargo, or even the ship. The *Sagatind* was a Norwegian steamer that had conveyed a cargo of liquor to the *Diamantina*, a British ship, about twenty miles from the New Jersey coast in 1925. An agent of the Internal Revenue Service had gone out to buy liquor and establish that the British ship intended to peddle liquor along the coast and had both vessels arrested. But Judge Hough of the District Court of the Southern District of New York would not find against them: "no such extension of territorial jurisdiction is created by the treaty," he declared. This was the central issue. Were treaties between the United States and other countries the law of the land or not? Could American courts find against nationals of foreign countries for smuggling?

The *Pictonian* was a British steamer taken fourteen miles from the New Jersey coast for making contact with rumrunners on the shore. When its crew were prosecuted in 1924 the District Court for the Eastern District of New York took the view that the laws of the United States applied to British subjects and ships since Britain had agreed to accept additional American jurisdiction over smuggling. However in the case of the *Over the Top* (1925), a British vessel arrested nineteen miles from the coast for selling liquor to small boats from the shore, the Connecticut District Court ruled differently. "It is not the function of treaties to enact the fiscal or criminal law of a nation," said Judge Thomas.

Since the invention of motion pictures audiences have wondered what happened to the parts edited out by various censors. They suspected censors took home with them clippings from the cutting-room floor. The same questions arose about confiscated alcohol. What did customs officers and agents do with impounded booze? Some was undoubtedly misappropriated, but much was, quite simply, poured away. It was flushed down toilets and emptied into rivers and the sea. When officers at Plattsburgh, New York, where confiscated liquor was stored in the federal building, were told to get rid of it in 1923 they just pitched bottles from the nearest window. Ten thousand bottles of beer and twenty-five hundred bottles of wine and liqueurs were thrown to the street below. The streets of the town ran with alcohol.

The second source of illicit alcohol was bootleg liquor.

The actual term "bootlegger" probably originated in Kansas and the Indian Territory in the early 1880s where the sale of alcohol was prohibited by acts of 1834 and 1836. When the owner of an illicit still came to town to sell his moonshine he carried it in pint bottles hidden in his boots. In the twenties the term was widely used to describe anyone who made, transported, or sold liquor illegally whether the original material was industrial alcohol or not.

The prohibition laws distinguished alcohol for drinking from commercial alcohol, alcohol denatured for use in industry, and sold under government license for fifty cents a gallon tax free. Professional bootleggers purified industrial alcohol by distilling it a second time. Irving Fisher estimated in his critique of 1926, *Prohibition at Its Worst*, that at least half of the alcohol drunk in the early twenties was produced this way. In 1910 less than 7 million gallons of denatured alcohol was produced for industry. In 1920, 28 million gallons were produced. By 1923 the amount was double that. In 1923, 81 million gallons were manufactured—an increase of 189 percent in six years, without a comparable increase in industrial production. How much denaturized industrial alcohol was diverted by bootleggers was a matter of speculation. James Doran, the chief chemist of the Prohibition Unit, told a committee of the House of Representatives in 1924 that out of 60 million gallons of industrial alcohol produced each year about 6 million went to bootleggers. By 1926 he had changed his mind and said the amount was between 12 and 15 millions. U.S. District Attorney Emory R. Buckner of New York said the amount was nearer 60 million gallons.

In the forty years to 1919 the government had seized an average of 1,553 illegal commercial stills. In the first six months of 1920 it seized 9,553 stills—an increase of 1,127 percent. In 1925 the federal government seized 17,854 illicit stills and General Lincoln C. Andrews admitted at best this was only one in ten of the stills in operation. And seizing stills in itself did not eliminate the problem. A commercial still costing five hundred dollars could produce between fifty and a hundred gallons of liquor a day at a cost of fifty cents a gallon. It could be sold for three or four dollars a gallon. The still could pay for itself in four days. If it were confiscated another could be purchased on credit of future sales. Moreover the government had control only of the initial processes by which industrial alcohol was made. It specified seventy-six chemical formulae for denaturing alcohol, awarding permits to businesses that issued an earnest of honest intentions. But it had no control over the sale and transportation of converted alcohol from manufacturer to wholesaler, retailer, and customer.

Moonshine was a variant on converted industrial alcohol. The term originated in the Appalachians in the eighteenth century. It meant alcohol distilled from a mash of sugar, water, yeast, and garbage. National prohibition turned it into big business based on corn sugar. The corn-sugar industry expanded from a production of 152 million pounds in 1921 to 960 million pounds in 1929. Dr. James Doran calculated in the *New York Times* on January 18, 1930, that for every one gallon of reconverted industrial alcohol there were seven or eight gallons of moonshine being drunk. The government's Wickersham commission of 1931 estimated that 70 million gallons a year were produced from corn sugar alone.

The extent to which domestic manufacture of alcohol would become a routine was not considered by the administration. "How about this home-brewing business, Doctor?" asked William Riis, a reporter of the *Kansas City Star*, in 1920, of A. B. Adams, chief chemist of the Treasury bureau that tested beverages. "Nothing to that," was the reply. "It's too much trouble for uncertain results. They may try it once or twice, but not more." Yet within the year millions of homes had equipment to make alcohol. For according to the new morality,

> Be it ever so humble
> There's no place like home
> —for BREWING.

After all, from the beginning of the twentieth century successive governments had issued a series of pamphlets advising people how to make alcohol from apples, bananas, barley, beets, oats, sugar, watermelon, and even potato peel. In addition the Women's Christian Temperance Union (WCTU) inadvertently gave the game away by organizing lecture tours of men from the Enforcement Unit to show women what a bad thing moonshine was and how alcohol was made. And shopkeepers did not have to advertise the illegal intention behind the legal sales of yeast, hops, other ingredients, and copper stills. But the hints they dropped were obvious. Preston Slosson, a contemporary historian of the twenties, saw one advertisement in a Washington streetcar for a store showing a procession of thirsty camels crossing a desert. In Detroit a shop sign read Malt and Hops—Try Ours for Better Results.

The situation was summed up in an outrageous pun:

> You may not have a fairy in your home
> Or a miss in your car—but feller!
> Everyone nowadays surely has
> A little maid in his cellar.

The illicit conversion of industrial alcohol and manufacture of liquor from novel materials was certainly ingenious. Yack Yack bourbon was made in Chicago from iodine and burnt sugar. Soda Pop Moon was manufactured in Philadelphia from isopropyl alcohol, a poison. Panther whiskey was produced from a combination of esters and fusel oil. These recipes had penalties. Careless bootleggers . did not always remove wood alcohol used to denature grain alcohol from the reconverted industrial alcohol they sold their clients. It was a poison that caused blindness and, sometimes, death. "Jake" made from Jamaican ginger, first in Oklahoma and later in the South, caused hundreds of deaths and a plague of paralysis, jakitis, or gingerfoot, to fifteen thousand people in 1930. Jackass brandy caused internal bleeding. Glycerine and oil of juniper were sometimes mixed into industrial alcohol and the product labelled "gin." When caramel, creosote, and prune juice were added it was called Scotch whiskey.

What deaths did occur were sensational enough. An unusually

large number of deaths were caused by alcoholism or alcoholic poisoning in December 1926 and January 1927. These deaths were
blamed on the government's callousness in having insisted on de-
naturizing industrial alcohol. Emmanuel Celler, a congressman of
New York, said it was like Lucrezia Borgia all over again. Within
four days in New York in 1928 thirty-four people died from wood
alcohol. From 1925 to 1929 forty people in every million died from
poisoned liquor. Senator James A. Reed of Missouri said, during
hearings of the Senate Judiciary Committee in December 1924, that
this was "enforcing prohibition by poison," and "the nearest approach to murder that a man can commit."

In the hue and cry over deaths from alcohol poisoning Dr.
James H. Doran said that wood alcohol was so obvious that anyone
who sipped it would realize he was drinking denaturized alcohol and
desist. It contained "distinctive odorous substances commonly
designated as pyroligneous compounds that, by their characteristic
odour and taste, at once disclose to the individual the patent fact
that the mixture or liquid is unfit for consumption." However on
July 26, 1923, he had been quoted by the *New York Times* as
saying,"It is impossible to detect wood alcohol except by a thorough
chemical analysis performed by a skilled chemist in a well-equipped
laboratory." As Richard Hofstadter explains, this part of prohibition
contained a terrible irony: "Before prohibition became law, the prohibitionists decried alcohol as a form of deadly poison. After prohibition was law, they approved the legal poisoning of industrial
alcohol, knowing full well that men would die from drinking it."

———◆◆———

The production of wine increased under prohibition. Prohibition officers calculated in 1930 that 100 million gallons of wine
were manufactured domestically each year. Clark Warburton estimated in 1932 that consumption of wine rose by two thirds during
prohibition. Although Californians who owned vineyards expected
prohibition would ruin them, things turned out very differently.
From 1920 to 1926 their sales of grapes, whether for eating or wine
making, doubled. And this led to the claim that "Andrew Volstead
ought to be considered the patron saint of the San Joaquin Valley."
For in 1921 the Internal Revenue Service had announced that heads
of families could make two hundred gallons of wine a year for home
use by obtaining a permit. There were, however, several cases on the
border between permissible and illegal wines. The Prohibition Unit

issued a statement on May 17, 1922, that dandelion wine was not legal because the dandelion was not a fruit.

Drys maintained that doctors were making a fortune by selling alcoholic prescriptions to their patients for real and imaginary illnesses. On July 4, 1920, six months after national prohibition, the *New York Times* reported that more than fifteen thousand doctors and fifty-seven hundred pharmacists had applied for licenses to sell alcohol. According to C. Stout in *The Eighteenth Amendment and the Part Played by Organized Medicine* (1921), more than half a million prescriptions for whiskey were issued by doctors in Chicago, and half of these were fraudulent. And according to *Statistics Concerning Intoxicating Liquor* (1933), an average of 10 million prescriptions for more than 1 million gallons of alcohol were issued every year of prohibition.

Wine could still be used in church communion. Permits to hold it were just as valuable as were permits to prescribe and permits to make industrial alcohol to people who wanted to exploit the law.

------◆------

Despite prohibition, beer and near beer were being drunk. Breweries were renamed cereal beverage plants, their product supposedly changed in substance from beer to near beer. Will Rogers said of it, "After drinking a bottle of this weak beer you have to take a glass of water as a stimulant." But the process of making near beer involved the manufacture of old beer with an alcoholic content of 3 or 4 percent and then a process to reduce the alcoholic content to the legal limit of 0.5 percent. In other words, a perfectly legal process was dependent on a first stage that was illegal, and that the government had to accept. In the first five years of prohibition 956,220,919 gallons of near beer were manufactured.

Beer could also be made from wort and malt by the addition of yeast. Production of wort and malt increased to six times its level before prohibition. Moreover the production of hops did not decline. The Association Against the Prohibition Amendment estimated that 15 million pounds of hops were sold in 1928, enough to make 20 million barrels of beer by traditional methods. Anheuser-Busch, a large brewery, complained that prohibition had made one of their plants, valued at $40 million worthless. The company had spent $18 million converting it to make a near beer, Bevo, which they could not sell: people could buy real beer from bootleggers.

For brewers who still wanted to manufacture real beer a novel situation existed. The brewers, who had the capital, the product, and the old managerial skills, cooperated with gangsters, who provided protection with new managerial skills and secured the permission of police and politicians. Since they also provided a front, whether as directors or personnel, they took the fall—legal liability. In Chicago the brewer Joseph Stenson and his three brothers took on the gangsters Terry Druggan, Frankie Lake, and Johnny Torrio as partners in the operation of five breweries—the Gambrinius, the Standard, the George Hoffman, the Pfeiffer, and the Stege—and, later on, four more. In New York William V. Dwyer, a sports promoter, and three other businessmen acquired the Phenix Cereal Beverage Company, the largest brewery in Manhattan, from the Clausen and Flanagan Brewing Company in 1923. In 1928 Dwyer was joined by another partner, Owen Victor Madden, "Owney the Killer," a paroled convict from Sing Sing who had once led the Gopher gang. Although Madden avoided publicity in general the product was known as Madden's No. 1 Brew until he returned to prison for parole violation in 1932. On an annual barrelage of 800,000 halves the Phenix brewery made a net profit of $7.4 million a year.

———◆———

While beer, wine, and spirits were still being consumed in their old forms, a new mixed drink, the cocktail, took its place at their side. The cocktail was a concoction of spirits and, sometimes, wine mixed with fruit juice or soda. It was served both inside and outside the home as a soft drink but its principal appeal lay in the hard liquor it contained.

Three hundred varieties of cocktail had existed before national prohibition. They included: the mint julep, a concoction of bourbon whiskey, Jamaica rum, crushed mint, sugar, and water; the Scotch highball consisting of Scotch with Appollinaris or seltzer; and the Orange Blossom, gin and orange juice. But such mixed drinks were consumed regularly by the upper classes only, especially at parties and in the most sophisticated hotels. Common saloons had served liquor straight. According to popular culture mixed drinks were effeminate. In David Belasco's play and Puccini's opera, *The Girl of the Golden West*, set in a California mining camp during the Gold Rush, the stranger Dick Johnson causes general astonishment by ordering whiskey with water at the bar. Even the schoolmarm, Minnie, rejoins that miners' drinks will curl his hair for him.

During prohibition, however, the cocktail was to become

popular because it was necessary. First, a mixed drink concealed the fact that alcohol was being included. Thus a drinker might, under duress, deceive a detective. Second, the alcohol used had, in all probability, already been cut or diluted. Cocktails therefore provided an element of choice about what was actually being drunk. Third, the mix masked the foul taste of reconverted industrial alcohol. Fourth, cocktails gave ample opportunity for youthful ingenuity in creating novel taste sensations. In the twenties when Old Mother Hubbard went to the cupboard it was to take a nip at her gin. And when the cupboard was bare it was most likely because her daughter had broken in before her to experiment with new mixtures.

Recipes ran a range from the sublime to the ridiculous, including the right royal mess. Some were named after places, such as the *Manhattan*, a mixture of rye whiskey and Vermouth with Angostura bitters and a slice of lemon, and the *Bronx*, consisting of two parts gin to one part Italian and French Vermouth with a slice of orange. Others were named after people: the *Renee and Howard Cocktail* was a mixture of Brandy, Creme de Cocoa, and fresh cream in equal proportions; the *Mamie Taylor* was Scotch and ginger ale served with a cherry. At least one was named after the decade: the *1920 Cocktail* contained half "Canadian Club" whiskey, a quarter Italian and a quarter French Vermouth with a dash of orange bitters. Others mixed the incompatible with the unpalatable. The *Silver Fizz* contained gin and seltzer water, lemon juice, sugar, and the white of an egg. The *Golden Fizz* mixed gin with both lemon and lime juices, sugar, and the yolk of an egg. Thus some commentators conclude that cocktails represented masochistic Puritanism, first punishing the palate with a poisonous taste before the alcohol reached and polluted the rest of the body. In this interpretation it was no longer the purity of natural products that satisfied public appetite but, rather, the impurity of unnatural mixtures. As a New York rhyme put it:

> *Who'd care to be a bee and sip*
> *Sweet honey from a flower's lip*
> *When he might be a fly and sail*
> *Head first into a good cocktail?*

In line with this notion and to counteract any residual idea that cocktails really were effeminate, some were known by hard, masculine-sounding titles that gave no clue about their fruity contents: in the *Rock and Rye* a tablespoon of Rock Candy syrup and the juice of half a lemon were added to rye whiskey; the *Jockey Club Cocktail* consisted of equal portions of Italian Vermouth and rye whiskey with the juice of maraschino cherries; the *John Collins* mixed gin and soda with lemon juice and sugar. All were served with ice, whether chipped, crushed, or in cubes.

———◄◆►———

If people wanted to drink outside their homes they did so in hotels and restaurants as they had always done. But they had a choice of two new venues, the speakeasy and the nightclub.

The word "speakeasy" was first used to mean an unlicensed saloon in 1889. H. L. Mencken thought that the word itself originated in Ireland as "speak softly shop." The speakeasy now replaced the old saloon. And its ambience gave the old saloon a restrospective respectability. The saloon had often been situated at the corner of the block; the speakeasy was located in a basement, a back room, or an upstairs apartment. Speakeasies often had special fronts. They varied from drugstores, coffeehouses, and soda fountains to barbershops and Turkish baths, and even the occasional funeral parlor. Instead of a swinging door the entrance was locked and had a peephole.

There was no free lunch. Indifferent food was sold at high prices; booze was sold at exorbitant prices, anything from twice to ten times the cost before prohibition. Speakeasies in New York paid $18.00 for a half barrel of beer containing fifteen and a half gallons. There were 150 glasses in every half barrel sold at twenty-five cents apiece. Thus the retail price of beer was $2.40 a gallon. What was passed off as wine cost seventy-five cents a quart or $3.00 a glass in cities.

The labels on bottles of spirits in most speakeasies were counterfeit. The contents varied from a fifth to a tenth part whiskey. Before prohibition bartenders opening a new bottle of whiskey would pour off the top of the whiskey to get rid of the fusel oil. After prohibition they just shook the bottle to distribute the fusel oil so as not to waste anything. Another dodge was cutting, dilution of whiskey with water, giving rise to a cynical rhyme:

> *Little drops of water*
> *That we used to think*
> *Were only made for chasers*
> *Are now the whole darn drink.*

PROHIBITION

According to the census of 1910 the number of saloon owners was 68,000. By 1917 it is estimated that the actual number of saloons was 150,000 while 10,000 stores sold alcohol for consumption off the premises. Maurice Campbell, a former prohibition director of New York State, thought that by the end of the twenties the number of speakeasies was 225,000. Grover Whalen, police commissioner of New York, told the *New York Times* of April 5, 1929, that the number of speakeasies in the city was 32,000. The number only fell to 9,000 by 1933 because of the depression. And Judge Talley of New York told the subcommittee of the Senate Judiciary Committee in April 1926 that throughout America there were three speakeasies for every old saloon. He added, more ominously, "They are a terrible menace as they have brought the sale of liquor into tenement and dwelling houses, and within the purview of children . . . Terrible fights are common in them, provoked by the raw liquor they sell and unavoidable absence of police supervision. There are more applicants for shelter and aid at the free Bowery lodging houses than before prohibition."

Women had been barred from many saloons before prohibition. During prohibition their appearance in speakeasies was no more illegal that that of their men, an initiation that accomplished a revolution in social mores. The evils of the old saloon were the same and worse in the speakeasy. A poll of speakeasy proprietors published in the *New York World* of March 31, 1930, was twenty to one against prohibition. They were in perpetual fear of raids and of padlocking, of gangsters' holdups and of protection rackets. They were social outcasts dependent on corrupt policemen and agents who drank too much of their liquor and extorted too much of their profit. Whereas at one time they had paid taxes, New York speakeasy owners now paid more than $50 million every year from 1920 in graft to policemen and prohibition agents. From 1923 the annual average was $59,840,000. Each first-class saloon paid $1,800 annually, only a little more than before prohibition when the state license was $1,500 and the federal license was $25. One speakeasy proprietor estimated his expenses at $1,370 a month in 1930. This included $400 in protection money to the police, district attorneys, and federal agents and $40 to the individual policeman on his beat every time beer was delivered.

The nightclub made its first appearance under that title in New York in February 1922 when a group of cafés around Broadway formed themselves into "clubs" as alternative entertainments to orange juice booths and movie houses nearby. The *New York Times* reported that the name "club" was "a part of the general scheme of surrounding patrons with the psychology of privacy and intimacy." Thus "the successful 'club' is full of booths and alcoves and cozy wall benches, which somehow contribute to the atmosphere of 'just us members.'" And "A club this season is not considered a real success unless there is a carefree tendency among the guests to toss remarks to each other from table to table." Barney Gallant, the owner of the Greenwich Village Inn and three other clubs in succession and who had the distinction of being the first man imprisoned for selling alcohol under the terms of wartime prohibition, agreed with this view when he said, "Exclusiveness is the nightclub's great and only stock in trade. Take this away and the glamour and romance and mystery are gone. The nightclub manager realizes that he must pander to the hidden and unconscious snobbery of the great majorities. It is because they make it so difficult of access that everybody is fighting to get into them."

During prohibition the specific character of nighclubs in New York was determined by their special entertainers: the torch singer Helen Morgan at her own Fifty-fourth Street Club; the comedian Jimmy Durante, "Schnozzola," at the Club Durant; revue artists Douglas Byng and Beatrice Lillie at the Sutton Club; the dancers Clifton Webb and Mary Hay at Ciro's; the Fokine ballet at the Mirador; Fred and Adele Astaire dancing to Emil Coleman's music at the Trocadero. This was the time of the so-called Harlem renaissance in which Duke Ellington and other talented black artists like "Snake Hips" Earl Tuckers, Don Redman, Florence Mills (the "Little Black Mosquito"), and Cab Calloway were promoted by Lee Posner, a Russian Jew, and brought mixed audiences to the Cotton Club, the Exclusive Club, Hoofer's Club, Club Cabaret, the Nest, Small's, and Connie's Inn there.

Not all the old saloons closed down. Sale of alcohol had only been one of their functions. Sale of snacks and use as a social center were the others. Thus the saloon could legitimately continue providing these by converting itself to a "drugstore," selling stamps, books, and hot-water bottles as well as salads, sweets, sodas, and ice cream. Moreover confectionery stores could also make the conversion to soda fountains. Charles Merz estimated there were thirty thousand soda fountains across the United States in the twenties. The soda fountain served drinks that were devoid of alcohol and perfectly legal. Their names promised more than they delivered, hinting at hard liquor or evocative of far-off places and things: New Orleans Fizz, Hawaiian Special, Mandalay Delight, Mary Pickford's Own, Stolen Hours, Bed of Roses, and Forbidden Fruit.

The means of prohibition enforcement was, supposedly, a federal agency. It was called the Prohibition Unit until March 3, 1927. Thereafter it was known as the Prohibition Bureau. Its first commissioner was John F. Kramer, an Ohio lawyer who had served in his state's legislature. He lasted eighteen months and was succeeded by Roy A. Haynes. Representative William D. Upshaw called him a man of "amazing genius and energy in organization." But it was in his four years' tenure of office that the unit became a center of corruption. The unit had none of the prerequisites for making a success of its job: good salaries to make graft superfluous; continuity of personnel; cooperation from government and the general public. The total appropriation for 1920 was minuscule, $2,200,000. And the average yearly sum throughout the twenties was small, $8,811,848. U.S. District Attorney Emory R. Buckner of New York estimated that to suppress bootlegging and the manufacture of hard liquor in New York State alone would cost $15 million a year. Taking into account the total population of the United States and the fact that it cost more to enforce prohibition in the sparsely populated areas, the national Association Against the Prohibition Amendment said the cost of adequate enforcement in the country as a whole would have been $2.25 billion a year. At the same time as it was expected to provide additional means of law enforcement the federal government had less revenue with which to do so. The revenue from beer and spirits in 1919 was $183,050,854. That source of revenue was truly dry even if beer and spirits still flowed. Opponents of prohibition estimated that the potential revenue from beer alone in 1926 would have been $1,874,500,000 without the Eighteenth Amendment, whereas the total federal income from taxes was only $1,350,000,000 in the fiscal year ending 1925.

The total number of agents in the Prohibition Unit, and its successor, the bureau, varied between 1,500 and 2,300 men and the entire staff was never more than 4,500. The rate of pay was between $1,200 and $2,000 a year in 1920, and $2,300 a year in 1930. In 1924 the Bureau of Labor considered that an average family of five required a minimum annual income of $1,920 to survive. Yet these paltry sums were what the government itself was prepared to pay its own agents. Nevertheless they were more than the other guardians of prohibition, customs officers, and policemen earned. In the early twenties the pay for customs and border patrolmen was $1,680 a year and out of this they had to provide their own uniforms. In time the sum was raised to $1,860. In 1927 it became $2,000 and in 1930, $2,100. In 1920 New York State Police were paid $900 a year and some maintenance. After eight years of service they were qualified for a maximum of $1,270. In 1924 the maximum salary was only $1,300.

Police, customs officers, and prohibition agents were expected to work hard for this pittance and to risk their lives against armed gangsters. It is hardly surprising that some fell from grace. A prohibition agent could certainly earn another $4,000 by looking the other way while a consignment of liquor was being ferried to its destination, especially during the night. In the first eleven years of the service 17,972 appointments were made but there were 11,982 resignations and 1,608 dismissals for various corrupt practices: bribery, extortion, corruption, embezzlement, and false reports. Most of them were among the rank and file. The figure represented one in twelve of the personnel of the Prohibition Unit. As Senator J. Harreld of Oklahoma pointed out in 1926 the average was no more than the number of apostles who had gone wrong. Within the American federal government it was a novelty.

The enforcement unit relied on the resourcefulness of individual detectives for making its pinches. Within two years two of the unit's agents were more famous than the rest: Izzy Einstein and Moe Smith, "as the master hooch-hounds alongside whom all the rest of the pack are but pups." Their detective devices were disingenuous and dazzling. Izzy and Moe disguised themselves as fishermen and football players, grocers and garage mechanics, sellers of haberdashery, hoses, and horses. They were credited with 20 percent of all cases brought to trial in the first two years of prohibition and by 1925 had arrested 4,932 people altogether.

"Have you heard the latest story," Izzy asked one barman.
"No, go ahead," was the reply.
"You're pinched."

A report appeared in the *New York Times* on their activities in April 1922:

Streetcar conducting seems remote from bootlegging, yet the tip that saloons near certain car barns were doing rush business took Izzy there. He appeared bright and early one morning dressed in all the regalia of a B.R.T. employee. He entered a saloon and laid a $5 bill on the bar.

"Can you give me a lot of change for this?" he asked. "I need it for my run."

The bartender also had use for small change.

"Why don't you buy a drink?" he asked. "That's the way to get change."

Izzy ordered a glass of beer.

"Why don't you take a good drink?"

Izzy ordered whiskey. He got $4.25 in change.

The bartender got arrested.

But while everyone laughed at Izzy and Moe they were also laughing at the law. Their colleagues resented their success and their seniors did not dare risk their landing one of the big fish, thereby reducing the corrupt profits of the Prohibition Unit. On Friday, November 13, 1925, Izzy and Moe were discharged.

In addition to individual detective work the Prohibition Unit's means of attack were the drive and the raid. The drive was a concerted effort by federal and state agents to pool resources for a large-scale offensive on bootleggers or rum runners in crucial areas—the Atlantic coast, the Canadian border. For instance, the climax of federal activity in New York was a drive of fifty-five agents on different parts of the Rum Trail from Plattsburgh to Albany in February, 1925. They seized liquor valued at $60,000 and arrested thirty-six people.

At best successive drives dispersed the enemy for a time; at worst they were downright failures. The local complement was the raid. Often the raids were illegal and the device of the tipover, indiscriminate destruction of everything in sight by axes and sledgehammers known as "the big keys," was blatantly so. John P. Smith, police commissioner of Detroit, defended this form of police action in support of the Prohibition Unit: "In this case we are dealing with law violators and we have to break the law to enforce it."

In the fall of 1922 the Prohibition Unit began to use the padlock in earnest to make sure speakeasies and factories that had been raided stayed closed. The Volstead Act defined a place that sold alcohol as "a common nuisance" and allowed the government to have it closed for a year by court order. The number of injunctions used to padlock factories and speakeasies rose from 466 in 1921 to 1,270 in 1922 and thence by stages to 4,471 in 1925. In New York 500 speakeasies were closed in thirteen months when the unit first began to use the padlock in the city. In Chicago a whole hotel of 125 rooms was once closed for selling liquor. In California, near Dyerville, a huge redwood tree with a still in its hollow had a padlock nailed to it. But although the padlock was effective as a device against speakeasies where liquor was sold it was not so effective against factories where liquor was manufactured. The personnel and sometimes the equipment could easily be moved. In addition the courts issued injunctions in only 35 percent of the cases brought to their attention.

The undercover work of federal agents brought the unit into great disrepute on a number of occasions. R. W. Merrick, the prohibition chief in northern New York, organized rum running by federal agents in 1925 in order to make contacts and clamp down on smuggling. He secured a promise from Federal District Judge Frank Cooper, who was severe to bootleggers in court, that if any of the agents were caught they would be released so that the scheme would not be discovered. Both Emmanuel Celler and Fiorello La Guardia, congressmen for New York, charged Cooper and Merrick with conspiracy to "entrap" bootleggers unlawfully. They called for Cooper's impeachment.

Even more notorious was the case of the Bridge Whist Club. Hitherto agents had incurred expenses in speakeasies as part of detective work. But in 1926 in the midst of a conventional law case about a leasehold it transpired that agents had rented 14, East Forty-fourth Street, New York, and established a speakeasy, the Bridge Whist Club, selling liquor there from November 1, 1925, to May 1, 1926. This speakeasy was an important source of information on smuggling and bootlegging. The wets criticized such misadventures as dangerous precedents threatening ordinary citizens with intolerable surveillance.

One clause in the Prohibition Enforcement Act exempted prohibition agents from sitting examinations for the Civil Service as prescribed in the Pendleton reform of the Civil Service in 1883. The general counsel of the Anti-Saloon League, Wayne B. Wheeler, knew that only by allowing a spoils system of political nominees in the unit could he hope to get Congress to pass the Volstead Bill. Politicians were anxious to build up their local political machines with a new type of patronage. Wheeler weighed up the advantages of an impartial unit outside his control against those of an imperfect unit within it. He knew he could monitor politicians' relationship with a unit of their own nominees and intimidate them if necessary. Thus he supported what he realized would be an inadequate unit to retain bargaining power with Congress. He was identifying the aims of the Anti-Saloon League with his own pursuit of power. The National Civil Service Reform League was blunt about Wheeler's motives: "Congressmen wanted the plunder and you let them have it. . . . You bought the bill with congressional patronage and paid for it not with your own money, but, far worse, with offices paid out of taxes levied upon the people."

———— ◆ ————

The difficulties of the unit were compounded by the hostility of the states to the federal law.

A few states held out against bone-dry prohibition. Wisconsin passed an act allowing the manufacture and sale of beer with 2.5 percent of alcohol. The drys said this violated the Volstead Act and took the state to court. However, the court at Milwaukee upheld the Wisconsin statute on March 1, 1920. In Massachusetts the legislature passed a bill permitting beer with 2.75 percent of alcohol on May 3. Governor Calvin Coolidge vetoed it despite the fact that wet candidates had defeated dry candidates in the municipal elections earlier that year—a demonstration of traditional northern wet standards. Both Maryland and New Jersey passed a 3.5 percent beer bill. Maryland also refused to concur with the federal government in enforcement of the Volstead Act and New Jersey filed a suit in the Supreme Court to have the Eighteenth Amendment declared null and void and prevent enforcement of the Volstead Act.

The most sustained opposition came from New York State where the Democrats declared against the Eighteenth Amendment. The lower house voted an investigation into the lobbying of the Anti-Saloon League and the legislature passed a 2.75 percent beer bill signed by Governor Alfred E. Smith—all in 1920. Later, as a result of public alienation from prohibition, the legislature repealed the state's enforcement law, the Mullan-Gage Act or Baby-Volstead Act of April 1921, by a narrow margin on May 4, 1923.

The states' abnegation of their responsibilities is most clearly indicated by the paltry sums they were prepared to pay for prohibition enforcement. The total for 1923 was only $548,629; in 1927 it was $689,855. This represented one 0.25 percent of their total expenditure. Only eighteen states contributed, and three—Missouri, Nevada, Utah—contributed less than $1,000. The largest contribution came from Ohio with $146,577. But thirty states contributed nothing at all, even though twenty-eight had previously passed state prohibition. These dry states obviously expected the federal government to take charge of a federal law. Thus the states spent on prohibition enforcement half of what they spent on the regulation of oil sales, a quarter of their expenditure on park maintenance, and an eighth of what they spent on enforcing fish and game laws.

Many states with industrial complexes had never adopted state prohibition: California, Connecticut, Illinois, Massachusetts, Missouri, New Jersey, New York, Pennsylvania, Wisconsin. The opposition of new immigrants to prohibition was particularly telling in cities that rejected state or municipal prohibition from 1917 to 1919: Boston, Chicago, Cincinnati, Cleveland, San Francisco, St. Louis, St. Paul. The hostility continued in 1920. Wet spots persisted along the eastern seaboard from Baltimore to Boston, in towns along the Mississippi and Missouri rivers, in tourist centers, Miami, New Orleans, Reno, San Francisco. The failure of prohibition to win the cities was crucial in the failure of the whole experiment. As Larry Engelmann says, prohibition "died on the city streets."

The impetus for enforcement depended on public interest. Once the governor of Pennsylvania, Gifford Pinchot, criticized the Philadelphia police for their apathy in 1923, the mayor employed Brigadier General Smedley D. Butler of the marines to clean up the city in 1924. With ruthless efficiency he made adroit use of policemen and firemen. But success was short-lived. Internecine feuds in the Police Unit and decline in public interest impeded his work. In September 1925, shortly before he returned to the marines, he admitted, "The path of law enforcement has been blocked by powerful influences, by legal machinery that should have been an aid, and by the invocation of technicalities." Thus of more than 6,000 people arrested in his second year of office only 212 were convicted in court. Butler concluded "enforcement hasn't amounted to a row of pins after the arrests were made." And the grand jury in Philadelphia discovered in 1928 that Butler's tough policy had halted bootleggers but briefly. He had just taught them to organize their industry more efficiently. The scale of bribery ascended. Fifteen policemen were dismissed for corruption when their bank deposits, totaling more than $800,000, were investigated.

The local commissioners who remained honest soon became exhausted. Their task of enforcement was beyond endurance. New York City had especially difficult tasks of enforcement, and no fewer than four administrators followed one another, each with different systems of organization, in the first eighteen months: James L. Shevlin, Frank L. Boyd, Daniel L. Chaplin, and Ernest Langley. The New York Police Department continued to suffer from inconsistent direction. Under Mayor Jimmy Walker it was headed by a whole series of police commissioners: George V. McLaughlin, a banker obliged to resign because Tammany Hall resented his raids on gambling houses; Joseph A. Warren, Walker's former law partner, who resigned because he did not have the stamina for the job; Grover A. Whalen, a department store executive whose predilection was for display rather than effect; Edward P. Mulrooney, a professional policeman, who resigned in 1933 to become chairman of the State Alcoholic Beverage Control Commission. The new mayor, John P. O'Brien, appointed another professional policeman, James S. Bolan who was acceptable to Tammany Hall, which got more than it bargained for when he revived the defunct vice squad. For, as Stanley Walker suggests in *The Night Club Era*, "What the law enforcement bodies of the large cities wanted . . . was not enforcement but a sort of safe regulation of the liquor selling traffic."

In the early days, when violation of the Volstead Act was a misdemeanor, bail was usually $1,000. After Congress made violations felonies and they became more flagrant bail was set at $2,000. First offenses usually carried fines of not more than $1,000 or six months imprisonment. Second and later offenses usually carried fines of between $200 and $2,000 and imprisonment of between one month and five years. The Jones Act of 1929 made violations a felony and provided maximum penalties of $10,000 fine or five years' imprisonment or both for the first offense. However, the national average of fines remained $130 and the average prison sentence was 140 days. Whereas the federal court of New York City had imposed fines of between $5 and $10 under the Volstead Act, under the Jones Act in exchange for pleas of guilty it levied fines of between $25 and $50. Although U.S. attorney George Z. Medalie persuaded federal judges they were cheapening justice, in 1931 the fines averaged between $100 and $250, a fraction of the legal limits.

Defendants were encouraged to plead guilty and thus avoid trial by jury. Their punishments were often negotiated by the defense attorney and the federal district attorney, and judges would accommodate their compromise in passing sentence. The mounting tide of prohibition cases was processed in cavalier fashion. Once Judge Howe disposed of 140 cases in a single "bargain" day. Albert Levitt found after eight years, "Local enforcement is with very rare exception very insincere" for bribery and corruption were widespread: "It is nothing unusual to find that the sheriff himself was a bootlegger or in quiet partnership with those who were. . . . Judges impose a light fine on some bootlegger brought before them for sentence and then retire to their chambers to drink the liquor which the same bootlegger has sold to them."

<hr>

However, it is insufficient to contrast the work of prohibition agents, local and federal, with public antipathy to the law and present the subject as a ridiculous dialogue in which the Prohibition Unit always came off worse. The law had a serious and disastrous side even beyond the deaths of hundreds of people and the crippling of thousands. As Representative George H. Schneider of Wisconsin put it in 1925: "Vice, crime, immorality, disease, insanity, corruption, and a general disregard for law, directly traceable to the unenforceability of the Volstead Act, are increasing with alarming rapidity." A proponent of prohibition echoed this view. Edwin C. Dinwiddie, formerly of the Anti-Saloon League but in 1925 at the National Temperance Bureau, said in November that year: "Cabinet officers, Senators and other legislators and leaders find it easy to disobey the law themselves and they have been known to use their influence to free their henchmen after they have been caught in the toils of the law." For prohibition was a significant part of the general social political and social scene of the 1920s.

"It was characteristic of the Jazz Age," said the novelist F. Scott Fitzgerald, "that it had no interest in politics at all." And indeed it is the social life and art of the twenties that have dominated everyone's idea of them. However, everything we know of the 1920s has an unexpected aspect, its relationship with recent events. The flapper, the nymphet with boyish figure and bobbed hair, who danced the Charleston and Black Bottom was a creature of the First World War before she became the representative symbol of the 1920s. H. L. Mencken described her and designated the term "flapper" as early as 1915.

The most crucial poem, *The Waste Land* by T. S. Eliot, was written in Europe. The alienation of the expatriates was as much against the stifling provincialism and plutocracy of America before 1917 as it was against the blaring commercialism after. The leading political commentators, Walter Lippmann and Reinhold Niebuhr, owe their inspiration more to the progressive period and the war than to the social and political tensions of the 1920s, as their first major books attest. However, this does not mean we must constantly turn to the war as a basis for interpreting the twenties. It means we must not be misled by the apparent finiteness of the decade. It may have a precise beginning with the Treaty of Versailles in 1919, the scoring of jazz, the invention of radio, and the coming of prohibition in 1920. It has an obvious ending with the Wall Street crash of 1929. And it is true that these boundary dates sharpen its profile. But the sluggish politics and feverish social life only make sense if we consider them beyond their individual interest as items in a catalogue. Prohibition was part and parcel of the twenties, embedded in the social and political structure of the United States. English television producer Daniel Snowman, in the first chapter of his *America Since 1920* (1968), has found a way through the maze of politics, problems, and personalities. From him we can deduce what prohibition reveals of its period.

Daniel Snowman discerns two tensions underlying the social, political, and economic events of the 1920s. One showed itself in political, economic, and religious intolerance, the other in social indulgence. Intolerance was exemplified by the trial of John Scopes, a biology teacher, in 1925 when the courts of Tennessee denied scientific evidence of Darwin's theory of evolution and asserted the literal truth of the origins of life described in Genesis. Intolerance was also exemplified by the prejudicial treatment of the Italian anarchists, Nicola Sacco and Bartolomeo Vanzetti, arrested on circumstantial evidence for the robbery and murder of a paymaster and his guard in South Braintree, Massachusetts, in 1920. They were tried and retried and eventually executed in 1927. Another illustration of intolerance was the demand of Congress that its European associates in the world war repay their loans yet used the Fordney-McCumber protective tariff of 1922 to deny them effective access to American markets so that they could not earn the necessary dollars to do so. The resurgence of the Ku Klux Klan and the immigration restriction of 1921 and 1924 are other examples. Indulgence showed itself in sexual license of townsfolk hell bent on pleasure, justifying their behavior by misinterpreting Freud, and in riotous speculation during the Florida land boom of 1925 and in Wall Street before the great crash of 1929. There was considerable political corruption principally in Harding's administration of 1921 to 1923 when his associates Harry Daugherty, Charles W. Forbes, and Albert B. Fall plundered, respectively, the Department of Justice, the Veterans' Bureau and the federal oil reserves at Teapot Dome, Wyoming.

Linking indulgence with intolerance is prohibition. Its inception was intolerant—fundamental rural and puritan values foisted on an increasingly urbanized society. Its adoption led to a self-destructive indulgence, the law of might above right at the hands of racketeers, bootleggers, and corrupt officials. The Federal Council of Churches of Christ summed up the situation in a pamphlet of 1925. The "virtual nullification" of prohibition signified "something more deep than administrative inefficiency and failure." Public tolerance of gangsters implied a lack of respect for law and order. Its disrespect developed inevitably into contempt for the conventional democratic processes.

—THREE—

THE REVENGERS' TRAGEDY

OF ALL THE CITIES IN THE UNITED STATES in which prohibition was derided and defied, one—Chicago—became, and has remained, much more notorious than the others. In Chicago the illegal trade in liquor during the twenties became a huge industry. It corrupted the police and city government. It led to a war of terror among rival gangs characterized by barefaced breaches of the law and crimes ranging from extortion and theft to white slavery and murder. In 1930 Major General Milton J. Foreman, returning from the Far East, told the *Chicago Post* of May 16 how the fame of Al Capone and other gangsters had spread to Java, Burma, and French Indochina: "People the world over believe they would be shot down by machine guns five minutes after their arrival in Chicago." Why especially in Chicago when the rest of America was also evading prohibition?

The significance of prohibition for Chicago lies less in what it was than in when it happened. Detroit, which was closer to Canada and more convenient for smuggling enterprises than Chicago, had its share of gangs, notably the notorious Purple Gang. And it was a crucial city in America's industrial economy with a volatile immigrant population. But it never acquired the reputation or the problems of Chicago. The difference is not that Detroit suffered state-imposed prohibition for two years before national prohibition came into effect, that it had already developed the capacity and complaisancy to confound the law without recourse to violent lawlessness. It is not that it had a dress rehearsal before the first night. The true difference lies in the nature of the Chicago underworld. Prohibition was imposed on Chicago at a crucial stage in the development of organized crime there. It was imposed at a time when a comparatively recent immigrant group, the Italian, was making its bid for full acculturation in, and control of, its new environment. That new environment was largely determined by organized and syndicated crime, hitherto the preserve of Jewish and Irish gangs.

———— ◆ ————

Joseph L. Albini in *The American Mafia* (1971) has distinguished between organized crime and syndicated crime. Whereas petty crimes, such as shoplifting, are the province of the individual, larger crimes, such as backmail, extortion, kidnapping, and hijacking, require organization. If the crime is politically motivated, like the guerrilla activities of John Brown at Harper's Ferry or the Ku Klux Klan, or, if it is psychologically motivated, like the terrorist activities of motorcyclist gangs, organization is a prerequisite. Organized crime and syndicated crime are not, however, synonymous. Organized crime is not dependent on a syndicate; but syndicated crime cannot exist without organized crime. It is the syndicates that provide illegal services, such as prostitution and gambling, or illicit goods, such as alcohol and narcotics. The syndicate exists to protect production and consumption, wholesale and retail. It does so by monopoly or by compromise, sometimes achieved by attack on a rival but always by the defense of bribing officials.

The Chicago underworld was well established, and its ranks of thieves, burglars, pickpockets, counterfeiters, prostitutes, and gunmen were organized in rings, long before the establishment of the police force in 1835. That the task of the police in combating organized crime was truly impossible can be easily demonstrated by a glance at the statistics. As late as 1854 there were only nine men in the force for a city with a population of eighty thousand. Crime syndicates were instituted after 1855, when the numbers of policemen rose to eighty and bribery became a prerequisite of organized crime. The most famous of the early syndicates was that of Roger Plant, whose vice resort was maintained with covert support from the police, whom he paid. Another syndicate was that of Mike McDonald, a Chicago gambling boss who ran a dive, the Store, and a newspaper, the *Chicago Globe*, in the 1870s.

It was in this period that the incipient friendship of political machines and gangs for mutual protection and profit held firm and grasped the government of several large cities. Politicians courting an ethnic group required the approval of the dominant gangster in the neighborhood. Organized crime was the prime source of funds, party workers, poll watchers, and illegal, but essential, sources of support. In exchange for his financial and physical protection of politicians the gang boss expected political protection for his own activities. However, ties of affection and ethnic solidarity were of more lasting consequence than any formal trade of services rendered. Mike McDonald's authority was such that he could ensure the election of Carter H. Harrison (Sr.) as mayor of Chicago in 1879.

In the early twentieth century the leading syndicate operators were Mont Tennes, who ran handbook gambling in thirty Chicago poolrooms from the Payne Racing Service of Cincinnati, and two aldermen from the First Ward. Michael Kenna, called "Hinky Dink" on account of his diminutive size, and John Joseph Coughlin, known as "Bathhouse John," not only provided political protection for syndicates but probably also owned saloons and dance halls in other people's names which hosted nefarious activities. Another alderman, Johnny Rogers, ran a gambling syndicate on the West Side and Jim O'Leary ran gambling on the stockyards on the South Side.

Their syndicates preyed on the new immigrants. But immigrants did not simply remain clients.

The immigrant from southern, central, and eastern Europe, having at first no facility in English, was deaf and dumb to his environment beyond the ghetto. But he was not blind nor deprived of his senses of touch and smell. The tenements, with their poverty and crime, were real enough and the affluence of the opulent plutocracy beyond was alluring. Most people in the city ghettos were "poor working stiffs"—artisans, shop assistants, or clerks—engaged for menial tasks at low fees. Some acquired an education and entered a profession. Some rose in business or politics, whether local government or labor union, where their ethnic origins could be put to commercial or electoral advantage. These entrepreneurs by and large were not considered respectable: they were closely linked with the demimonde of sport, particularly boxing, and nightlife and entertainment.

Organized crime was, therefore, an important part of acculturation for some groups. It provided the most rapid route of escape from ethnic slums. A typical ghetto pattern was for three sons to become, respectively, a boxer, a gangster, and a politician, and this is what happened to the three Miller brothers of Chicago's West Side Jewish ghetto.

Gangsters were genuinely respected in lower-class immigrant neighborhoods. They were gregarious and generous and their morality was imbued with sentimentality in local myths, which transformed them into Robin Hoods robbing the rich to aid the poor. They were heroes to be admired. Davy Miller himself said, "Maybe I am a hero to the young folks among my people, but it's not because I'm a gangster. It's because I've always been ready to help all or any of them in a pinch."

But there was another sense in which gangsters' wealth was shared. Many people supplemented their wages with part-time work for criminals. Taxi drivers, hotel bell boys, policemen, janitors, and shoeshine boys, among others, helped bootleggers and prostitutes ply their wares. Defense lawyers, tax accountants, bailbondsmen, bailiffs, policemen, and judges provided expert support for criminals that could be both legal and illegal.

In general parlance the gangsters' businesses, whether syndicates or organizations, were rackets. The term "racket," meaning an extortionate means of raising money, originated in the late nineteenth century. Courtenay Terrett in *Only Saps Work* (1930) notes its resemblance to the rack, an instrument of slow torture; to the biblical word *raca*, meaning contemptible and worthless; and a Levantine drink, *arrack*. It was certainly a vaudeville term for an easy way of making a living. In Italian *ricatto* is the word for blackmail. But its first English association with criminals was in New York during the 1890s. Gangsters held gala benefits for social and political clubs that were so boisterous and rowdy that the noise and commotion really was a racket. They compelled businessmen to buy blocks of tickets for these galas. But they had no interest in whether or not the ticket holders turned up at the event, hence the system of extortion by racketerring. In the early twentieth century the term came to mean, precisely, obtaining money for protection by threats, and by the 1920s, more generally, illegal buying and selling of a particular commodity. The din from Chicago dives was described as a racket in the local press.

F. L. Hostetter of the Employers' Association in Chicago circulated a report on the protection rackets there on December 10, 1927. He listed twenty-three separate lines of business exploited by racketeers including window cleaning, machinery moving, cleaning and dyeing, ash and rubbish hauling, dental laboratories, groceries and delicatessens, and garages. He believed, "The gunman and gangster are, at the present time, actually in control of the destinies of over ninety necessary economic activities." The Employers' Association of Chicago estimated that the annual cost of rackets was $136 million in increased prices passed on to the customer, about forty-five dollars per person.

The most notorious racket was that of the laundering industry. Simon J. Gorman became "czar" of the laundry business as labor secretary of the Chicago Laundry Owners' Association, the Chicago Wet and Dry Laundry Owners' Association, the Chicago Linen Supply Company, the Chicago Hand Laundry Owners' Association, and the Laundry Service Association of Chicago, all of which had agreements with the Teamsters' Union.

The Irish predominated in labor racketeering—a natural result of their importance in organized labor—and gambling syndicates. The first base was ownership of a saloon. Irish saloons were exclusively for male society and provided prostitutes and gambling for men's pleasure. Thus they adopted more easily to the ambience of the underworld than, for example, the old German beer gardens, which provided recreation for the whole family. Many senior police officers were Irish and had risen by attaching themselves to various political factions. As Mark Haller, the criminologist, explains, "A complex system of Irish politicians, gamblers and police shared in the profits of gambling, protected gambling interests and built careers in the police department or city politics." But the Irish monopoly could not last indefinitely. Prohibition provided an opportunity for others. By the end of the 1920s racketeering and bootlegging were almost synonymous in everyday speech.

———————◆◆———————

The most influential transitional figure between the prewar and postwar worlds of syndicated crime was Jim Colosimo.

"Big Jim" Colosimo entered the United States as a child. An immigrant from southern Italy, from either Abruzzi or Calabria, he had a varied career as a pimp, thief, and even streetsweeper in the Levee. The Levee was the central district for crime and vice in Chicago, situated between Twenty-second and Eighteenth streets to the north and south and between Wabash and Clark in the west and east. Colosimo organized other streetsweepers in the First Ward into a voting bloc, and thus his authority was recognized by the political machine of Alderman Michael ("Hinky Dink") Kenna and John Joseph ("Bathhouse John") Coughlin, under whose protection he flourished.

Colosimo's business success in the Levee began with his marriage to a madam, Victoria Moresco, in 1902. In partnership with Maurice Van Bever, he organized brothels, gambling houses, and saloons, one after the other, until he had virtual control of the Levee. His chain of brothels alone provided him with an average annual income of $600,000.

Colosimo's successes attracted the rapacity of *La Mano Nero*, the Black Hand. Fred J. Cook and Gaia Servadio, historians of the Mafia, assume that *La Mano Nero* was a criminal conspiracy associated with the Mafia. Others, like Joseph L. Albini and Francis A. J. and Elizabeth Ianni, describe it as a limited, if crude, form of extortion that started in Italy. According to them, small, unattached *cosche*, or gangs, sent extortion notes to Italian businessmen threatening bombing attacks unless ransom money was surrendered and signed them with the emblem of a black hand. This particular protection racket was confined to Italians and widespread among them. For instance, in May 1915 there were fifty-five Black Hand bombings in Chicago. Thus, in the natural course of things, as his business flourished, Colosimo became a target of Black Hand demands. At first he accommodated them. But he was not, then, a tolerant man and, in 1909, he called in his wife's nephew from New York, Johnny Torrio, to deal with the Black Hand decisively. Torrio arranged ambushes for the Black Handers while they were collecting the loot and the demands petered out.

By 1910 the Levee was so notorious that it had become a target of progressive reformers. To placate public protests the Democratic mayor, Carter H. Harrison, (Jr.), determined to clean it up. Privately he opined that a single center for prostitution and gambling was the optimum way of keeping the lid tight on urban vice and crime. He knew that closing down the Levee would disperse criminal elements throughout the city, and, indeed, this was what happened. Johnny Torrio, however, was less disturbed by these attempts at reform from the respectable middle class than the changing pattern of social behavior of Colosimo's affluent clientele. Torrio believed that the future of organized vice lay in the suburbs rather than the city center, anyway, not on account of progressive reform, but as a result of the increasing number of cars on the roads. Between 1908 and 1913 the number of automobiles in the United States was to increase ten times to 1,192,262. And opulent clients preferred to travel in their cars to the suburbs for their pleasures rather than to the downtown areas. The suburbs were out of reach of busybody municipal reformers, accessible to the new, reckless rich, and poorly policed.

By the time of the second reform wave in Chicago of November 1912, Colosimo and Torrio had secured the compliance of the "boy mayor," John Patton, of the incorporated village of Burnham, eighteen miles from the Levee, and established a roadhouse there. It was open twenty-four hours a day: in the first year it took nine thousand dollars a month. Colosimo and Torrio also acquired the Speedway Inn and put "Jew Kid" Grabiner in charge. Both the Burnham and Speedway inns were only a few feet from the Indiana line. In the event of a raid the prostitutes could get across before the police had time to arrest them. In addition Torrio established a vice resort in Stickney, a village eight miles west of the Levee, at the Shadow Inn. And whereas Torrio took half the profits of the Burnham and Speedway inns, he took complete profits of his own saloon at 2222 South Wabash Avenue, the Four Deuces.

Colosimo's world was apart from, and subversive of, the established order of society. Politics was undermined not only by criminal activities but the mutual friendship of criminals and politicians that broke down the clear line between right and wrong, legality and criminality, private profit and public morality. The connecting bond between gangster and politician was ward politics, which depended on intimacy and personal loyalty. These friendships made a political machine work but undermined the essential impartiality and formality of government. Colosimo's various enterprises were now so extensive he no longer depended on the political patronage of Coughlin and Kenna. Instead they depended on him.

Sated, Colosimo turned over the actual running of his illicit businesses to Torrio and concentrated on a sideline, Colosimo's Café, opened in 1910 at 2126 South Wabash Avenue. He was interested more in its social cachet than its cash returns. The underworld could scarcely be distinguished from the world of show business. The celebrities at Colosimo's included John Barrymore, Amelita Galli-Curci, Mary Garden, Al Jolson, John McCormack, Luisa Tetrazzini, and Sophie Tucker. The entertainment was a mixture of cabaret, jazz, and songs from operettas.

At his café Jim Colosimo met a young soprano, Dale Winter, whom he promoted, fell in love with, and planned to transform into an opera singer. He left his wife and they were divorced on March 20, 1920. She married a gangster twenty years younger than herself, Antonio Villani. He married Dale Winter three weeks later. "This is the real thing," he told his nephew. "It's your funeral," Torrio was supposed to have replied. Colosimo's infatuation with a good girl weakened his reputation and resolution.

In 1920 Torrio urged the illicit liquor trade on Colosimo. He believed prohibition could provide a new frontier of crime. Colosimo showed none of the foresight he had demonstrated in 1912. Torrio sensed the opportunities for wealth and power bootlegging and speakeasies could provide. He also appreciated the hazards. He was most concerned about the danger of internecine feuds among the gangs, and in anticipation of such antagonism he wanted a prearranged and amicable apportionment of territories. What was required was the old forcefulness of Colosimo, hitherto a most eminent man in the underworld, to bring the others to heel. This Colosimo could no longer supply.

Jim Colosimo was shot and killed in the vestibule of his restaurant on May 11, 1920. The fatal bullet had penetrated his right ear. Although he had left home that day with $150,000, when the police examined the body they found only small change in his pockets. Colosimo was supposed to have a fortune worth $500,000 but it had, apparently, dwindled to a mere $67,500 in cash and bonds, jewelry—mainly diamonds—valued at $8,894, and fifteen barrels of whiskey. The principal beneficiary was not his new wife, whom he adored. The second Mrs. Colosimo learned she should have waited a year after the divorce to marry. The first Mrs. Colosimo was awarded $12,000, the second Mrs. Colosimo only $6,000. Thus Dale Winter returned to the stage and succeeded Edith Day in the operetta *Irene* on Broadway. The bulk of what was found of Jim Colosimo's fortune went to his father, Luigi. However, the real beneficiary was Johnny Torrio.

Almost certainly Colosimo was the victim of his nephew's rapacity. Of course the truth never emerged. Torrio was protected by *omertà*, the code of silence among the peer group which preserved the guilty from exposure. The name derives from *omu*, a word in Sicilian dialect meaning man. *Omertá* was the way of proving one's manliness by silence. Another gangster, Dion O'Banion, sarcastically referred to it as "Chicago amnesia."

On the day of the murder, police intercepted the New York gangster, Frank Uale or Yale, in Chicago as he was about to board a train for New York. He was soon released for lack of evidence of complicity but rumor spread that he had been paid ten thousand dollars by Torrio to dispatch his unfortunate uncle. Torrio's ascendancy was aided by his able lieutenant, a friend of his New York youth, recently arrived in Chicago. The friend was Al Capone.

In his life-style Colosimo had set the pattern for gangsters of the future. Colosimo was the prototype of the boss who was a natty dresser, enjoyed wearing diamonds and cultivated a style of wide-brimmed hats. This boss did not necessarily carry a gun but was always surrounded by bodyguards who did. He was the man whose wealth depended in part on prostitution and who might himself have a mistress but who usually had an almost morbid attachment to his wife and family. Colosimo, his nephew, Johnny Torrio, and Torrio's rival, Dion O'Banion, were all devoted to their wives, and Al Capone doted on his son. These, too, were the men who aspired to high society and the worlds of fashion and entertainment, who sometimes developed a legitimate sideline such as Colosimo with his café and O'Banion with his flower shop, as an expression of spontaneous, sentimental yearning for a lost world from which they were excluded by the harsh exigencies of their chosen profession.

Even in his death Colosimo set a precedent as potent as his life-style. Although George Cardinal Mundelein refused Christian burial to Colosimo's body, supposedly because he had been a gangster, Father Philip F. Mahany implied in the *Chicago American* that the real reasons were Colosimo's absenteeism from church services and the fact that he was divorced and had married again. Nevertheless, a Presbyterian, the Reverend Pasquall De Carol, officiated at a private ceremony in Colosimo's home on Vernon Avenue. The funeral procession to Oakwood cemetery on May 14, 1920, was splendid.

Colosimo's funeral inaugurated a whole series of ostentatious funerals in which almost as many cars were used to carry the floral tributes as to ferry the mourners. The mourners themselves included a host of civic dignitaries and leaders of allied and rival gangs, who had probably had a part in the murder of the deceased. Colosimo's funeral brought together representatives of the goverance of Chicago

outside the Gold Coast: eight aldermen, three judges, a congressman, and three singers of the Chicago Opera and nine resort
keepers. Professional politicians realized that their presence at gangsters' funerals attested to their close connections with the deceased
and therefore attended them assiduously. Johnny Powers never
missed an important funeral in over thirty years as a ward boss.

But if Colosimo's style had set a pattern for the future his particular form of influence was doomed. His assassination brought one
era of the underworld to an end. The succession of Torrio inaugurated a new one.

Prohibition was an upheaval for American society in general. In
Chicago it was a secondary disturbance compared with the competition of immigrant groups in organized crime. Its importance lies in
the fact that it provided a new incentive for all immigrants and for
the Italians a unique opportunity that would not recur. They could
break the Irish monopoly.

A principal argument of both progressives and prohibitionists
before 1920 had been that easily available liquor impeded the assimilation of immigrants. Ironically, the reverse was true, but the existing acculturation to a world of crime was not what progressives and
prohibitionists intended for immigrants. Even more ironically, under
national prohibition this perverse sort of assimilation became more
likely than before.

According to the census of 1920, 2,701,705 people were living in
Chicago, of whom as many as 1,946,298, about 72 percent, were
first- or second-generation immigrants. The ethnic composition of
these new Americans was: Slavic and Lettic, 28.1 percent; German,
23.5; British, 18.4; Scandinavian, 9.7; Jewish, Magyar, Armenian,
9.5; Latin and Greek, 8.5; and mixed or unknown, 2.3. It was from
the ranks of these struggling immigrants that the new master criminals would emerge.

A study of the leaders of organized crime in Chicago during
prohibition by William F. Ogburn and Clark Tibbits showed that
none were both native and white or of native and white parents: 31
percent came from Italian backgrounds; 29 percent were Irish; 20
percent were Jewish; and 12 percent were black. Moreover these
ethnic groups now associated with organized crime were composed
of recent migrants who had come from those places most hostile to

government. The Italians had fled feuds in southern Italy and Sicily; the Irish excoriated British rule in Ireland; the Jews had been subject to purges in Russia and eastern Europe; and the blacks had been denied political, social, and economic equality in the American South. "There was," says Mark Haller, the criminologist, "a relationship between the cultural factors that sanctioned violence and private revenge in Europe and the factors that sanctioned the violence with which Italian bootleggers worked their way into a central position in Chicago's organized crime." Italians from the south and Sicily had the highest rate of murders in Europe.

The Italians' preeminence in the organized subversion of prohibition depended on a unique combination of American and Italian cultural values in a special situation. The new gangsters retained some of the cultural values of southern Italy: devotion to parents and family; indifference to a weak and alien political system; zeal for individual honor that had to be maintained at all costs. They also retained the lessons their ethnic group had learned in the new culture: superiority of local interests to all others; ethnic solidarity based on ties of kinship; the code of silence. But they learned, too, from the new culture around them that, as far as society was concerned, the recent immigrant had no past and, for his future, crime could ensure heroic status. In this novel situation the ethnic ghetto provided the base, the street-corner gangs of the second generation provided the organization, and widespread political and municipal corruption provided the example for the young gangster. Italian gangsters were more single-minded than the others. And their most basic instinct, a lust for revenge at all costs, while it corruscated them, confirmed their complete dedication to their ends.

In the 1920s the new gold was the amber hue of whiskey.

In 1920 the Terrible Gennas, a gang of six Sicilian brothers on the South Side of Chicago, had developed sufficient political weight from a career of payroll robbery and service to political bosses to seek and obtain a government license for handling industrial liquor. The Gennas (Sam, Vincenzo, Pete, "Bloody Angelo," Antonio, and Mike the Devil) bought seven thousand dollars' worth of denatured alcohol from federal sources and, from a three-story warehouse at 1022 West Taylor Street, distributed a small quantity for legitimate uses. The bulk was distilled a second time, colored and flavored to resemble whiskey, brandy, and other spirits, and sold at six or three dollars a gallon.

Although the liquor was poisonous, the Gennas' plant on Taylor Street could not begin to meet the demand for it. To do so they revolutionized the local economy. Local inhabitants were persuaded to install copper stills in their kitchens, and given corn sugar and instructions on how to extract alcohol. They were paid fifteen dollars a day for their complaisant "cooking." Tony Genna later instituted a change in the bootlegging industry from household to factory manufacture by substituting alcohol recooking for proper distilling from mash. Distilling was a small-scale process by which one gallon of alcohol was produced from ten gallons of mash. Moreover, it could be easily detected by the authorities by its smell. By comparison, recooking was cost effective: it produced nearly double its original volume.

In addition to local production large quantities of beer and whiskey were imported from Joliet, Illinois, from Ontario, and from the states of Florida, Georgia, Kentucky, and Michigan. In early 1923 Chicago breweries were producing eighteen thousand barrels of beer a week. The wholesale price varied between thirty and sixty dollars a barrel but the usual price was fifty dollars. The annual wholesale value of beer was about $28 million. ·

On October 19, 1923, Puro Products, or West Hammond brewery, was tried for violation of the Volstead Act in the name of W. R. Strook, a former federal marshal, who admitted ownership of one half of the shares, and Timothy J. Mullen, an attorney, who held one share of the stock. The trial exposed new arrangements in the brewing industry in general and Johnny Torrio's part in them in particular. For it was the base of Johnny Torrio's syndicate. Brewers who wanted to stay in the business were taking on gangsters as partners to peddle and protect their product. Joseph Stenson and his brothers had already acquired Terry Druggan and Frankie Lake as partners in their five breweries (the Gambrinius, the Standard, the George Hoffman, the Pfeiffer, and the Stege). In 1920 they also took on Johnny Torrio as a fourth partner and he persuaded them to buy four more (the Manhattan, the Best, the Sieben, and the West Hammond). They sold beer at fifty dollars a barrel and this fee included protection for the speakeasy proprietor.

There were about six thousand establishments in Chicago licensed to sell soft drinks under regulations provided by city ordinance. The license fee was about a tenth of that paid by saloonkeepers before prohibition. Of course, the new establishments were really saloons. They charged seventy-five cents a glass for whiskey and twenty-five cents for beer, whereas before prohibition those prices had been, respectively, fifteen cents and five cents.

The police were not slow to appreciate the new position. Charles C. Fitzmorris, Chicago's chief of police during the early years of prohibition, declared, "Sixty percent of my police are in the bootleg business." Police captains received a bribe of five dollars a barrel from gangsters for each barrel sold in their district. The total of bribes paid to police officers and public officials during the twenties was at least $5 million a year and perhaps more than $10 million.

In the beginning prohibition opened opportunities for all sorts of individuals and groups, not only the Italians. By the mid-1920s certain coalitions of interest were clearly visible. Once organized prostitution was dispersed throughout the city, the Jews, who had hitherto remained on the periphery of the Chicago underworld, began to operate vice resorts on the South and West sides. Before and during prohibition their main function, however, was to provide support services for organized crime. They acted as bailbondsmen, as fences, as defense attorneys. In each category their share was disproportionate to the size of their ethnic group.

Some of the bootleggers were Irish, one set of O'Donnell brothers on the far West Side and another on the South Side. The West Side O'Donnells were William ("Klondike"), Myles, and Bernard. The South Side O'Donnells were Ed ("Spike"), Steve, Walter, and Tommy. Southwest of the stockyards was a joint Polish and Irish gang led by "Pollack" Joe Saltis and Frank McErlane. On the near North Side a major group of former burglars and footpads was led in turn by men from different ethnic groups: Dion O'Banion (Irish); Earl ("Hymie") Weiss and George ("Bugs") Moran (Polish); and Jack Zuta and the Gusenberg brothers (Jewish).

O'Banion was born in Aurora, Illinois, but raised in the North Side's Little Sicily, "Little Hell." Once an Irish shantytown called Kilgubbin, it had been infiltrated by Sicilian immigrants at the turn of the century. It surpassed the Levee for vice and crime, and every year there were at least a dozen and sometimes a score of violent deaths. O'Banion joined the Market Streeters, a gang of youths, graduated to slugger for the *Chicago Herald Examiner* during the newspaper circulation wars, and became an inexpert safecracker. Then he, too, acquired a share in the Sieben brewery, along with the original owner, Joseph Stenson, and Stenson's new partner, Johnny

Torrio. Whereas Colosimo had enjoyed his café, the lighter side of O'Banion's character was expressed by his fond partnership in a flower shop at 738 North State Street. It was a profitable sideline, of course, for O'Banion supplied the grand funerals of assassinated gangsters with their masses of wreaths and floral tributes. Apart from this the only thing warm about him was his "sunny brutality," his delight in killing.

The major Italian bootlegging gang associated with John Torrio and Al Capone was based on firm foundations of vice and gambling resorts on the South Side. It was not entirely Italian, since it included Frankie Lake and Terry Druggan (Irish), who organized brewing for them, and Jack Guzik (Jewish), who was their principal business manager.

Bootlegging was Torrio's main business and he took full advantage of the situation whereby many different municipal governments shared the metropolitan region of Chicago. Hence Torrio concentrated on control of the suburbs: Cicero, Burnham, River Forest. With the aid of Capone he established himself as Colosimo's successor. Other suburbs—Stickney and Forest Park—became resorts for vice, and their officials, Joseph Z. Klenha (village president of Cicero), Theodore Svoboda (police chief), as well as Sheriff Peter B. Hoffman and State's Attorney Robert E. Crowe, proved subservient to Torrio, as Bathhouse John and Hinky Dink had been to Colosimo.

If Colosimo was a transitional figure in the American underworld Torrio was the first of the new master criminals. John Kobler in his biography of Al Capone describes him as "a criminal far ahead of his time. He anticipated by at least two decades the organization gangster who would forgo personal vendettas, stooping to murder only as a practical necessity . . . who, guided by corporation counsel, would funnel unlawful profits into lawful channels until, a millionaire, his financial stance was indistinguishable from those of reputable businessmen."

Torrio approached other gang leaders with a simple proposition. Their traditional interests in extortion and robbery, with their piecemeal profits, did not justify the risks compared with the immense profits to be had from bootlegging. The prerequisite was the principle of territorial integrity. Bars and brothels within one gang's territory should buy only from their particular beer concessionaire. Despite the various ethnic, political, and commercial rivalries, Torrio kept the gangs at peace for about three years. The gangs had their specialties. Torrio's syndicate handled beer; O'Banion's North Side gang smuggled whiskey from Canada; the Gennas distilled spirits. Since they needed to provide their clients with both beer and spirits they agreed each could also serve the other. Torrio and O'Banion exchanged liquors and the Gennas afforded safe passage through Little Italy for Torrio's beer trucks.

But in 1923 everything began to go wrong. The thieves fell out. Their old rivalries were intensified at the prospect of fantastic profits, and the explosion came when they needed one another most.

———————◆◆———————

In 1923 the corrupt administration of William ("Big Bill") Thompson, mayor since 1915, was challenged and everything changed. William E. Dever was the candidate of reformers of both Republican and Democratic parties, although he stood as a Democrat. Dever had served the city council as a lawyer and the superior and appellate courts as a judge. Thompson withdrew from the primary elections and Dever was elected mayor.

Dever was not a convinced dry but was determined to enforce the law because it was the law. Like other reformers he was dismayed by so much blatant corruption. Dever saw that more than prohibition was at stake when he said, "The supreme issue is the cynicism that has taken hold of the body politic." He understood the complex character of the Chicago electorate and its conflicting interests and that, whatever the merits of prohibition, it made a great deal of difference what people thought of it: "Everyone knows that there is an unparalleled contempt for law and order, and that it is because public officials have not been enforcing the law." As Henry Barrett Chamberlin explains, his mayoralty produced turmoil: "The transfer of authority caused a revolution in the underworld; the old system of protection was destroyed. None could be sure he was 'in' anywhere; therefore competition was free and easy."

On June 1, 1923, Morgan Collins, the new chief of police who cooperated closely with Dever, transferred seventeen captains and three lieutenants from one precinct to another to break their ties with, and usefulness to, the underworld. These transfers upset the status quo of the underworld and caused an upheaval in it. Then on August 6, 1923, there were more than eight hundred arrests for violations of the liquor laws in soft-drink parlors as part of the Dever-Collins campaign to clean up the city.

Johnny Torrio needed to increase orders to keep his breweries busy and began to invade the territory of the South Side O'Donnells. At first, the South Side O'Donnells could not challenge Torrio successfully and the two operations ran side by side. But after the pardon and release of their leader, Spike O'Donnell, from Joliet Penitentiary, Illinois, in mid-1923 they would not accept this situation indefinitely.

When Torrio offered saloonkeepers beer at a reduced rate of forty dollars a barrel, the South Side O'Donnells competed openly with him for the territory, fighting his allies there, the Saltis-McErlane gang. They sold a better beer and tried to cut in on his enclaves in the Stockyards and New City. Torrio cut his prices, selling beer for less than ten dollars a barrel. The O'Donnells retaliated by threatening saloonkeepers who bought from Torrio. Thus began the first beer war. One of their strong-arm gorillas, Jerry O'Connor, was shot dead on the night of September 7, 1923, at the saloon of Joseph Klepka, 5358 South Lincoln Street, during his tour to terrorize saloon owners. Two men were arrested but the police chief, Morgan Collins, had to let them go for lack of evidence. On September 17, 1923, "Georgie" Meghan and George ("Sport") Bucher, henchmen and beer drummers for the O'Donnells, who had said they would reveal the names of O'Connor's murderers, were themselves killed in separate incidents.

Dever began to revoke more and more licenses. On September 28, 1923, he revoked the licenses of sixteen soft-drink parlors, on September 29 he revoked thirteen more, and on September 30 another thirty-four. In the first two days of October he revoked eighty-nine and eighty licenses and continued until on one single day almost two hundred parlors were closed. By law anyone whose license was so revoked could never have it restored if the charges against him were upheld. Moreover the parlors could not be used for any purposes for at least sixty and perhaps ninety days after the license had been withdrawn. When they were reopened they could only be used for a completely different and legal purpose. Whereas there had been sixty thousand saloons open at the beginning of the year, by December 1, 1923, the soft-drink licenses of two thousand had been revoked. Another three thousand had closed on account of poor business and only one thousand remained open under careful police scrutiny. On the whole the Chicago press supported Dever's policies, and the newspapers that did not praised his courage. Soon speakeasies replaced the supposed soft-drink parlors.

Open warfare between the gangs began with a hijacking incident. Two bootleggers, Morrie Keane and William Egan, planned to invade Torrio's territory in December 1923. One night they came from Joliet with three truckloads of beer and were stopped at the Sag, a lonely slope, by Torrio's men, Walter Stevens, Daniel McFall, and his ally, Frank McErlane. After they had secured the beer the gunmen took them for a ride. They forced Keane and Egan into McErlane's car, riddled their bodies with bullets, and dumped them by the side of the road. McErlane was subsequently arrested, held in the Sherman Hotel rather than a police station, and released.

The conclusion of the beer war was a complete triumph for Torrio. His enemies, the South Side O'Donnells, were all imprisoned at one time or another and two were indicted. Torrio went free. His man, Daniel McFall, was arrested for the murder of Jerry O'Connor, released on bail, and then disappeared. Torrio's influence was so great that he could even obtain pardons for the convicted panderers Harry and Alma Cusick from Governor Len Small. Harry Cusick was a crucial man in Torrio's empire. He was the payoff man in downtown Chicago. It was his office in the Loop that actually paid those police still faithful to him for protecting his vice resorts.

———◆———

Despite his victory, Torrio looked, as always, to the future. Torrio had long recognized the importance of the suburbs for the stability of organized crime. Now they were crucial if the attempts at reform were to be evaded successfully.

Hitherto, Cicero, a dormitory town of sixty thousand residents, had been politically corrupt but comparatively free of vice and crime. Torrio and Capone had already done business there and made a deal with the West Side O'Donnells, whose fief it was. In 1924 Torrio and Capone chose Cicero as a base beyond the reach of Dever and Collins. To secure it in perpetuity they needed to ensure the victory of their political allies, Joseph Z. Klenha, the village president, and Boss Eddie Vogel, in the elections of 1924. However, they were faced with extraordinary competition. In April 1924 the corrupt Democratic machine decided to challenge Klenha. Previously he had controlled Cicero in elections contested between the Citizens' party and the People's party. Beer runners eager to take control of supplies away from Torrio allied themselves with the Democrats. To help them the election commissioner, Anthony Czarnecki, simply struck the names of three thousand known Republicans off the electoral role; he discharged the official clerks, judges, and watchers and appointed new ones in their place.

However, neither Torrio nor Capone refrained from counterattack. On the Monday before the polling day, Thursday, their gunmen beat up William K. Pflaum, the Democratic candidate for clerk, and opened fire on his office. To ensure the election of the Republican ticket they instigated a reign of terror on polling day. Henry Barret Chamberlin described the events: "Automobiles filled with gunmen paraded the streets, slugging and kidnapping election workers. Polling places were raided by armed thugs and ballots taken at the point of the gun from the hands of voters waiting to drop them into the box. Voters and workers were kidnapped, brought to Chicago, and held prisoners until the polls closed." One worker, Stanley Stanklevich, was held prisoner; another, Michael Gavin, was kidnapped and shot in both legs.

Judge Edward Jarecki ordered seventy patrolmen, two for each of thirty-five precincts, and five squads from the detective bureau and nine flivver squads to Cicero to drive the gangsters away and restore peace and order. Frank Capone, one of Al's brothers and a Torrio man who ran the Four Deuces Saloon, was killed in one fracas. His funeral was even more splendid than Colosimo's

A month after the notorious Cicero elections Torrio and Capone opened the Hawthorne Smoke Shop. Situated next to the Hawthorne Inn, it was an illegal betting shop operating under different names at different times. An average of $50,000 worth of bets a day were placed on horse races and the net profits were above $4 million a year. The number of gambling establishments in Cicero rose to 161.

———————◆—————

If Torrio was satisfied with the general scheme of things, the Terrible Gennas and the North Side gang were not. They were ambitious, predatory, and remorseless and openly challenged one another's rights. In early 1924 the North Side gang hijacked $100,000 worth of Canadian whiskey from a West Side railroad yard and then stole 1,750 barrels of bonded spirits from a Sibley warehouse. O'Banion then went further and hijacked a shipment of the Gennas worth about $30,000. They were only restrained from killing him in return by Mike Merlo, president of the *Unione Siciliana*, a key organization in the social and criminal world of Italian immigrants of the 1920s.

In May 1924 O'Banion told Torrio and Capone that he wanted to sell them his share in the Stenson Sieben brewery for half a million dollars, and retire to Colorado. He admitted he dreaded the revenge of the Terrible Gennas. However, when Torrio and his men went to collect beer from the brewery on May 19 they met an unpleasant surprise. That day a police squad, led by Chief Morgan Collins and Captain Matthew Zwimmer, raided the Sieben Brewery and seized thirteen truckloads of beer. They arrested many gangsters, all of whom gave aliases but all of whom were recognized as representatives of different gangland territories: Johnny Torrio and Nick Juffra of the South Side, Dion O'Banion of the North Side, Louis Alterie of the Valley gang, Spike O'Donnell of the South Side. Among police and prosecutors, press and public, it was assumed that Torrio and O'Banion were the real operators of the Sieben plant.

Torrio deduced that O'Banion had known about the raid, had swindled him by inviting him there, and was, perhaps, in league with the police. Thus he initiated the first assassination in the revengers' tragedy.

Within the Italian immigrant community there existed two conflicting attitudes toward revenge. Both church and law condemned private revenge as an attempt by man to usurp the prerogative of God and the state. But everyone knew that the state's power to punish was poorly coordinated and often inefficient. Not only immigrants but native Americans as well knew that recourse to law for injuries sustained was both the sign and method of the weak. If private revenge was not sanctioned by the letter of the law it was supported by the spirit of personal honor. Thus there were three sorts of wrongs for which Italian communities would condone acts of retaliation: an injury committed treacherously; a wrong for which legal redress was out of the question; murder. Even in Italy in the late twentieth century Article 587 of the Italian Penal Code made special provisions for "homicides with honor as the motive."

On November 8, 1924, Mike Merlo, president of the *Unione Siciliana* in Chicago, died of cancer. The last opposition to the elimination of O'Banion was silenced. When Frank Yale, the New York head of the *Unione Siciliana*, attended Merlo's Chicago funeral he approved Angelo Genna as Merlo's successor. On November 10, O'Banion was killed in his own flower shop by three people he thought had come for flowers for Merlo's funeral. The Cook County coroner noted in the margin of the court record of the inquest: "Slayers not apprehended. John Scalise and Albert Anselmi and Frank Yale suspected, but never brought to trial." Hymie Weiss, who assumed leadership of the North Side gang, surmised that Torrio, Capone, and the Gennas had planned the assassination and that Mike Genna (not Frank Yale) had accompanied John Scalise and Albert Anselmi, new Sicilian immigrant killers, to carry it out.

Dion O'Banion was buried without a church service but in great state; his casket alone cost ten thousand dollars. The criticisms of churchmen like Dr. Thompson and Dr. A. J. McCartney, aghast at such ostentation for a criminal, did not deter a great throng from attending. Traffic along the north and east streets of the Loop was halted for twenty minutes while the cortege passed.

After a holiday in the South and the Caribbean Torrio returned to Chicago in January 1925 to stand trial in the Sieben brewery case. On January 23 he pleaded guilty and the federal judge, Adam Cliffe, allowed him five days to settle his affairs before passing sentence. On January 24 he and his wife, Ann, and his chauffeur, Robert Barton, were ambushed and fired upon in front of his house. Torrio was wounded in the jaw, the right arm, and the groin. For a time his condition was critical. He was held at the Jackson Park Hospital under maximum security by both police and Capone linked together in the common cause of preserving his life. He had escaped with his life only because the chambers of his assassin's gun were empty when it was time to make a getaway. Peter Veesaert, the seventeen-year-old son of a janitor, who watched the ambush from the doorway of an apartment building, identified Bugs Moran of the North Side gang as the man who had fired the first shot and had the courage to do so face to face. Moran was never indicted.

Within three weeks Torrio had recovered sufficiently to leave the hospital and reappear in court on the same day. The crime was Torrio's second proven conspiracy offense and it could carry a penalty of five years' imprisonment. However, Torrio was sentenced to only nine months in Du Page County jail and fined five thousand dollars. Edward O'Donnell was given eight months in Kane County jail and fined two thousand dollars. Two of the negligent policemen, Joseph Warszynski and Joseph Lanenfield, whose insignia Collins had torn off after the raid, were both imprisoned for three months. Other leading gangsters were given similar sentences. Cases against the twenty-three other defendants, including the other two policemen, were dismissed.

O'Banion's case, of course, had ended with his death. But not his cause. Torrio had unintentionally instigated more than the murder of O'Banion. Against his own political principles he instituted a blood feud between his syndicate and the North Side gang. Though he had been spared by chance and Capone would be spared by strategy, successive leaders of the North Side gang would be eliminated and the cycle of retribution would continue up to and beyond the St. Valentine's Day Massacre of 1929.

The murder of O'Banion also led to a feud between the Terrible Gennas and the North Side gang and this weakened Torrio's prestige. His treaties were wrecked beyond repair. Some gangsters, such as the South Side O'Donnells, had never really conceded Torrio's authority. Others, like O'Banion, had chafed at the bit. Although Torrio had dominated the underworld by his ruthless intelligence the Sieben brewery case damaged his prestige further. It made clear to public, police, and criminals that the new mayor, William E. Dever, and the chief of police, Morgan Collins, were not under his control. Dever's attacks on crime had upset the balance of power in the underworld. They invalidated the operation of Torrio's system. Torrio's personal prestige ensured his control of the Chicago gangs but depended on his remarkable record of immunity from prosecution. Now he had been arrested, indicted, tried, convicted, and sentenced.

In Page County jail, Waukegan, Torrio lived in comparative luxury under heavy security—blinds made of steel mesh so they would be bulletproof and constant patrols outside the cell. But in March 1925 at a gang conference in his cell Torrio transferred all his holdings to Capone. He expected no compensation or immunity for his retirement. But these possessions were by no means secure even for Capone. After his release in October 1925 Torrio and his wife immigrated to Italy. Torrio's methods of keeping gangsters at bay had failed. Capone was left to shift for himself. His methods, too, might fail. But they would have to be different to succeed.

—FOUR—

THE NEAPOLITAN SHRUG

THERE IS NOTHING MORE DISAPPOINTING than anticlimax. Chicago of the mid and late 1920s had all the ingredients necessary for novels, plays, and films in the gangster, crime-thriller, and whodunnit genres—all but one. When the story of Al ("Scarface") Capone is written for stage and screen, the audience can arrive late without fear of disappointment. They will certainly discover who did it: but they will not know what it is that he did. Spectators attending from the beginning will not know either. For, to this day, no one who has written about him knows for certain. That is to say, the many crimes of murder imputed to him remain a mystery. Circumstantial evidence and motives for the successive elimination of North Side gang leaders and other rivals abound. So, too, do alibis. In accumulating an empire of bootlegging, racketeering, prostitution, and gambling interests Capone was consistent in his criminal methods: bloody, bold, and resolute. But on the surface Scarface passed off everything with a shrug. Of only one of his most heinous crimes was he the actual perpetrator. He usually instigated death from a distance and then dismissed the deed. In shrugging off responsibility, in claiming

77

close ties with the recently deceased, he was conforming to an age-old tradition of Naples, his parents' home.

As early as 1593 the English writer Thomas Nashe noted this characteristic in his *The Unfortunate Traveller:* "The Neapolitan carrieth the bloodiest mind, and is the most secret fleering [sneering] murderer: whereupon it is grown to a common proverb, I'll give him the Neapolitan shrug, when one intends to play the villain, and make no boast of it." This was *omertà* with a vengeance. Despite his sustained conviction that he was one of the new men, Capone's methods were more mediaeval than modern, although they were contemporary also—like Mussolini's and Hitler's. Hence Bertolt Brecht in his *The Resistible Rise of Arturo Ui* was to parody the rise of fascism by setting a version of Hitler's story in Chicago's gangland.

Al Capone was the third of nine children of Gabriel and Teresa Caponi, Neapolitan immigrants to New York. He was almost certainly born in Brooklyn on January 17, 1899, although some of his biographers believe he was born in Italy, either in Naples itself or in Castel Amara, near Rome. Unlike other Italian gangsters he rarely paraded his ethnic origins. And he flatly denied an Italian nativity. For instance, Eleanor Patterson, a journalist of the *Washington Herald,* on January 18, 1930, reported her reception by Capone in his Miami home and his annoyance with the idea of returning to Italy: "What for should I live in Italy for? Why should I? My family, my wife, my kid, my racket—they're all in Chicago. I'm no Eye-talian. I was born in New York thirty-one years ago." He said his name was pronounced, "Ca-pone—just 'pone'—no 'e' in it." Like Buonaparte after he became Napoleon of course. In time Capone became an embarassment to his own ethnic group. The social historian Humbert S. Nelli explains that after the St. Valentine's Day Massacre of 1929, his most notorious crime, the Italian-language papers refused to print the name of Al Capone and covered the massacre without implying it was part of the beer wars in Chicago.

Wherever his birthplace, the social ambience in which he grew up was certainly the street-corner gangs and their feuds in New York City. Many leading gangsters in the 1920s had started as young thugs in New York: Johnny Torrio and Al Capone of Chicago, Abe Bertnstein and Harry Fleisher of Detroit's Purple Gang, and Charles ("King") Solomon of New England all graduated from the Lower East Side. Suspected of two murders and indicted for a third—the killing of "St. Louis Shorty" Woeifel on April 5, 1919,—Capone fled

New York to join Torrio, his old friend, who had moved to Chicago in 1909.

In the Roma Inn, a brothel in the Colosimo-Torrio syndicate, Capone was first employed as a towel boy, that is to say he had to keep the beds clean. Later his card read, "Alphonse Capone, second hand furniture dealer, 2220 South Wabash Avenue." And the premises, next to the Four Deuces, really were filled with junk. For eventually Capone managed the Four Deuces, and took a quarter of the profits from Colosimo's chain of brothels, about twenty-five thousand dollars in 1920. His first crimes in Chicago to come before a court were keeping a disorderly house and keeping slot machines, respectively cases 23031 and 23032, to which he pleaded guilty on April 14, 1921, and was fined a total of a hundred and fifty dollars with twenty dollars costs by Judge Friend. In these cases and for the murder of Woeifel in New York he was indicted under the name of Al Brown. To his friends he was "Snorky."

But his most common title was Scarface. Capone's three facial scars were the result of an attack by Frank Galluccio at the Harvard Inn, Brooklyn, years earlier. One was oblique, extending four inches across his cheek below his left ear; another was vertical, extending two and a half inches on the left side of his jaw; the third was oblique, extending two and a half inches on the left of his neck. Years later he made Galluccio a bodyguard in a spontaneous gesture of forgiveness. But he was still embarrassed by the scars and ashamed of how he had received them. Therefore he pretended they had been caused by shrapnel piercing the skin during the war when he was in France. Of course, he had never fought in the services at all.

———◆———

After the blood feud with the North Side gang of the late Dion O'Banion was instigated by Torrio, who then withdrew from the fray, Capone inherited Torrio's position and determined, like his predecessor, to establish a federated system of organized crime between all interested parties. The gangs realigned for a time. The Irish, Polish, and Jewish gangsters of the North Side fell in with O'Banion's successor, Hymie Weiss (born Wajiechowski). So, too, did the West Side O'Donnells and the Saltis-McErlane gang, which had once sided with Torrio. The Sicilians and the Gennas and Terry Druggan and Frankie Lake threw in their lot with Capone. Outsiders, like Ralph Sheldon's gang, took advantage of the ebb and flow in the underworld and changed sides back and forth. This was the period of the beer wars.

Between 1922 and 1926, 215 gangsters were killed in Chicago in the course of their internecine feuds. Another 160 were killed by the police. In 1926 between January and October 42 gangsters were killed inside city limits, another 54 were killed in Cook County—all by gangsters—and 60 others were killed in affrays with the police. Then the rate of killings increased. Between 1927 and 1930, 227 gangsters died, many of them on the city streets.

The gangs' weapons were two: the machine gun and the bomb. The machine gun was developed by Brigadier General John T. Thompson in 1920, too late to be used in the trenches of the First World War. Weighing eight and a half pounds, it was light enough to be carried by a child. It could fire up to a thousand 45 caliber pistol cartridges a minute. In Chicago it was first adopted by the Saltis-McErlane gang. In 1923 the Model 21A "tommy gun" with a twenty-cartridge capacity box was sold for a hundred and seventy-five dollars. No legislation was passed against possession of tommy guns until the late twenties and the average price steadily increased to reach five thousand dollars. It was Bugs Moran of the North Side gang who took the credit for inventing murder by motorcade, gunmen and their cover men in half a dozen cars enfilading their victims—raking them with fire along the whole line of vehicles. And Louis Alterie (or Leland Varain) of the same gang developed death by rented ambush—renting an apartment within range of an address to which the victim was enticed and shooting him on arrival. By 1925 bombs were as likely to be used by gangsters trying to eliminate a rival as machine guns. This form of terrorism was superior to gunning victims down. It involved no special skill or courage, posed little danger for someone escaping quickly by automobile from arrest or prosecution.

The beer wars of the 1920s eliminated some gangs, attenuated others and strengthened the grip and power of Al Capone in the city. His gang comprised the most deadly fighters and most efficient organizers.

The Capone syndicate, with its hierarchical organization, had much in common with a Neapolitan predecessor, the *Camorra*. The *Camorra*, the Quarrel, of Naples perhaps had its origins as long ago as the sixteenth century but did not exist in its structure of twelve centers and many subcenters and ranks of *camorrista, piccinuto* (lad), and *giovinutto onorato* (respected youth) until about 1820. Like the Sicilian form of Mafia it offered services—protection, prostitution, and gambling. And it was highly structured with an elected *capintesta* (chief), a *caposocieta* or *capintrito* (section chief), who had his own *contajuolo* (secretary), *contarulo* (accountant), and *capo carusiello* (cashier).

Capone was referred to in the files of Jack Zuta, whoremaster, as "the big boss." Besides Capone the gang was led by Jake Guzik, his accountant and business manager. Behind his back he was called "Greasy Thumb." His treasurer, Frank Nitti—the Enforcer—provided Capone's link with the *Unione Siciliana.* Tony Lombardo was his senior adviser, *consigliere.* Capone's brother, Ralph ("Bottles"), controlled sales of liquor—the only member of his family who played a prominent role in the gang. The liquor distributors were Charlie Fischetti and Lawrence ("Dago") Mangano. Frank Pope and Peter Penovich controlled gambling houses, and Michael ("Mike de Pike") Heitler and Harry Guzik (at first) controlled the brothels. Hymie ("Loud Mouth") Levine was the chief collector. Louis Cowan, a newsdealer, provided the gang with bail in case of arrest. His security came from real estate given to him by Capone for that purpose. James Belcastro, once a Black Hander, organized bombings.

From 1925 Capone's headquarters was a suite of fifty rooms in the Hotel Metropole in the First Ward, 2300 South Michigan Avenue, convenient for city hall and the police department. Capone paid bribes to the police of about $30 million a year: his own payroll listed about half the force.

Organization was necessary not only to make huge profits but also to preserve life. After an abortive attempt on his life on January 12, 1925, Capone was determined to take maximum precaution to ensure his survival. He ordered a special limousine from General Motors at a cost of thirty thousand dollars. It had a steel-plated body and gas tank, windows half an inch thick, a secret gun compartment in the back seat, and a movable rear window from which shots could be fired. It weighed seven tons. His bodyguards were legion. They included: Phil d'Andrea, who could slice a quarter in midair with a rifle shot; Jack White, who fired with his left hand because his right had been shattered by a falling brick in his youth; Samuel McPherson Hunt, known as "Golf Bag" because it was in a golf bag that he hid his shotgun; Antonio Leonardo Accardo alias

Joe Batters; Felice De Lucia alias Paul Ricca, "the Waiter"; Sam Giancana, "Mooney"; Murray Llewellyn Humphreys, known as "the Camel" after his overcoat; "Machine Gun" Jack McGurn, born Vincenzo De Mora; Frank Rio alias Kline, the most loyal of all.

———————◆———————

Beyond the obvious mysteries associated with Al Capone—the assassinations of other gangsters—lies a more crucial and more impenetrable one. Control of the underworld depended on holding a prominent place in the aristocracy of Italian-American crime that was to become the American Mafia. The war of attrition between rival gangs takes on a more ominous significance than the unending round of gang killings at first suggests. The contest for local authority that each of these implies was probably less important in itself than the struggle for national monopoly underlying them. Capone was undoubtedly a player in this scenario. But his role is easily overlooked. Was he a Mafioso, or a rival to the Mafia, or a complaisant colleague? What does become clear with hindsight is that Capone was fighting a war on two fronts: the feud with the North Side gang along a chain of command—Dion O'Banion, Hymie Weiss, Vincent ("Schemer") Drucci and George ("Bugs") Moran; and the contest for control of the *Unione Siciliana.*

Organizations already existed that could be transformed into an American Mafia, and the *Unione Siciliana,* originally a legal fraternity for Sicilian immigrants, was one. The Chicago lodge, founded in 1895, had forty thousand members in thirty-eight district lodges during the 1920s. In 1925 its name was changed to the Italo-American National Union. Some writers, like Fred J. Cook in *The Secret Rulers* (1966), equate the Mafia with La Mano Nero and the *Unione Siciliana.* Yet to categorize the *Unione Siciliana* as an organization interested in racketeering from its inception is to judge only with the benefit of hindsight. Other writers are more circumspect. According to Rudolph J. Vecoli's unpublished study of Italians in Chicago before the First World War the *Unione Siciliana* was one of the few Italian organizations that contributed to the White Hand, the society aimed at the elimination of Black Hand extortion. (In New York, however, its infiltration by gangsters like Ignazio Saietta—"Lupo the Wolf"—gave it a dual character. Not only did it support Sicilians by respectable means but it was also linked with vice, extortion, kidnapping, and racketeering.)

Above: Maine was the first state to prohibit the manufacture and sale of alcohol, in an act passed in 1851. As this 1855 cartoon shows, the result was negligible. *(Library of Congress)*

Women constituted an essential part of the prohibition movement, especially after the founding of the Women's Christian Temperance Union in 1874. This 1874 print illustrates the appeal of a self-conscious metaphor. *(Library of Congress)*

PROFIT

—Good Housekeeping.

The 2,000,000 children in bondage to toil is an outrage against our civilization, but the millions enslaved by the licensed liquor traffic is the foulest blot upon our nation's honor.

Excessive Death-Rate In Drinking Homes Cost 2,407 Children Their Lives

(Statistics, 19,519 children in 5,736 families.)

SERIES G. No. 21.

THE AMERICAN ISSUE PUBLISHING CO., Westerville, Ohio

The caption of this cartoon is aimed at the capital cornered by the liquor interests, the point being not the profit to business but the price paid by the poor—alcoholism, disease, hunger, and social dislocation. *(Library of Congress)*

This Anti-Saloon League poster is a reminder that the temperance movement gained from the spread of scientific information on the detrimental physiological effects of alcohol. *(Library of Congress)*

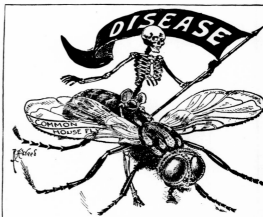

ALCOHOL---The Great Enemy

The fly, through its germ-spreading proclivities, is said by government experts to cost the nation more than $150,000,000 a year, besides the cost in loss of human life. But we've a greater enemy. In the years 1900-08, 33,000 men, from twenty-five to sixty-five years of age, were reported to have died in the United States, in the "registration area" alone, from alcoholism and from hardened liver due to alcoholism,— 11,000 more than died from typhoid fever.

Thirty-Six States Can Stop It By Constitutional Amendment

Series G. No. 16.

This cartoon of two children orphaned of parental care and proper sustenance by the saloon was aimed by the Anti-Saloon League at progressive consciences. *(Library of Congress)*

Daddy's in There---

And Our Shoes and Stockings and Clothes and Food Are in There, Too, and They'll Never Come Out.
—*Chicago American.*

WANTED--A FATHER; A LITTLE BOY'S PLEA
JULIA H. JOHNSON

A shy little boy stood peering
  Through the door of a bright saloon;
He looked as if food and clothing
  Would be thought a most welcome boon.

And one of the men, in passing,
  As if tossing a dog a bone,
Asked, "What do you want this evening?"
  In a rude and unkindly tone.

"I am wanting"—the boy's lips trembled—
  "I am wanting my father, sir."
And he gazed at the little tables
  Where the careless onlookers were.

It was there that he saw his father,
  But the man only shook his head,
And the boy, with his thin cheek burning,
  Ran away with a look of dread.

Oh, the fathers—the fathers wanted!
  How the heart-break, and bitter need,
With the longings, deep and piteous,
  For the wandering children plead.

May the children's call arouse them,
  May the fathers arise and go
With the young souls waiting for them,
  For the little ones need them so!

SERIES G. NO. 23.

The American Issue Publishing Co.
Westerville, Ohio

A TOAST

—Apologies to Mirror and New York World

ALCOHOLIC UNFIT--"Here's to the Guy that went in My Place!"

"SEVENTY-SIX PER CENT of the young men who applied for enlistment were rejected because unfit to serve -- from their own drink habits, or their parents"--COL. MAUS

Your Boy Fill the Place of a DRINKING SLACKER ?

SERIES G. POSTERETTE No. 52. 3c doz., $6. 100; $2 per 500. Attractive Quantity Rates
AMERICAN ISSUE PUBLISHING CO. WESTERVILLE, OHIO.

During the First World War the Anti-Saloon League identified drinking with decadence. Here a young man about town is too gin-sodden to fight, his courage sapped by too many cocktails. *(Library of Congress)*

Carry Nation with Yale students in 1902. She did not realize that the tumbler of water in her hand would be taken for a glass of whiskey, or that a cigarette and smoke rings would be drawn in before the Yale *Record* published the photo. *(Yale University)*

William Jennings Bryan (left) and Henry Ford, foremost opponents of prohibition who were brought together in 1915 to publicize Ford's "Peace Ship" and protest against the Great War. *(Library of Congress)*

THE PRESIDENTS OF PROHIBITION

Clockwise From Top Left: At the height of his international prestige in 1919, Woodrow Wilson was powerless to prevent the introduction of national prohibition. *(Portrait by Sir William Orpen; Library of Congress)* As senator from Ohio, Warren G. Harding supervised passage of the Eighteenth Amendment through Congress. *(Library of Congress)* When Calvin Coolidge succeeded Harding the press purveyed his puritan values and personal asceticism as a guarantee of poitical integrity. *(Library of Congress)* Herbert Hoover implied that he and the Republicans were responsible for the affluence of the 1920s, so he was blamed for the Wall Street Crash and the collapse of economic security. *(Library of Congress)* The election of Franklin D. Roosevelt in 1932 initiated the final, triumphant campaign for the repeal of national prohibition. *(Library of Congress)*

Wayne Wheeler, general counsel of the Anti-Saloon League, was the acknowledged architect of national prohibition and unacknowledged arbiter of congressional debates and administrative decisions on the subject. *(Underwood & Underwood; Library of Congress)*

Senator James A. Reed of Missouri, a staunch opponent of prohibition, who led the B-E-E-R group in Congress against Wheeler and, later, Bishop Cannon. *(Library of Congress)*

Whiskey still impounded during the 1920s. *(Library of Congress)*

Dismantling an illicit still. *(Library of Congress)*

The continuous war between Coast Guard and rumrunners was extremely bitter. The *Seneca*, a Coast Guard cutter, captured a rumrunner, the K-13091, on March 27, 1924. *(Library of Congress)*

The four-inch cannon on board the *Seneca*, which showered two men with shrapnel before capture was effected. *(Library of Congress)*

The possibilities of its subversion were inherent in the political climate of Chicago in which the ward machines and the underworld were inextricably associated. John Landesco in *Organized Crime in Chicago* (1929) notes that from 1916 there were so many Italians in Chicago that wards formerly dominated by the Irish became politically uncertain. Politicians seeking office had to court the Italian bloc. The *Unione Siciliana*, being a large association of Italians, offered politicians a bridge between their machines and the electorate.

The presidency of the *Unione* thus became a highly influential position and, therefore, highly coveted. Power rested in the ability to make and control political appointees. Anthony D'Andrea was both president of the *Unione* and an Aldermanic candidate. Other presidents, such as Mike Merlo and Antonio Lombardo, were allied with bootleggers. Thus the *Unione* had access to the political machine and the underworld.

Capone, who was denied the office because he was not Sicilian, continuously sought the cooperation of the *Unione* presidents and determined to place his own nominees in the office. Thus many murders really did kill two birds with one stone, a temporary nuisance and a permanent rival in the struggle for ultimate power. A crucial part of strategy both for Al Capone and the North Side leaders was the elimination of the Terrible Gennas. The fall of their house was as precipitous as their rise but even bloodier. Angelo was killed by members of the North Side gang led by Bugs Moran and Schemer Drucci on May 25, 1925; Mike was killed on June 13 by John Scalise and Albert Anselmi, who had joined Capone; and Tony was killed by Giuseppe Nerone, *Il Cavaliere*, supposedly one of the Gennas' gang, on July 8. The surviving brothers fled. Sam and Pete hid outside Chicago and Jim went to Sicily.

The motive of Weiss and the North Side gang was revenge for the murder of O'Banion. Capone's motives were more complex. He planned to control the *Unione Siciliana*, even though he could never become president, by securing that office for Antonio Lombardo, who was Sicilian and therefore eligible. To do this he needed to eliminate Angelo Genna, who had succeeded Mike Merlo in 1924 and, if necessary, the other brothers. However, his plan miscarried and Samoots Amatuna succeeded Angelo Genna. Thus he, too, had to be eliminated. With this the North Side gang and West Side O'Donnells would concur. Calling a truce to their feud with Capone's gang Schemer Drucci and Jim Doherty, acting for all three gangs, murdered Samoots in a barbershop on November 13, 1925.

Once the Gennas had fallen their position at the center of the alky cooking industry was taken over by Joseph, Dominic, and Tony Aiello and their six brothers, who had entered the bootlegging business as sugar distributors. Since one reason for the war was competition among bootleggers for production and consumption of alcohol, the change of one team did not end the fray. The Aiellos were, in time, to prove as hostile to Capone's organization as the Gennas had been. And, again, the specific bone of contention was control of the *Unione Siciliana.*

But the elimination of the Gennas had, nevertheless, served its purpose. By now it is quite likely that the *Unione Siciliana* was infiltrated with gangsters to such an extent that its benevolent side had been clouded by its malevolent majority. From time to time its respectable side was celebrated. When the Italian ambassador, Giacomo de Martino, arrived in Chicago on January 24, 1927, he was met by, among others, Antonio Lombardo, Capone's *consigliere,* as a prominent member of the *Unione* demonstrating ethnic loyalty. Thus the criminal side used the official side as a front for its own purposes.

Denis Tilden Lynch in his *Criminals and Politicians* (1932) assuming that the Mafia and the *Unione* were one and the same thing, cites from the testimony of a repentant mafioso about the means of induction. The account contains the sort of features of initiation commonly associated with secret and subversive societies: "The oath of the Unione Siciliana compels obedience to the boss under no less a penalty than death. As a candidate is about to take the obligation he is led to an altar where the only object is a dagger, the hilt resting on the altar; then he rests his hand on the point of the dagger, palm downward, and repeats the words of the oath after the chief of the lodge."

———————————◄◆►———————————

Burrasca, originally meaning storm or quarrel, came to signify gang warfare when one gang invaded another's territory. The Saltis-McErlane gang waged a beer war on the South Side first with the South Side O'Donnells and, second, with the Ralph Sheldon gang, which had split from them. And on the West Side the Klondike O'Donnell brothers waged war with Al Capone. And it was their internecine rivalry that brought the full glare of publicity on Chicago gangsters by the press.

THE NEAPOLITAN SHRUG

One murder marked what Henry Barrett Chamberlin of the Illinois Crime Survey describes as the beginning of "intense public interest in organized crime." Until the murder of William McSwiggin in 1926 information was meted out to the public by the mass media sporadically. Though people could see the impact of prohibition around them in their neighborhoods, their appreciation of its impact on the city as a whole was incomplete. The McSwiggin murder changed all that. The myth that the dogs of the underworld killed only their masters and themselves was also exploded by the murder.

An assistant state's attorney, William ("Little Mac") McSwiggin, twenty-six years old, was mowed down by machine gun fire from a motorcade of five cars in front of the Pony Inn, 5613 West Roosevelt Road, on April 27, 1926 at 8:40 P.M. Slain with him were two known gangsters, James Doherty and Thomas ("Red") Duffy. Their association was especially odd since McSwiggin had recently prosecuted Doherty unsuccessfully for the murder of Eddie Tancl. Doherty and Duffy had spent the day with Myles and Klondike O'Donnell as ballot watchers for State's Attorney Robert E. Crowe. The success of Crowe's candidates in the Republican primary elections was being contested by Senator Charles S. Deneen of Illinois, whose own nominees had been defeated. The recount had confirmed the victory of Crowe's men.

At six o'clock McSwiggin had joined Duffy, the O'Donnells, and Doherty first in Doherty's car and then in the O'Donnells' Lincoln sedan; so, too, had Edward Hanley, a former police officer. As soon as the machine gun fire started Hanley and the O'Donnells saved themselves by diving to the ground behind their Lincoln sedan parked in front of the saloon. Although Duffy, Doherty, and McSwiggin were badly wounded, the survivors did not dare take them to a hospital and risk an investigation. Duffy was so badly hit that they left him to die on the street whence he was rescued by a passing motorist who did take him to a hospital. There he died the next morning. But McSwiggin and Doherty were taken away only to expire in the car. Their bodies were then dumped in the lonely prairie outside Berwyn. They, too, were discovered and taken to the morgue by police at about ten o'clock.

Public interest in McSwiggin's murder was widespread. There was a general belief that a solution to that mystery would provide a clue to answer all questions connected with the beer war and the alliance between the underworld and politics. In fact as events unfolded it became clear that questions would be raised but answers to them denied. On May 5, 1926, the *Chicago Tribune* discovered that secret warrants had been issued for the arrest of Al Capone and that the state's attorney, Robert E. Crowe, believed Capone himself had led the assassins. Capone himself disappeared for a time and remained in hiding, probably in New York. It was therefore upon Crowe that the whole affair devolved. The law occupied the center of the stage.

Robert E. Crowe had become chief justice of the Cook County Criminal Court in 1919 at the age of thirty-eight and he was first elected state's attorney in 1921. During his tenure of office he increased the budget to $100,000, added an extra thousand men to the police department and increased the number of judges from six to twenty. His own staff comprised fifty police officers and seventy assistant state's attorneys. But the increase in personnel did not result in a greater number of convictions. In his first two terms 349 people were murdered of whom 215 were gangsters, victims of their own beer wars. Yet only 128 people were convicted of murder and none of these were gangsters. No one was convicted for any of the 369 bombings in the same period. Indeed the number of convictions for major crimes fell: it was 2,309 in 1921, the year Crowe took office, and 1,344 in 1923.

Crowe's attitude to crime and punishment was cynical. Frequently accused of conspiring with gangsters to subvert the reform program of Mayor William E. Dever, he consistently criticized prohibition: "The town is wet and the county is wet, and nobody can dry them up . . . for every dive in the county there are two in the city, and everybody in Chicago knows it except Dever." He knew he could not turn back the tide: "Why don't I get busy and stop it? For the simple reason that I am running a law office, not a police station. . . . I will not be both arresting officer and prosecutor."

Despite this philosophy Crowe felt threatened by the chain of evidence relating his office to alleged poll frauds and gang rivalry that was being made public in the wake of the McSwiggin murder. Thus he determined to put on a display of disinterested duty. He offered a reward of five thousand dollars out of his own pocket for information leading to the arrest of the murderers. He declared, "a war to the hilt against these gangsters." And he authorized raids on speakeasies, brothels, and gaming houses. Fully conscious of public suspicion about his personal involvement, he anticipated open opposition. He petitioned Judge William V. Brothers to create a special grand jury to be directed by the state's attorney general, Oscar Carl-strom. Crowe was, however, determined to control everything from behind the scenes. In order to cover his traces he, Carlstrom, and Brothers, with the Cook County coroner, Oscar Wolff, appointed a distinguished prosecutor from Indiana, Joseph Roach, as a special state's attorney for the inquest. Though he was certainly allowed to investigate the affair, Roach's special skills were never used. The dossiers he assembled on gangsters were ignored by the authorities.

Nevertheless interlocking interests between the underworld and politicians were discovered in the course of raids launched by Crowe on Capone's gambling houses and brothels, the Ship, the Stockade, the Hawthorne Smoke Shop, and twenty-two others. The special prosecutor, Charles A. McDonald, came across canceled checks that had passed between gangsters and public officials in Cicero. They were clear evidence that Capone had allied himself with public of-ficials several years earlier and could operate his nefarious businesses with impunity. And, years later, the ledgers seized in 1926 from the Hawthorne Smoke Shop were to bring about his downfall.

The murder of McSwiggin also marked the beginning of active public revulsion against what prohibition had done to Chicago. The day after the Stockade was sacked, on May 16, 1926, a part of Forest View Vigilantes from the West Suburban Citizens' Association set fire to it. So great was Capone's unpopularity that they could do so with impunity. When the fire brigade arrived it was only to make sure the flames did not engulf buildings nearby. They could not spare the water to douse the flames on the Stockade.

Different interpretations were put on McSwiggin's murder. Judge William V. Brothers said McSwiggin was a martyr killed in the performance of his duties in revenge for his fearless prosecutions of gangsters. The fact that he was with gangsters when he was killed simply suggested that he was gathering information from them. A more sinister version of this explanation was put forward by the *Chicago Daily Tribune* of August 26, 1926. This was that the murder was a political rather than simply a criminal assassination. Accord-ing to this interpretation McSwiggin was killed with his underworld allies for his part in the primary elections as an agent of Robert E. Crowe. A second interpretation put forward by Joseph Klenha, mayor of Cicero, was that McSwiggin was killed as a result of mis-taken identity. His death was an accident of the beer war between rival gangs. His assassins were really after the two O'Donnell brothers. A variant on the story of mistaken identity was that Al Capone had killed McSwiggin instead of his archenemy Hymie Weiss.

This theory of mistaken identity in the beer war was the most persistent of all. The Capone gang was no longer the acknowledged beer concessionaire of Cicero. For instance, although Harry Madigan's saloon, the Pony Inn, was close to Capone's Hawthorne Inn, he was buying his beer from the O'Donnells. They asked for fifty dollars a barrel whereas Capone charged sixty, and theirs was better beer. Other saloonkeepers followed Madigan's example. Thus the authority to levy protection now rested with the O'Donnells. They took McSwiggin with them on a round of saloons to convince the keepers that the balance of power really had shifted. McSwiggin was widely known and his prestige was recognized. The police discovered a list of sixty Cicero saloons in one of Duffy's pockets while he was in the hospital. Many of the saloons on the list had a pencil mark at the side. The list disappeared mysteriously and when it was recovered the pencil marks had been erased. The Capone gang knew the O'Donnells were making the rounds of the saloons but did not know McSwiggin was with them. When they set out to eliminate the O'Donnells it was McSwiggin who was hit.

There were no fewer than seven separate investigations by different juries: the coroner's jury, a federal grand jury, and five special county grand juries.

The first session of the coroner's jury was held in secret supposedly to anticipate interested gangsters from obtaining crucial information that they could manipulate to obstruct justice should they be tried. More than two hundred saloonkeepers were obliged to testify and reveal from whom they obtained alcohol and to whom they paid a protection fee. This information was not given to the newspapers nor the federal grand jury, appointed later. Although it was not able to solve the mystery, the first of the special county grand juries presented a final report on June 4, 1926, that found, "A conspiracy of silence among gangs and intimidation by threats to murder witnesses make it almost impossible to solve the killing of gangsters by their rivals and of innocent bystanders." As Henry Barrett Chamberlin said, "The cardinal feature of the rule of organized crime was the paralysis of justice." In Sicilian terms it was, quite simply, omertà.

The federal grand jury was more positive and on May 27 indicted members of both the Capone and O'Donnell gangs. It named

Al Capone and his brother, Ralph, Frank Smith, Charles Fischetti, and Peter Payette and William, Myles, and Bernard O'Donnell and Harry Madigan, the saloon owner of the Pony. They were charged with violating the Volstead Act.

The O'Donnell brothers at first refused to testify, but when compelled on May 28 they said they had gone to Cicero with McSwiggin on the day he was murdered to recover a bulletproof vest that had been stolen from a friend, Albert Dunlop. On July 29 Al Capone gave himself up to federal agents but was immediately exonerated of any complicity in the murder. Capone denied any association and told a reporter, with his customary shrug: "Of course, I didn't kill him. Why should I? I liked the kid. Only the day before he got killed he was up to my place and when he went home I gave him a bottle of Scotch for his old man." And he added more ominously, "I paid McSwiggin and I paid him plenty, and I got what I was paying for."

Illinois law limited the life of a special grand jury to a single month. Thus if the investigation was incomplete at the end of a month another jury had to be appointed. Robert E. Crowe used this practice to delay exposure. The second, third, and fourth grand juries were subject to delaying tactics, diverted to the disclosure of another murder, and deflected to a study of election frauds. Al Capone was arrested a second time under suspicion of complicity but discharged when all indictments for voting frauds were declared unconstitutional by the Illinois Supreme Court.

The only positive accomplishment of the fourth jury was to return indictments against forty election officials of the Forty-second Ward, all of which were subsequently quashed by the Illinois Supreme Court. On August 5 Charles McDonald, the former judge acting as a special prosecutor, ordered the opening of the Cicero ballot boxes in order that "Judges and clerks may be compelled to testify against bosses to save themselves from jail. If we can get them talking about election crookedness, we will get them talking about the spoils of election. If, as we believe, the stakes in that election were beer privileges, we may be abe to prove it. If we can prove that, we can create a situation in which many will be willing to tell on each other to save themselves. And if the underlings ever start confessing we may get the murderers of McSwiggin."

The father of William McSwiggin, Sergeant Anthony McSwiggin of the police department, said the murderers were Al Capone, his bodyguard, Frank Rio, one of his gunmen, Frank Diamond, and a suburban beer runner, Bob McCullogh. It was, he added, no case of mistaken identity: Edward Moore and Willie Heeney had relayed to Capone the information that William McSwiggin, Doherty, and Duffy were in Cicero just before the murder took place. In asking Justice Thomas J. Lynch to empanel a fifth grand jury McDonald claimed, "I know who killed McSwiggin, but I want to know it legally and be able to present it conclusively. Neither Sergeant McSwiggin nor anyone else has at any time given me or my assistants the name of any one witness who would appear before the grand jury and identify Al Capone or any other person as the murderer." New clues had been found and new witnesses were available. But, "It is necessary to keep the names of these witnesses secret. The moment any of the witnesses learn that they are wanted, they disappear, or are even killed."

In addition to its main investigations the fourth jury had been diverted to another crime, the murder of John ("Mitters") Folley by Joe Saltis and his chauffeur, Frank ("Lefty") Koncil, on August 6, 1926, for selling beer in Saltis-McErlane territory. Much later, on November 7, they were acquitted. In a report Judge Charles A. McDonald left press and public in no doubt about the reasons:

> Prior to the trial two of the states's important witnesses disappeared, the immediate members of their families either refusing or being unable to give any information or clue as to their whereabouts.
>
> After the selection of the jury and the introduction of some of the state's evidence, one of the jurors selected to try the case became violently insane, necessitating the discharge of the entire jury and the selection of another in its stead. . . .
>
> Certain of the state's witnesses testified to having been threatened with violence in the event they testified against the defendants, and of having been approached with offers of bribery for either withholding their testimony or testifying falsely.

———————————◆———————————

During the McSwiggin investigations of 1926 the second of the beer wars was at its height. Though they might unite temporarily to remove a common nuisance like Samoots Amatuna, the Capone and Weiss gangs neither forgot nor forgave.

The North Side and Capone gangs fought a pitched battle in front of the Standard Oil Building, South Michigan Avenue on August 10, 1926, and then an action replay in the same location on

August 15, 1926. The North Side gang then laid siege to the Hawthorne Inn, Cicero, on September 20. In retaliation the Capone gang rented a room at 740 North State Street, next door to the flower shop of Dion O'Banion and William Schofield, which still served as a front to Hymie Weiss's headquarters. And there they mowed down Hymie Weiss, his chauffeur, Sam Feller, and bodyguard, Paddy Murray, on October 11, 1926.

In his display of grief to the press after the murder of Hymie Weiss Capone repeated his now familiar gesture of the Neapolitan shrug. "That was butchery. Hymie was a good kid. He could have got out long ago and taken his and been alive today. . . . Forty times I've tried to arrange things so we'd have peace and life would be worth living. Who wants to be tagged around night and day by guards? I don't for one. There was, and there is, plenty of business for us all and competition needn't be a matter of murder, anyway. But Weiss couldn't be told anything. I suppose you couldn't have told him a week ago that he'd be dead today." The torch of vengeance in the North Side gang now passed to Bugs Moran, and Schemer Drucci.

But for the time being there was an armistice. On October 21, 1926, the gangs agreed to a truce, which is sometimes reported as having taken place at the Morrison Hotel and sometimes at the Hotel Sherman. The peacemaker, Maxie Eisen, persuaded them to divide Chicago according to their traditional territories. Each gang would have exclusive wholesale and retail rights for beer and whiskey in a particular area.

The North Side gang led by Schemer Drucci and Bugs Moran, Eddie Vogel, Julian ("Potatoes") Kaufman, Frank Citro, and Peter Gusenberg would control territory from Lake Michigan on the east and north to the surburbs and on the south and west from the Chicago River to the Wisconsin state line. The Saltis and Sheldon gangs divided the South Side of Chicago from south of the Chicago river to the Indiana state line and from Lake Michigan on the east to the small towns of the west. In this arrangement Sheldon acquired a strong position partly on account of the advocacy of Capone's representative, Antonio Lombardo, and partly because Saltis and McErlane were in jail, awaiting trial for the Foley and Koncil murders, and unable to speak for themselves. Capone's territory was to include the far West Side and the western suburbs, Chicago south of Madison Street.

Of course the gangs could not hold fast to this agreement and several chafed at Capone's bit. There were many murders and minor misdemeanors still. But the Morrison Hotel truce held together while the gangs united in support of Big Bill Thompson's campaign for reelection.

Thompson's previous tenure of office as mayor, from 1915 to 1923, had been utterly corrupt. Yet now Thompson entered the Republican mayoral primary in the fall of 1926 and secured a majority of 180,000 votes against reform candidates—a record to that time. The reform administration of William E. Dever had by no means wiped Chicago dry. Thompson was not even going to try: "I'm wetter than the middle of the Atlantic Ocean. When I'm elected, we'll not only reopen places these people have closed, but we'll open ten thousand new ones." Thus it was in the gangsters' interests to support him in the hope of untold future profits.

The relationship between gangster and politician was most obvious during elections and sometimes during recounts later. Capone contributed $200,000 to Thompson's campaign in spring 1927. Money was ladled out to Thompson workers from a bathtub in the Hotel Sherman filled with packets of five-dollar bills. He also supported Thompson with a range of techniques of bribery and terrorism. Thompson's slogan was "America First," fourteen years before it was taken up by an isolationist pressure group in the early months of the Second World War: "What was good enough for George Washington is good enough for Bill Thompson. . . . I want to make the king of England keep his snoot out of America! America first, and last, and always!" Capone's slogan was more to the point: "Vote Early and Vote Often."

Gangsters had refined the electoral techniques of the brewers before the First World War to ensure the successes of their allies. Their techniques now included:

1. Padding the register with fictitious names to enable the casting of fraudulent votes on polling day.
2. Abuses of the suspect notice provisions of electoral laws—both failing to disqualify people registered irregularly and also disqualifying people legally registered on the pretense that they had not answered some official inquiry.
3. Kidnapping election officials and substituting partisan officials in their place.
4. Failure of election officers to initial ballots so that they could be invalidated if it suited the gangsters.
5. Altering ballots after they had been cast.

6. Altering totals of votes cast on the tally sheets.
7. Substituting fraudulent ballots and tally sheets for the originals, which were then destroyed.
8. Allowing nonresident vagrants to make false statements about their length of residence and also paying them to vote under fictitious names.
9. Stuffing ballot boxes with fraudulent ballots.

Thompson won the election of May 5, 1927, by a majority of 83,072 votes against the incumbent, Dever. This victory with all its implications for future profit and plunder was perhaps less pleasing to Capone than the unexpected elimination of an archrival, Schemer Drucci. And Capone was actually rid of one of his most deadly enemies by the police. On April 4, the day before the election, Detective Dan Healey and other officers picked up Schemer Drucci for organizing the destruction of the offices of Alderman Dorsey R. Crowe, who supported Dever. In a struggle in the squad car Healey shot Drucci dead.

Subordinate gang leaders were alternately complaisant and antagonistic to Capone. Guerrilla warfare continued. The death of Drucci did not determine the demise of the North Side gang. When Bugs Moran took command he joined with the Aiello brothers, Christian ("Barney") Bertsche and Ed Zuta in a war of attrition against Capone and Lombardo. The conference at the Hotel Morrison of October 21, 1926, had accomplished an armistice. It had not produced a binding treaty. Although the beer wars were brought to an end, the rivalries and tensions that caused them continued.

In this situation public reaction toward gangsters and politicians had reached the point of nausea.

Politics in American society during the twenties operated according to deals and favors cemented by friendships. During prohibition there was little noticeable difference between legal and illicit business and the smart operator who handled either well was much admired. Americans within and without the law were tolerant of other people's behavior and business provided there was no interference in their own. Thus there was no clear division between the economic and political confines of gangsters and machine bosses and the social world at large. Office seekers in the Chicago of the 1920s were not motivated by political opportunism, for power itself rested with the gangsters. The office seekers were ambitious only in their avarice. Their store of moral tags trotted out to cover inaction, their lore of proverbial wisdom poured out to justify self-seeking were not, of course, related to any deeply felt principles. The gulf between political rhetoric and political reality unintentionally exposed a society where social, legal, and moral restraints had been eroded. People became disgusted not so much at the behavior of gangsters, alone or in their packs, as at the process they represented, the disintegration of a whole social order.

Bloody-minded though they were, the gangsters were sensitive to public opinion. With the exception of Capone they became less prone to ostentatious display. And the splendor of Chicago's funerals, the most potent image of the relationship of politics and crime, declined between the funeral of Mike Merlo, head of the *Unione Siciliana*, on November 10, 1924, and that of Big Tim Murphy, shot in West Rogers Park on June 20, 1928. At Merlo's funeral the honorary pallbearers included William E. Dever, mayor of Chicago; Robert E. Crowe, state attorney; four judges including Anton Cermak, subsequently mayor. In comparison, Murphy's funeral was not attended by any officials or politicians of importance. This decline reflected growing public unease of the relationship between politicians and gangsters and also the changing nature of that relationship itself. Whereas machine politics and criminal rackets were once linked by common professional interest, as the profits increased so the financial incentive superseded ties of friendship.

After years of painful acquiescence the public had had enough. Its resentment burst in the primary and state elections of 1928.

The Republican primary election for state and county offices of April 10, 1928, was known as the "Pineapple Primary" after the numerous bombing and shooting incidents between pro- and anti-Thompson gangsters. Diamond Joe Esposito favored Circuit Judge John A. Swanson as a replacement for Robert E. Crowe as state's attorney and in support agreed to run for Republican committeeman. He was shot and killed on the street by Capone's agents on March 21, 1928. Octavius Granady, a black lawyer and rival candidate to Boss Morris Eller for Republican committeeman for the Twentieth Ward, was killed on polling day. All the old devices were used by Capone in support of Thompson's candidates. On March 7 five of the six candidates for committeemen of the Twenty-fifth Ward were taken from their homes at gunpoint and forced to sign withdrawal notices to remove them from the ticket.

94

THE NEAPOLITAN SHRUG

It was the clergy that first announced that the public had had enough. On Easter Sunday, April 4, 1928, Catholic priests, Protestant ministers, and Jewish rabbis denounced the whole corrupt system: "We have a governor who ought to be in the penitentiary. . . . Ours is a government of bombs and bums. . . . Grant that we may be awakened to a sense of public shame." Despite the fraudulent way in which corrupt officials collaborated with the Thompson machine by adding false votes to its candidates and subtracting true votes from its rivals not a single Thompson hack was reelected in the primary of April 10. More than 800,000 votes were cast whereas about 430,000 votes had been predicted. The governor, Len Small, the state attorney, Robert E. Crowe, sank with the others. Thompson's own tenure of office would last until 1931 but his prestige was shattered and he retired, leaving the actual running of affairs to an acting mayor, Samuel Ettelson.

In the autumn of 1928 Frank Loesch, president of the Chicago Crime Commission, appealed to Al Capone to stay clear of the election itself, which followed the primary, and to persuade other gangs to do the same. Capone knew an honest election would yield returns inimical to his interests, but the experiences at the primary elections convinced him the Thompson machine was doomed. He had weathered the vicissitudes of politics under different administrations and, in all likelihood, could do so again. After all, he was at the height of his power.

Either directly or through his affiliates Capone had come to control the greater majority, perhaps 70 percent, of Chicago's rackets. Of an estimated $105 million in gross profits he took in 1928, about $10 million came from racketeering. The plumbers' union alone surrendered $200,000 every year to the Capone gang. It was estimated that two thirds of all unions in Chicago paid Capone tribute.

When Morris Becker, an independent dry cleaner, refused to cooperate with the Master Cleaners' and Dyers' Association and raise his prices to give them a cut in 1928 his main plant was bombed. Fifteen officers of the association, including its business agent, Sam Rubin, were indicted by the state attorney, defended by Clarence Darrow, and acquitted for lack of testimony. Becker would still not give in and, since the law was no protection, turned to Capone for support. Their alliance, the Sanitary Cleaning Shops, was perfectly legal. It retained the old price scale and obliged the association to do the same.

In the summer of 1928 Capone moved his headquarters in Chicago from the Metropole to the Lexington across the street, a ten-story hotel where he occupied the whole of the fourth floor and most of the third. Cash was stored in Capone's hotel rooms in padlocked canvas bags until it was deposited in bank accounts under fictitious names. To guard his wealth and his person he had an army of between seven hundred and a thousand men, machine gunners or sluggers or bombers.

On the brink of monopoly control of politics and crime Capone was nevertheless forced to continue his war on two fronts: the feud with the North Side gang and the war of Sicilian succession.

When Tony Lombardo attained the presidency of the *Unione Siciliana* his rival, Joseph Aiello, spread the news that he would pay fifty thousand to anyone who would eliminate Al Capone. The Aiello brothers hired a series of assassins to kill Capone and each of them was foiled and rubbed out. The feud ended temporarily when Aiello sought police protection from a new chief of detectives, William O'Connor, and on November 22, 1927, escaped temporarily to Trenton, New Jersey, with O'Connor's blessing. His brothers, Tony and Dominic, went with him.

The war of Sicilian succession for control of the .*Unione Siciliana* broke out when gangsters dominant in either New York or Chicago began to vie with one another for complete control of both wings. In 1928 Frank Uale (or Yale) was the head of the New York wing. Frank Uale dominated Brooklyn rackets. He was also hired by industrialists to break strikes. His particular racket was extortion of shopkeepers whom he intimidated into buying bad cigars. The term "Frankie Yale" meant a cheap smoke. Yale was also a lieutenant of Guiseppe Masseria, also called Joe the Boss. Both of them had sided with Antonio Lombardo in the struggle in the Chicago *Unione.* Yet Capone suspected Yale of double-crossing him and hijacking his liquor. He feared that Yale might transfer his support from Lombardo to Aiello and suspected that the theft of liquor was a sign of a change of heart.

Yale was killed on July 1, 1928, after he lost a car chase in Brooklyn to assassins armed with sawed-off shot guns, machine guns, and revolvers. The revolvers were traced to Parker A. Henderson, son of the mayor of Miami, and thence to Al Capone, for whom he had bought them, and who had acquired a house in Miami. Yale's funeral in Brooklyn on July 5, 1928, was the most splendid ever in New York and probably more so than those of Colosimo, Merlo, and O'Banion in Chicago. One wreath bore an inscription, the threat, "We'll see them, kid."

According to Denis Tilden Lynch it was not only Capone who was involved. Yale was as much a nuisance to Ciro Terranova, the Artichoke king. At a banquet for Albert H. Vitale, a magistrate, given by the Tipecano Democratic Club at the Roman Gardens, in the Bronx, New York, on the evening of December 7, 1929, seven gangsters entered. They relieved fifty-three of the sixty guests of $2,000 in cash, and jewelry worth $2,500. The seven guests who were not robbed were also gangsters with records. Inspector Joseph J. Donovan later testified that the robbery was staged by Ciro Terranova. The Artichoke king wanted to retain a contract held by a Chicago gunman for the murder of Frank Yale. Terranova had agreed to pay $20,000 for the murder but had only paid a first installment of $5,000 and was delaying a full settlement. The unknown gunman said if he did not come up with the rest of the money he would turn the contract over to the police. Terranova had invited him to the banquet for Vitale where the robbery was staged in order to seize the contract. The story came out when Daniel J. Iamascia, designated to take the rap for the thefts, jibed at the payment of only $1,000 to keep quiet. Thus the story broke.

Terranova disappeared for a time, and the police were unable to link him with the Yale murder. However, the murder contract bore the signature "Ciro Morello," the name of his stepbrother, which he sometimes used as an alias. He was charged with instigating the robberies at the banquet but freed later. Thus the murder of Yale, and also of his associate, Frank Curto, about the same time, and the consternation in the underworld indicate more was at stake than punishment for offending Al Capone. Like so many assassinations of the period it consolidated the aristocracy of crime by eliminating a fractious criminal. Thus it is possible that Yale was a pawn in some sort of move between Terranova and Guiseppe Masseria—Joe the Boss.

The war of the Sicilian succession, intensified by the murder of Frank Yale, continued. Antonio Lombardo was killed with his bodyguard on Madison Street, Chicago, on September 7, 1928. He was the fourth *Unione* president to be assassinated since the murder of Anthony Andrea in 1921. His successor was Pasquale Lolordo. But the war did not last forever. Self-preservation was as keen an instinct as vendetta, and there was a truce of sorts. Probably the first national summit meeting of organized crime in the United States took place at the Hotel Statler, Cleveland, on December 5, 1928, when twenty-seven gang leaders from Chicago, St. Louis, Buffalo, New York City, Gary, Newark, and Tampa met to discuss the future of the *Unione Siciliana* and the national distribution of whiskey. Capone, who was not Sicilian, did not attend. But Torrio, out of retirement, did.

◄◄►►

The notorious climax of Chicago's gang warfare was the St. Valentine's Day Massacre of February 14, 1929. It was the climax of the feud instigated in 1924. Seven members of the North Side gang, now led by Bugs Moran, were mowed down by machine gun fire in a warehouse of the S-M-C Cartage Company at 2122 North Clark Street, Chicago. The gang was lured there by an offer of a hijacked truckload of Old Log Cabin, an expensive Canadian whiskey, which the Purple Gang of Detroit provided for the Capone syndicate. The North Side gang was asked for fifty-seven dollars a case. Frank and Pete Gusenberg, James Clark (or Kashellek), Adam Heyer, Al Weinshank, Reinhardt H. Schwimmer, and Johnny May were waiting there at 10:30 A.M., where a Cadillac with a driver and four passengers arrived. The passengers, two of whom were wearing police uniform, entered the warehouse. Four members of the North Side gang, Bugs Moran, Ted Newberry, Willie Marks, and Henry Gusenberg, arrived late. They saw the Cadillac, suspected a raid or trap, and stayed away. After the shooting the killers emerged from the warehouse. The two men dressed as police officers directed the other two from behind with their guns as if they had arrested them and were taking them to a police station.

Even by Chicago standards the massacre was so heinous that the Chicago Association of Commerce offered a reward of $50,000 for information leading to the arrest and conviction of the murderers. A group of independent citizens offered $10,000, the city council offered $20,000, and the state's attorney offered $20,000—a total of $100,000. Both Moran in Chicago and Capone in Miami accused each other of organizing the crime. The police investigated the alibis of the noted assassins of John Scalise, Albert Anselmi, and Jack McGurn but were unable to come up with any conclusive evidence. (Two members of the grand jury examining the murders, Burt E. Masse [foreman] and Walter E. Olson, were so disturbed by the inability of police scientists to analyze bullets, bullet wounds and marks, and various weapons found in a garage three miles away that they provided funds for the establishment of a scientific crime detective laboratory at Northwestern University in 1930 especially for the study of forensic ballistics.)

In time the consensus of opinion among police and public was that Al Capone had conspired to eliminate Bugs Moran, who was his most deadly rival, and, perhaps, the whole North Side gang. Like other assassinations of the period the murders served a double function, satisfying the requirements of a blood feud and preparing for some sort of consolidation of crime to which these gangsters would be an impediment. Thus the St. Valentine's Day Massacre brought together the two fronts of Capone's feud with the North Side gang and his contest for control of the *Unione* and what it represented in a common war. There could be no consolidation without peaceful agreement of all parties. And there could be no peace with the North Side gang.

To make sure of his target Capone had placed three observers in different rented apartments on Clark Street. Their task was to summon the assassins by phone when they saw Moran arrive at the warehouse. In its most crucial essential the plan miscarried. The observers mistook Al Weinshank, who bore a resemblance to Bugs Moran, for the leader and called the killers before Moran had actually arrived. First the two phony policemen obliged the North Side gang to surrender their weapons and then the four intruders proceeded to annihilate them even though their principal prize had escaped. The victims were at first taken in by the disguise of police uniforms, for the assassins were strangers from out of state. John Kobler in *Capone* accepts the testimony of Al Karpis of the Barker gang, who met Capone years later in Alcatraz, that John Edward ("Screwy") Moore, also known as Claude Maddox, drove the Cadillac for the murderers, Fred ("Killer") Burke, George Ziegler, Gus Winkler and ("Crane Neck") Nugent. He also believes that the whole operation was planned by Jack McGurn for Capone. Whatever its significance the St. Valentine's Day murders sent a standard in massacre that was new in gang warfare.

The sequel to the St. Valentine's Day Massacre and prelude to the next conference of gangsters in Atlantic City in May 1929 was the elimination of Albert Anselmi, John Scalise, and "Hop Toad" Giunta in the so-called Hammond murders. After the St. Valentine's Day Massacre, which, for a time, everyone assumed they had perpetrated, Anselmi and Scalise were arrested and thrown into prison with Jack McGurn. There they tried to entice him away from Capone and into the nucleus of a new gang of their own. It is possible that their factiousness represented not only individual fantasies of self-aggrandizement but also a developing and sustained challenge that would upset the criminal consolidation of the near future. Giunta's place in the scheme is a matter of dispute. John Kobler believes it was Giunta who, with the authority of the *Unione Siciliana*, enticed Scalise and Anselmi first. According to Denis Tilden Lynch it was Giunta who tipped off Capone about Anselmi and Scalise, and Capone decided to eliminate him because he did not want anyone around to whom he was beholden. But it is just as likely that the assassinations again served a double purpose, punishing treachery and preparing for a new order by discarding probable obstacles to its establishment. Although Al Capone's methods seemed very different from Johnny Torrio's, it is possible that their fundamental objectives were the same.

The way Capone conspired to eliminate Scalise, Anselmi, and Giunta and carried out the execution combined political showmanship, Sicilian hospitality, Renaissance statemanship, and mediaeval torture. Frank Rio, alias Kline, pretended to quarrel with Capone in public and thereby induced Scalise and Anselmi to betray themselves. They fell into the trap and told Rio that the Aiello brothers were still offering fifty thousand dollars to anyone who could eliminate Capone. They asked him to join them. On May 7, 1929, Scalise, Anselmi and Giunta were invited to a banquet for sixty at the Hawthorne Inn, Cicero, and afforded a sumptuous display of hospitality. After the meal Capone turned on his special guests: "Three great men. Three great double-crossers. I'm going to show you how double-crossers in this outfit are punished." Taking a baseball bat Capone smashed their heads, arms, and shoulders, one after the other. Then they were riddled with bullets. Their corpses were ferried away by car and discarded over the Illinois state line.

———————◆◆———————

The arrangements made between gangsters at Cleveland in 1928 were provisional. In any case the meeting was probably confined to Sicilians and Sicilian-Americans. Its successor at the President Hotel, Atlantic City, New Jersey, from May 13 to May 16, 1929, was open not only to Sicilian and Italian but also Jewish and Irish gangsters. The Sicilian monopoly had been broken. Al Capone and Johnny

Torrio attended, and with them Capone's bodyguard, Frank Rio, his treasurer, Frank Nitti, and his business manager Jake Guzik. Frank Costello presided over the Atlantic City conference. A member of the family of Giuseppe Masseria—Joe the Boss of New York, Terranova's ally—he was also *consigliere* to Salvatore ("Lucky") Luciano, a pivotal figure of the 1930s. What took place is a matter of conjecture, but it seems that the Atlantic City peace pact was partly designed to end gang warfare in Chicago. Chicago's North and South Side gangs would merge with the Capone syndicate.

It is possible, furthermore, that the conference established territories in a loose federation of criminal syndicates across the nation. By the power of might the local boss who proved himself most efficient became head of his territory. Gangs were to unite and forbear feuds. In future there would be no executions without hearings and no depositions without due deliberation. The old *braggadocio* would be buried. In future the cultural code would be self-effacement. Fred Cook believes that a one million dollar fund was established from a pool of resources to be used for the bribery of politicians and public officers on a massive scale.

It was also decided that the *Unione Siciliana* would be reorganized from head to foot with a new national president. The previous truce had, after all, achieved nothing in that quarter. Pasquale Lolordo, successor to Lombardo as *Unione* president, was killed in his turn in February 1929 by Joseph Aiello, who finally achieved his ambition and became president of the association. Yet Capone was still determined to regain control. Long after the Atlantic City conference, Aiello himself was shot and killed, on October 23, 1930. Capone's candidate, a macaroni manufacturer, Agostino Loredo, succeeded and, after a year, was killed in his turn.

Despite the arrangements at Atlantic City, Capone was still threatened by Moran, who had not attended the conference, and by scattered Sicilian allies of Scalise, Anselmi, and Giunta, anxious to avenge their deaths. At the presumed peak of his career, with his rivals supposedly broken, he did what Torrio had done four years earlier.

In Chicago Capone never carried a gun. In Philadelphia he did so to get arrested as he came out of a movie theater at 8:15 P.M. on May 16, 1929. His bodyguard, Frank Rio, was arrested with him. They were charged with unlawful possession of firearms, and at 10:25 A.M. on May 17 a hastily convened grand jury returned three bills of indictment against them both. They were tried before Judge

J. A. Walsh at noon and at 12:20 P.M. pleaded guilty. A sentence of one year in Moyamensing prison was passed immediately. In the end Capone served most of the sentence in Holmesburg County prison, Philadelphia.

The mayor of Philadelphia, Harry A. Mackey, advised reporters on May 17, 1929, that Capone had planned his arrest and imprisonment in Philadelphia to protect his life from other gangsters. This was why he was so uncharateristically submissive. There was no search for concealed weapons. No warrant. No protest of innocence. No denial of identity. No offer of bond or bribe. "Hello, Shooey—here's my gun," was all he said to Detective James Malone when he was arrested. The speed of his indictment, trial, conviction, and sentencing had set a record. He was supposed to have told Major Lemuel B. Schofield, Philadelphia's director of public safety, "I've been trying to get out of the racket for two years but I couldn't do it. Once in, you're always in. The parasites trail you begging for favors and dough. You fear death and worse than death; you fear the parasites of the game, the rats who would run to the police if you didn't constantly satisfy them for money." During Capone's captivity Torrio was regent. Capone was set free on March 16, 1930, but his days were numbered.

———— ◆ ————

Actress and screenwriter Mae West once observed, "There are no withholding taxes on the wages of sin." The fall of Al Capone illustrates her point. His legend ended ironically. He was eventually foiled by the authorities not on account of his syndicated bootlegging, racketeering, prostitution, and gambling but for failing to file tax returns. In March 1929 Walter Strong, publisher of the *Chicago Daily News*, and Frank Loesch, chairman of the Chicago Crime Commission, persuaded President Herbert Hoover to prosecute Capone, if not to redress the criminal conditions he had imposed on Chicago then at least to reinstate the authority of the federal government above the underworld.

Andrew Mellon, secretary of the treasury, decided that Capone could be harassed on account of his bootlegging activities, a field in which the federal government had more authority than the states. A special detail of the Prohibition Bureau, the "Untouchables," nine men led by Eliot Ness, was recruited to compile evidence against Capone and his allies for conspiracy to violate the Volstead Act. Although personally incorruptible as far as money was concerned,

Ness and his team courted publicity, inciting the press to report and record his raids, and thus undermined their own attempt to dry out Chicago.

Not content with the first strategy, Mellon pursued a second. This involved a sphere of activity peculiar to the government, income tax evasion. Thus Elmer L. Irey, chief of the Internal Revenue's Enforcement Branch, was to accumulate evidence of Capone's evasion of income tax. He had never filed an income tax return nor paid any direct taxes. Irey's special agents, Frank Wilson and Arthur Madden, devised a way of ascertaining income and tested it on gangsters who had falsified their tax returns. In turn a series of gangsters were indicted, tried, and convicted: Manley Sullivan (1927); Terry Druggan (1928, sentenced 1932); Frank Lake (1928, sentenced 1932); Ralph Capone (1929); Jake Guzik (1929). Capone could scarcely credit the capture of his own brother: "The income tax law is a lot of bunk. The government can't collect legal taxes from illegal money." But he was concerned.

The investigators of the Internal Revenue Service had to prove a true disparity between the wealth of expenses and tangible assets and any records of income, such as accounts or ledgers. In Capone's case this would be difficult. Al Capone never opened a bank account or owned property in his own right. He paid cash for everything and never signed checks. The only way Frank Wilson and his team could deduce his earnings was by collecting circumstantial evidence of his worth and expenditures and making a tally of his actual expenses and assets.

Of all the documents confiscated from Capone's establishments the most crucial were three black ledgers of the period 1924 to 1926 seized in a raid at the Hawthorne Smoke Shop after the murder of William McSwiggin in 1926. They showed how in one eighteen-month period Capone's syndicate had accrued profits of more than half a million dollars. The entries were written by at least three different people. From various scraps of evidence Wilson discovered in November 1930 that one author was Lou Shumway, once cashier at a brothel, the Ship. In February 1931 he was traced to Miami and prevailed upon to return and give evidence voluntarily. The alternative would have been a subpoena, notice to Capone of a new threat, another nuisance to be eliminated.

At this critical juncture Capone's tax lawyer, Lawrence P. Mattingly, surprisingly, volunteered a written admission of his client's tax delinquency: $26,000 in 1926, $40,000 in 1927, and about

$100,000 in 1928 and 1929. However, Wilson was not going to be satisfied with this underestimate. Capone spent at least $100,000 a year. Although Mattingly stated that the admission was made "without prejudice," it was interpreted as a confession and retained for use in the trial—which now seemed inevitable.

It transpired that most of the offenses that could be proved were for 1924. Under a statute limiting prosecution of tax offenses to within six years, the government would be barred from prosecuting its case after March 15, 1931. A grand jury was summoned. It indicted Capone on March 13 for tax offenses in 1924. The verdict was not made public until investigation for the other years, 1925 to 1929, were completed. A federal grand jury assembled again but this time openly on June 5, 1931. It now added twenty-two counts, covering the years 1925 to 1929, to the first indictment. The income the Internal Revenue Service could prove Capone had earned was $1,038,655.84. Its tax assessment was $219,260.12, and therefore the possible fine was as much as $164,445.09. On June 12 a special grand jury returned a third indictment. It charged Capone and sixty-eight other people with conspiracy to violate the Volstead Act. The total of the maximum sentences for all three indictments would be thirty-four years.

With his customary sangfroid Capone met newspaper reporters on July 29 in the Hotel Lexington. "I've been made an issue and I'm not complaining. But why don't they go after all these bankers who took the savings of thousands of poor people and lost them in bank failures? How about that? Isn't it lots worse to take the last few dollars some small family has saved—perhaps to live on while the head of a family is out of a job—than to sell a little beer, a little alky?"

The actual trial lasted from October 6 to October 17, 1931. A principal argument for the defense was that Capone lost heavily at race tracks and thus had never possessed great wealth, that his gambling losses had to be deducted from his gambling winnings to discover his true wealth. In his summing up for the prosecution U.S. attorney E. Q. Johnson refuted the likelihood of Capone's largesse to the poor and needy: "Who is this man who has become such a glamorous figure? . . . He has been called Robin Hood by his counsel. Robin Hood took from the strong to feed the weak. Did this Robin Hood buy eight thousand dollars' worth of belt buckles for the unemployed? Was his six thousand dollar meat bill in a few weeks for the hungry? No, it went to the Capone home on Palm

Island to feed the guests at nightly poker parties. Did he buy twenty-seven dollar shirts for the shivering men who sleep under Wacker Drive?"

The jury found Capone guilty of only five of twenty-three separate charges. But it was enough. He was sentenced to a total of eleven years in prison and fined fifty thousand dollars and charged thirty thousand dollars in costs—a record for tax avoidance to that time. The third indictment, for violations of the Volstead Act, was not pursued.

Thus with the death of one legend, Capone's immunity from the law, another was born. The worst crime according to American law is not treason but tax evasion. It is the one offense that will not go unpunished. You may get away with murder but not without paying your income taxes.

The cellars that now awaited Capone were dungeons. Capone's first months of imprisonment were spent in the county jail pending an appeal. On May 14, 1932, he was transferred to the Atlanta Penitentiary, where he was set to work as a cobbler, and thence, on August 18, 1933, to the newly opened prison of Alcatraz. Assigned the fatiguing duty of working the laundry mangle, he was now the butt of others' jeers, "the wop with the mop."

Capone's career had, since 1925, been set out on a course of retaliation against the North Side gang. It was inevitable that the ensuing, wearisome cycle of retribution carried out in plot and counterplot would conclude with madness and death. Insanity was one of the penalties of players in the tragedy of revenge, something realized by Greek dramatists, Renaissance playwrights, and Italian opera composers. And it was Capone's fate.

For many years he had hidden his illness, neurosyphilis, contracted in the late twenties and never treated. But it was becoming progressively worse. And on February 8, 1938, it was clear Capone was going out of his mind. His central nervous system was damaged beyond repair and he spent the last eleven months of his main sentence in a hospital ward. He was too ill to serve the extra year's sentence in Cook County jail and, on January 6, 1939, was removed to the federal correctional institution at Terminal Island, near Los Angeles. Jake Guzik said of him, "Al is as nutty as a fruit cake." On his release he was able to eke out a few years of comfort in the comparative obscurity of his Miami home. Penicillin stabilized a condition it could not cure. Capone died after a bout of bronchial pneumonia and a brain hemorrhage on January 25, 1947.

—FIVE—

BEST CELLARS

THE SOCIAL ABANDON AND GAIETY OF THE 1920s was celebrated in the song and expression "Makin' Whoopee." It was used variously to describe: a tourist soaking himself silly in a nightclub; a countryman out on the town; an errant husband on the loose; and, more ominously, a banker speculating recklessly. Its result, according to F. Scott Fitzgerald, was "A whole race going hedonistic, deciding on pleasure." He also said in his *Echoes of the Jazz Age* (1931) that the profligacy of the period was perpetrated by "the generation whose girls dramatized themselves as flappers, the generation that corrupted its elders and eventually overreached itself less through lack of morals than lack of taste."

If asked to select only one feature of social life that contributed most to the special character and legend of the Roaring Twenties most people would probably settle for the rise and fall of gangsters. The world of literature provided its share of best sellers—especially the thick books used to secrete bottles of booze. But the underworld provided the best cellars of all; its protagonists proved the most persuasive salesmen. Crime provided as many heroes and heroines for mass idolatry as spectator sports and motion pictures. Several, like

106

the stars of sport and screen, rose in public esteem through natural talent combined with a flair for publicity, an innate sense of timing and good luck. Many were not gangsters but excited attention as associates of successful bootleggers and racketeers. Some, like Texas Guinan, were celebrated for their bizarre behavior. Others, like Joe E. Lewis, engaged sympathy for surviving overwhelming odds.

Texas Guinan was the most celebrated nightclub hostess of the day. Born Mary Louise Cecilia Guinan, she did indeed come from Waco, Texas. Throughout the decade at various clubs (and once in partnership with Larry Fay) she insisted she did not have to sell alcohol to make money and pretended she did not do so. Her clients, she claimed, if they drank, did so from their own hip flasks and bought only mineral water and ginger ale at her clubs. Charged by Emory R. Buckner, the district attorney of New York, for violating the liquor laws, she managed to get herself acquitted and said the publicity acquired was worth a fortune. She capitalized on it by opening a revue, "The Padlocks of 1927," in the Century Theater, New York. She herself appeared in public with a necklace made of padlocks. Her cry of "Hello, suckers" to her clients conveyed her special brand of opportunistic candor. She was, for a while, adored by a public anxious to adopt the part she had conferred on them. Her showgirls were "Guinan Graduates" and one danced with a boa constrictor.

But the underworld was not joyous. Its macabre and malevolent side was illustrated by the fate of singer and comedian Joe E. Lewis. Lewis was widely known for his act at the Green Mill, a North Side cabaret in Chicago, owned by Danny Cohen. In the fall of 1927 Danny Cohen offered "Machine Gun" Jack McGurn a 25 percent interest in the Green Mill if he could persuade Joe E. Lewis to renew his contract there. Lewis was earning $650 a week as the star of the show but he had been offered $1,000 and a proportion of the cover charge to appear at the rival New Rendezvous Café owned by Joe Fogarty. Despite threats from McGurn Joe Lewis opened his act at the New Rendezvous on November 2, 1927. On November 10 Machine Gun struck. He wanted to destroy Lewis by making him a cripple. Lewis was assaulted by three gangsters in his bedroom. Two of them fractured his skull with the butts of their guns. The third pierced the singer's jaw with his knife and sliced open the left side of his face to his ear. He slashed Lewis's tongue and vocal cords a dozen times. Joe E. Lewis came round and got up. He underwent six hours of surgery at Columbia Memorial Hospital. He survived, but it took him almost a year before he was able to speak and to read and write again. It was ten years before he recaptured his former success on the stage, this time as a comedian only. Perhaps out of shame, Al Capone, who was McGurn's patron, gave Lewis $10,000 after his ordeal.

Stories about Texas Guinan, Joe E. Lewis, and other associates of criminals are myths of the underworld. They have been propagated by legends surrounding the inception of a national criminal syndicate, the Mafia, and the introduction of a special vocabulary, first into the underworld and then society at large.

———————◆◆———————

The more exacting analysts among recent historians, Joseph L. Albini in *The American Mafia* (1971) and Gaia Servadio in *Mafioso* (1976), agree that the term "Mafia" can only be used with any certainty to describe a certain type of criminal organization after May 11, 1860, when Giuseppe Garibaldi annexed Sicily for Victor Emmanuel II of Piedmont-Savoy. It was not unitl 1950 that the Senate Committee on Interstate Commerce in Organized Crime, headed by Estes Kefauver, declared that the Mafia existed at all. And it was not until 1963, when Joseph Valachi testified before another Senate committee, that the expressions "Cosa Nostra" and "Mafia" were commonly regarded as synonymous. Joseph L. Albini concludes that "all the so-called evidence for 'Cosa Nostra,' 'The American Mafia' or any form of national, formally structured criminal organization lies only in the massive confused and contradictory assumptions of those who purport to have demonstrated its existence."

In 1863 Giuseppe Rizzotto's play *I Mafiusi di la Vicaria (The Heroes of the Penitentiary)* dramatized life in the large prison in Palermo, Sicily. It was extremely popular, and its focus on the *camorristi* of organized crime introduced the term *Mafiusi* to press and politics. *Mafia*, derived from it, was soon adopted by Italian society as a designation for all sorts of organized crime. *Mafioso* or *maffioso* came to denote affiliation with the Mafia.

In Sicily between 1820 and the year of revolutions, 1848, societies had developed to sustain the interests of the landowning bourgeoisie and aristocracy against the resentment of the peasants. The Sicilian Mafia was neither one society nor several but a prototype, what Francis and Elizabeth Reuss Ianni in *A Family Business* (1972) call a "generic model." *Mafia* was commonly used to describe a whole series of protective societies of different regions: *Mano Fraterno; Oblonica; La Fratellanza; Fratuzzi; Fontana Nuova; La Scattialora;* and others. There was probably no centralized system of authority, which was why the Mafia was so difficult to attack. It was hard enough to define.

To some the Mafia was a benevolent organization, robbing the rich to give to the poor. Certainly peasants venerated brigands. Whether they were their beneficiaries is another matter. If the poor were not robbed it was perhaps because they had nothing worth stealing. It is just as likely that Mafia was a system of executing crime by extortion, force, and intimidation with an organization to provide immunity from prosecution through various forms of legal and political protection. The mafioso, like latter-day American political and criminal bosses, moved in the demimonde.

One historian, Herbert Asbury, believes the Sicilian Mafia was present in America in New Orleans as early as 1869. But most others agree that it was the Hennessy (or Hennessey) case of 1890 that led to press and public speculation about a Mafia in the United States.

A series of macabre murders in New Orleans was traced to a vendetta between rival gangs of dock racketeers, that of Antonio and Carlo Matranga (brothers from Palermo) and that of the Provenzano brothers (Joe, George, and Pete). David Hennessy was the superintendent of police investigating the case. After an attempt on the lives of seven members of the Matranga gang on May 6, 1890, Joe and Pete Provenzano were tried and convicted of conspiracy to murder. Several policemen testified on behalf of the Provenzano brothers, and Hennessy, who was friendly with them, tried to intervene and settle the dispute between the two gangs. After their conviction the Provenzanos were granted a new trial for October 22, 1890. Hennessy indicated that his new testimony would disclose information about a secret society of Italian immigrants, the Mafia. He did not live to tell his tale. On October 15, 1890, he was killed by five armed men on the streets of New Orleans.

In the public outcry following the assassination of their chief of police nineteen Sicilians were indicted for conspiracy or murder. Of these eight escaped and were allowed to elude prosecution, five had their trial postponed, and six were actually tried. But the jury acquitted three outright and was undecided about the other three. Public speculation about bribery and intimidation of the jurors was rife. On March 14, 1891, when the birthday of the Italian king, Umberto I, was being celebrated by Italian-Americans throughout the United

States, a lynch mob took the eleven defendants from jail, mowed down nine of them with a variety of firearms, and hanged the other two from lampposts.

One of two grand juries investigating the murder of David Hennessy confirmed "the existence of the secret organization styled *Mafia.*" The press was not slow to gather clues and speculate on the cause of public concern. For instance, the *New York Tribune* of March 23, 1891, said,

> Not only in New Orleans but generally in large cities throughout the country, Italians of criminal antecedents and propensities are more or less closely affiliated for the purpose of requiting injuries and gratifying animosities by secret vengeance. These organizations, in common speech and belief are connected with the Mafia . . . Through their agency the most infernal crimes have been committed and have gone unpunished. They have succeeded in keeping their existence and doings wrapped in mystery and darkness, and in the opinion of thousands who condemn the New Orleans Mob, a branch of the order is immediately responsible for the crimes which the mob avenged.

When extortion by *La Mano Nero*, the Black Hand, led to widespread terrorization and lawlessness on New York's East Side at the turn of the century the police department created a special Italian squad under Lieutenant Giuseppe (or Joseph) Petrosino, a Neapolitan immigrant, to break up syndicated crime. He ascertained the whereabouts of hundreds of Italian and Sicilian illegal immigrants and had them deported. It was said that in one year, 1907, he made over seven hundred arrests personally. He identified his archenemies: Enrico Alfano, or Erricone, whom he supposed head of a transplanted Camorra; and Ignazio Saietto"Lupo the Wolf"—head of a new American Mafia. His chance to prove his theory came in 1907 with a new wave of Black Hand terrorism. His break came with the appeal for help from an Italian merchant, Joseph Trano, who was a victim of extortion demands. In August Petrosino set a trap by marking the ransom money. Thus he traced and captured Vincenzo Abadezza, one of Lupo's men, and eight others. The police confiscated two notebooks from the gangsters and discovered details about the organization of the Mafia and the names of some of their victims. If Petrosino was pleased with his solution to the problem of *La Mano Nero* in New York he was dismayed at the punishment of the offenders. Abadezza was sentenced to only two-and-a-half years' imprisonment and his fellow defendants received much shorter terms.

Undeterred, Petrosino pursued his investigations—this time in Italy. In Rome and Naples in 1909 he gathered information on known criminals who had immigrated to the United States. However, when he went on to Sicily he was assassinated there in Palermo on the night of March 12 and 13, 1909. Most writers, such as Norman Lewis in *The Honored Society* (1964), ascribe the instigation of the assassination to Don Vito Cascioferro, supposed head of the Mafia in Sicily. He himself boasted of the deed. Two anonymous letters to the police, one of March 13, 1909, and the second of March 16, named Petrosino's assassins and attributed the instigation of the murder to Cascioferro. Cascioferro, however, went free until 1926, when he was interned in Mussolini's purge of the Mafia. Whatever the circumstances Petrosino's death was intended as a warning to others as well as the elimination of a threat to the Mafia.

Cascioferro, a native of Palermo, had been a temporary immigrant to the United States in 1900, living first in New York and later in New Orleans. Suspected of the murder of Benedetto Madonia, or Morris, an Italian he stabbed and cut into pieces, which he stuffed into a barrel, he fled America and returned to Palermo. Petrosino's biographer, Arrigo Petacco, writing in 1974, makes a considerable claim for Cascioferro's importance: his principal task in America, argues Petacco, "was to establish an organizational structure for the Palermo-New York circuit, which until then had consisted of relations between persons rather than between groups." Cascioferro was "the pivot" in the alliance of the Mafia and *La Mano Nero:* "it was he who created the vast empire of crime, with permanent, solid interconnections, that exists today."

As Francis and Elizabeth Reuss Ianni explain in *A Family Business*, the conditions that had led to the formation of Sicilian *Mafie* had their counterparts in the cities of the United States. In the Italian ghettos the family was just as important as it had been in Sicilian villages, poverty was just as endemic, and the immigrants' inability to assimilate themselves into American society resulted in social tension and conflict. But the American Mafia took time to develop, just as the Sicilian Mafia and Neapolitan Camorra had taken time. Immigrants had come over as individuals and not as members of a cohesive social group with well-defined aims. Without established systems of authority and friendship the Mafia could not exist, and the chance of achieving this in the new environment was undermined by the system of education in American schools, with its emphasis on individualism rather than family loyalty.

However, in the twenties everything changed. Benito Mussolini, Fascist prime minister of Italy from 1922, directed Cesare Mori, prefect of police, to disband the Sicilian Mafia. Although he did not succeed in exterminating it, two thousand mafiosi were tried (sometimes for crimes committed more than twenty years previously), convicted, and imprisoned. The leaders probably escaped and they and their subalterns either joined the Fascists and submerged their identities—while retaining their style—or emigrated to the United States.

The other development was the introduction of national prohibition in America. Bootlegging was not only a source of profit but also provided a basis for organizing immigrants in gangs. It was the second generation of Italian immigrants who were especially attuned to both Italian individual abilities (such as producing alcohol) and American social needs (consuming it). The successful American bootlegging gang supplied the sort of hierarchical structure and family loyalty that had been disrupted by the processes of acculturation in American society. Thus the Italians could gain most. The conception of a new form of syndicated crime and the reception of new Sicilian mafiosi like John Scalise and Albert Anselmi in their flight from Mussolini's purges led to the inception of a new Italian-American Mafia. At the end of the 1920s the Atlantic City conference, the Wall Street crash, and the Castellammarese War provided a leavening to make the mixture rise and ensure its stability.

———————◆▶———————

The chain of events in Chicago leading to the Atlantic City Conference at the President Hotel from May 13 to May 16, 1929, is comparatively easy to follow and interpret. However, New York was as important in the national organization of syndicated crime as Chicago. But much less is known about it. The train of events from New York to the Atlantic City conference is more a matter of conjecture than certainty. The facts are part of criminal history. But many were never recorded; others have become obscure. New York received much less publicity than Chicago, although internecine feuds between rival political factions and competing gangs were a feature of its social life. Battles were fought with machine guns on the streets; assassinations were consummated at banquets. If the body count seemed smaller in New York than Chicago this was because most deaths occurred in suburban ambushes or in deserted speakeasies and restaurants. They were rarely caught in the glare of press publicity.

Yet the pattern of gangster politics was similar in both cities. In Chicago Johnny Torrio was the criminal leader ahead of his time who tried to forge alliances between different ethnic groups lest the incredible profits of prohibition be wasted in feuds. Arnold Rothstein in New York, the man who "fixed" the World Series in 1919, saw the advantages of Torrio's system. But he trusted other gangsters much less, not because he had doubts about their loyalty to him but rather because he knew about their greed and cupidity, their ethnic rivalries and political affiliations, all of which were subversive of order. Thus he preferred to enjoy a profit from the periphery by subsidizing others' rackets in bootlegging, prostitution, and gambling, and letting them feud.

Rothstein inculcated his views in a new breed of master criminals. He employed Frank Costello, Salvatore Luciano, and Meyer Lansky, among others, and urged them to imitate Torrio and cultivate the image of successful businessmen and maintain a low profile to police, press, and public. Rothstein was killed in the Park Central Hotel on Seventh Avenue in November 1928 for failing to honor gambling debts. For a time it seemed that his precepts died with him.

The competition for political control between the Irish and the Italians that had erupted in Chicago before the 1920s had already broken into a guerrilla war in New York after the death of Charlie Murphy, boss of Tammany Hall, in 1924. The principal contenders for power were James J. Hines (Irish) and Albert C. Marinelli (Italian). Since the new boss, George Olvany, was a nonentity, Hines and Marinelli competed openly for control of the Hall. Each had forged links with the underworld. Hines and his faction with Arthur Flegenheimer, alias Dutch Schultz, and Marinelli with Guiseppe Masseria, Salvatore Luciano, and Frank Costello.

Giuseppe Masseria was the most prominent of self-styled bosses in the Italian-American underworld of New York. Behind his back Joe the Boss was called Joe the Slob by his enemies. Slovenly, uncouth, semi-literate, he owed his preeminence to an ability to outwit and survive his rivals. Unlike other famous hoodlums he was already an adult when he immigrated to New York and allied himself with Ignazio Saietta—Lupo the Wolf—in East Harlem. When Lupo was convicted of counterfeiting and sentenced to thirty years' imprisonment in 1920 Masseria took over. In the crucial first year of prohibition he dispatched his only rival as leading Italian bootlegger, Salvatore Mauro. But Masseria could not rest in peace. A new rival, Umberto Valenti, signaled his ambition to supersede him by murdering Vincente Terranova, the younger brother of his ally, Ciro Terranova, the Artichoke king. Masseria planned revenge but his scheme misfired. When he tried to eliminate Valenti on May 8, 1922, at the so-called curb exchange on Grand Street—where bootleggers consummated their transactions—a melée ensued. Four passersby were injured. One of Joe's bodyguards, Silva Tagliagamba, was fatally wounded. At an action replay on August 9 Joe the Boss escaped unhurt and earned increased status. The opposing gangs met at a spaghetti house on East Twelfth Street on August 11 for a conference. And there Valenti was eliminated.

Despite his gross personal behavior, Masseria cultivated the techniques of Rothstein, to live in the shadows and exercise power without appearing to do so. Besides his alliance with Ciro Terranova in the Bronx he formed others with Frankie Yale and, later, Anthony Pisano and Joe Adonis, alias Joseph A. Doto, in Brooklyn and Salvatore Luciano and Frank Costello in Manhattan.

✗ Frank Costello was born Francesco Castiglia in Cosenza, Calabria, in 1891. When his family immigrated to New York in 1895 they settled in East Harlem. His most individual characteristic was his voice. A badly executed operation to remove his tonsils and adenoids damaged his vocal cords. Thereafter he could only speak in a rasping whisper, which turned every sentence into an ominous threat.

Salvatore Luciano was born Salvatore Lucania in Lercara Friddi, part of Palermo, Sicily, in 1897 and came to New York with his family in 1906. They settled in a neighborhood composed of Italian, Sicilian, and Jewish ethnic groups on the Lower East Side. Luciano began his criminal career by selling protection to Jewish children on their way to school. But he graduated to the distribution of narcotics and was indicted and convicted of trading in heroin in 1916 and 1923. He belonged to the new generation of Italians and Sicilians who formed alliances based on common interests with men from different ethnic groups. Thus his closest ally was Meyer Lansky, a Jew. Born Meyer Suchowljansky in Grodno, Poland, in 1902 he, too, immigrated to New York with his family in 1911. An exceptional mathematician, Lansky began his career in organized crime as an automobile mechanic who provided gangs with fleets of souped-up trucks and cars before he entered the bootlegging industry. His partner was Benjamin ("Bugsy") Siegel and their gang was known as the Bug and Meyer mob.

Luciano and Lansky wanted to smelt gold from the molten ores of the melting pot. They were interested only in a syndicate that was run like a conventional business corporation. To them profit and efficiency counted for more than ethnic ties. Any syndicate of crime would, like the society it served, have to be a pluralistic organization containing and absorbing different ethnic groups.

With Johnny Torrio, Rothstein had tried to forge a national syndicate based on sectional cooperation between different groups. He organized a central buying office to procure alcohol for wholesale and retail. It came from Canada, the West Indies and even England and Scotland. It was distributed throughout the United States. By 1927 the syndicate, known variously as the Big Seven and the Seven Group, enjoyed a monopoly of the liquor traffic on the North Atlantic coast from Boston to Baltimore. It was to be the prototype of national syndicates based on any illicit trade. The monopoly was absolute. Rivals were given no quarter. As Fred J. Cook explains in *The Secret Rulers* (1966): "Since the East Coast mobs held control at the neck of the liquor bottle, so to speak, theirs was the decisive voice in determining whom they would do business with." And according to Rothstein's principles its success depended on cooperation between these different ethnic groups—Italian, Irish, Jewish—rather than internecine competition. The names of the leaders indicate as much: Salvatore Luciano; Waxey Gordon, Owen Madden, and William Dwyer—Rothstein's heirs; the Bug and Meyer mob led by Bugsy Siegel and Meyer Lansky; Louis ("Lepke") Buchalter and Jacob ("Gurrah") Shapiro; Frank Costello and Dandy Phil Kastel; Abner ("Longy") Zwillman of Newark; and Charles ("King") Solomon of Boston.

In the underworld the success of the Big Seven was held up as a model to be imitated elsewhere. Moreover, gangsters looked to their future. Even before the Wall Street crash many expected repeal of prohibition. Thus they prepared to consolidate their interests in traditional sources of wealth, the old services of providing prostitutes and gambling, the old disservices of drugs and racketeering. In order to take stock of a changing situation they met in Atlantic City. The conclave was representative of crime throughout the nation: from Chicago came Al Capone and Jake ("Greasy Thumb") Guzik; from New York Salvatore Luciano, Lepke Buchalter, Joe Adonis, Dutch Schultz, Frank Scalise, and Albert Anastasia; from

Boston King Solomon; from Cleveland Moe Dalitz, Louis Rothkopf, Chuck Polizzi, and Big Al Polizzi; from Detroit Abe Bernstein of the Purple Gang; from Philadelphia Nig Rosen, alias Harry Stromberg, and Max ("Boo-Boo") Hoff; from Kansas City John Lazia of the Pendergast machine; from New Jersey Longy Zwillmann.

Nucky Johnson was the host of the conference, which was presided over by Frank Costello. Its immediate problem was Chicago, both the collapse of thieves' honor there and the publicity surrounding Al Capone. For his part Capone was expected to lie low, to accede to voluntary imprisonment. More ominously, gangsters attending planned to eliminate those who stood in the way of a new national syndicate or who would not accept its authority. The old guard was conspicuous by its absence from the conference. The so-called Mustache Petes did not attend.

The determination of the new men to eliminate the old guard deepened after the Wall Street crash, an event as crucial to the underworld as to the rest of society. In the depression gangsters' clients, shorn of their former affluence, could not afford their special services. Because of recession the gangs were once more in competition with one another. Rivalries that had become submerged in the revelry of the Roaring Twenties once more burst into the open. Especially notorious was the feud between Giuseppe Masseria and Salvatore Maranzano in New York. The settlement of their so-called Castellammarese War was synonymous with the institution of a Mafia on a national scale.

Salvatore Maranzano had arrived on the scene much later than any of the other leading gangsters. A native of Sicily and a failed priest, he immigrated to New York after the First World War. In addition to bootlegging and racketeering he had a front, a real estate business, the Eagle Building Corporation, in the Grand Central Building. But his most lucrative interest was an immigration racket designed to defeat the restrictive acts of 1921 and 1924. He despised Masseria for being an uncouth peasant. Masseria despised him for being a pedantic snob. Maranzano had the stereotyped and contradictory characteristics of a Mafia don. He was both generous and parsimonious, benevolent and malevolent.

Masseria and Maranzano headed rival but loose coalitions. That around Masseria still included Vito Genovese and Frank

Costello. It was led by Italians who were not from Sicily and was allied with men who were not even Italian and quite likely to be Jewish. The other, around Salvatore Maranzano, included Joe Bonanno, Joe Profaci, and Gaetano ("Tom") Gagliano. It was composed of men who were not only prominent in the *Unione Siciliana*, and therefore Sicilian, but also some of whom, like Bonanno and Stefano Magaddino, came from the town of Castellammare del Golfo in the west of the island.

For a time Luciano declined to ally himself with either Masseria or Maranzano. But eventually he threw in his lot with Masseria. His alliance was cynical and he began to work for Masseria's overthrow after the elimination of Maranzano. In league with him were Costello, Genovese, and Lansky. In 1929 Luciano earned a unique place in the mythology of the underworld. On October 17 he returned from a one-way ride. He was discovered by the police on the sidewalk of Hylan Boulevard, Staten Island, where he had been left for dead. He had been kidnapped by Maranzano's gang after drugs or, possibly, information—the names and intentions of his assailants are still not known. They had hoisted him from a tree by his thumbs and tortured him with cigarette burns, razor blade cuts, and beatings. He refused to yield the information and was abandoned to die. But he lasted until a police car took him to a hospital. His wounds were so extensive that he required fifty-five stitches and he carried the scars for the rest of his life. The front muscles of his right eyelid were severed and thereafter the lid drooped, giving him a baleful expression. Despite his ordeal he refused to tell the police what had happened. "I'll take care of this in my own way," was all they could get out of him. He lived on as "Lucky" Luciano. The reasons why he was kidnapped and assaulted remained secret. His survival became a legend.

The first victim of the Castellammarese War was Gaetano ("Tommy") Reina. Masseria resented Reina's monopoly of ice distribution in New York, even though Reina was supposedly in his own coalition. When Reina made plans to change sides from Masseria to Maranzano Masseria had him killed. He was assassinated in the Bronx on February 26, 1930, shot full in the face. Reina's lieutenants Gaetano ("Tom") Gagliano, Dominick ("The Gap") Petrilli and Tommy ("Three-finger" Brown) Lucchese would not accept Masseria's choice of Joseph Pinzolo as their new boss. They continued the secret negotiations with Maranzano begun before Reina's assassination. And in September they had Pinzolo killed in the office of the California Dry Fruit Importers, his front, in the Brokaw Building, Broadway.

This assassination led to open warfare. The alliances and, therefore, the antagonism stretched beyond New York. Thus Maranzano's allies included Stefano Maggadino in Buffalo and Joseph Aiello in Chicago, a sworn foe of Capone. Maranzano had Masseria's allies, Alfred Mineo, Steve Ferrigno (or Fennuci) and Joseph Catania (or "Soldier Joe" Baker) rubbed out one by one. During the course of the Castellammarese War about sixty gangsters were killed. Police in league with Masseria were so disturbed by unwelcome publicity attending the feuds that they persuaded him to try and bring them to an end. This was also the advice of other underworld leaders.

Luciano and his friends, trusted by both sides, offered to put other gang leaders out of their misery by murdering Masseria. In return they expected Maranzano's acceptance of Luciano as the new head of the Masseria gang and a guarantee that no reprisals would be taken against those who had fought on either side in the Castellammarese War. Masseria's other allies, Frank Livorsi, Ciro Terranova, and Vito Genovese, were brought over to Maranzano's side.

Although Joe the Boss could outrun his enemies, he could not outwit his friends. After lunch together at Gerardo Scarpato's restaurant in Coney Island on April 15, 1931, Lucky absented himself for a few minutes and Masseria was then dispatched by assassins who had entered the dining room. The assassins were Vito Genovese, Joe Adonis, Albert Anastasia, and Bugsy Siegel. Masseria slumped forward, his blood staining the tablecloth. His card game had been interrupted. In his hand was grasped the ace of diamonds.

Maranzano thus succeeded in achieving supreme control for a time. Some historians date the founding of the America Mafia to Maranzano's decisions implemented at a secret meeting of unknown date. They believe Maranzano thought he was carrying out Julius Caesar's ideas for a semi-military organization. He instituted criminal governance by a chain of command from a supreme boss of all bosses, to family bosses, and underbosses. The head of a family was the *capo* and below him were a *subcapo*, then *caporegime* lieutenants, each in charge of a *regime* crew. Maranzano of course would be *capo di tutti capi*.

In order to anticipate wasteful feuds families would be apportioned regional areas. Gaia Servadio lists the cities that were the new centers of syndicate crime: Boston, Buffalo, Chicago, Cleveland,

Detroit, Kansas City, Los Angeles, Newark, New Orleans, Philadelphia, Pittsburg, San Francisco, Miami, and Las Vegas. Havana in Cuba would remain open to all. New York City would be divided among five families: the old Masseria gang now led by Frank Costello and Salvatore Luciano with Vito Genovese, *subcapo;* the old Reina gang led by Tom Gagliano with Thomas Lucchese, *subcapo;* the Maranzano gang divided into two families, one led by Joseph Profaci and the other by Joe Bonanno; and in Brooklyn a coalition of Philip and Vincent Mangano with Albert Anastasia, *subcapo.*

According to the self-confessed mafioso Joseph Valachi, the new system was established by, and celebrated in, a banquet somewhere in the Bronx that lasted five days. It had the subsidiary purpose of raising funds to the tune of $115,000. And of that $6,000 came from tickets purchased by Al Capone.

However, the war was not yet over. The Castellammarese demanded another bloodletting. Maranzano himself supposedly said, "We have to go to the mattress again." He meant he would resume warfare and told his henchman, Joseph Valachi, that his new list of people to be eliminated included Capone, Costello, Genovese, Luciano, Mangano, Joe Adonis, and Dutch Schultz. They did not wait to be hit. This younger generation agreed that the only way to penetrate Maranzano's line of defense was to use Jewish gunmen, unknown in New York, disguised as federal agents working for the Internal Revenue Service. The day of reckoning would be called "the Night of the Sicilian Vespers."

On September 11, 1931, four men pretending to be income tax inspectors entered Maranzano's Park Avenue office. Two held his guards in one room while the others tried to eliminate Maranzano quietly—that is, without firing a shot. The assassins were unable to finish Maranzano by strangulation, stabbing his torso, and slitting his throat. When none of these sufficed they killed him with bullets, then they and the disarmed guards in the next room fled the scene.

Maranzano's murder was only the first of between thirty and forty killed that day and the next across the United States. They left Lucky Luciano supreme chief with Vito Genovese as his *subcapo.* As is the case with everything associated with the Mafia historians argue about what was achieved. Some believe that Lucky never occupied supreme power. Richard Hammer in *Playboy's Illustrated History of Crime* (1975) believes he did so by denying himself full recognition: "Knowing the fate of others who aspired to supreme rule and who publicly boasted of their new position, he categorically rejected the title and its implicit powers. . . . What Luciano recognized was that in spurning the title publicly, in showing himself modest, just one of the boys, the power and the position would devolve upon him in fact." Other historians believe the purges of September 1931 ended the power of the Mafia and established the authority of the *Unione Siciliana*. However, there is agreement that Luciano established a new underworld court of six judges before whom anyone suspected of a capital offense in Mafia or the *Unione Siciliana* could be tried. As a gesture of good faith Luciano and Genovese also went to Chicago and explained the reasons for the purge before Capone and the other leading gangsters at a conclave in the Congress Hotel. They exposed Maranzano's intention of eliminating allies, rivals, and adversaries and exculpated themselves. Lucky was unanimously elected chairman of the national underworld commission.

Under Luciano the syndicate, or Mafia, exploded its traditional boundaries of recruitment. Lucky realized that the Wall Street crash, which had brought incipient tensions in the underworld to a head, would, in the long run, also provide it with greater stability. It gave gangsters a golden opportunity to compensate themselves against future losses in the inevitable demise of prohibition. They could now enter legitimate business with honest citizens who had lost their assets. They alone could provide funds for needy businessmen. For instance, in 1931 Frank Costello formed an association with the Mills Novelty Company of Chicago, the largest manufacturers of slot machines. With a partner, "Dandy" Phil Kastel of New Orleans, he established a whole series of companies such as the Tru-Mint, the Village Candy, and the Monroe Candy companies. Their machines were placed in bars, candy and cigar stores and stationery shops across the country.

The Chicago conclave of 1931 was not the end of the matter. Over the next three years subsequent meetings were held in Cleveland, and New York. Representatives from syndicates in New York, Chicago, Cleveland, Minneapolis, Boston, Philadelphia, Miami, New Orleans, and New Jersey sometimes met in the new Waldorf-Astoria Hotel, New York City. The hotel was one of several residences of Lucky, who lived there under an alias, Charlie Ross. Ross appeared to be a respectable businessman. On the advice of Aaron Shapire, a Fifth Avenue lawyer, this criminal syndicate took the National Recovery Administration of June 16, 1933, as its model with a commission governing the operation and development of the principal syndicates.

Twentieth-century gang leaders had forged a political and economic system beyond, but subversive of, existing society. Yet they had done so within an American tradition. The industrial magnates of the nineteenth century, people like Andrew Carnegie in steel, John D. Rockefeller in oil, Gustavus Swift in grain, Henry Havemeyer in sugar, and others, also defied law and subverted justice to achieve their monopolies, industrial combinations outside the existing political and economic system. They transformed the various processes of the Industrial Revolution into their own rackets, graced with terms like "trusts," "pools," and "holding companies." Like the bosses of syndicate crime they emerged as leaders in the Gilded Age because they were smart operators. Their methods of suborning government and persuading the public were not very different from those of Johnny Torrio and Al Capone, Arnold Rothstein and Lucky Luciano. The railroad magnate Cornelius Vanderbilt was openly contemptuous of the law: "What do I care about the law," he said, "H'ain't I got the power?" He and other robber barons manipulated stocks and shares in their own interests, outwitted public authorities and gave no quarter to labor. Both robber barons and bootlegging gangsters were quite prepared to fight wars to get their way. And when a comparatively small number of monopolies emerged, strengthened at the expense of those that had failed, the remaining robber barons and bootlegging bosses were prepared to make peace with one another.

———◄•►———

According to popular myth gang bosses were bound to lose. Lucky Luciano was prosecuted by New York District Attorney Thomas E. Dewey for organizing rings of prostitutes, which took in twelve million dollars every year. He was indicted with eleven others on April 2, 1936, on more than sixty charges. His trial began on May 13 and lasted for three weeks, at the end of which he was convicted and sentenced by Judge Philip J. McCook to between thirty and fifty years at Clinton State Prison, Dannemora. However, the syndicate itself was intact. On January 3, 1946, he was set free on parole. The services he had rendered the state through the syndicate during the Second World War were being rewarded by Dewey, now governor of New York.

In 1939 Johnny Torrio stood trial for evading income tax to the value of $86,000 in the period from 1933 to 1935. In the course of the trial the quiet man of crime changed his plea to guilty and was sentenced to two-and-a-half years' imprisonment at Fort Leaven-worth.

———————◆▬————————

Public fantasies about the underworld were fostered by press speculation concerning the Mafia. They were fed by a new and developing vocabulary of crime. By the end of the 1920s there were several hundred words and phrases with special meanings in regular use among gangsters. Perhaps speech was superfluous in the underworld. Might was right. Deeds spoke louder than words. The criminal dictionary began with arson, bombing, and corruption and went on to include all forms of terrorism and intimidation. Yet the survival of the fittest in the city jungle, with its maze of competitive interests, depended on more than brute force. To ensure protection from rivals, traitors, and the authorities, communication in code was essential.

The new vocabulary that provided it was, like the professions it served, a product of a particular urban milieu. Words came from the languages of recent immigrants and racketeers, from farmhands and factory workers, from docks and dice games, from prostitution and penal servitude. Although the code was practical, it was also picturesque.

Gordon L. Hostetter and Thomas Quinn Beesley remarked on the development of underworld slang in *It's a Racket* (1929) and provided a "Glossary of Hoodlum Language." They found that some words were of foreign derivation. *Mokker*, a criminal boss, was a corruption of the Danish *Mokke*. *Mack*, a pimp, was a shortened form of the French *macquereau*. The sea provided a series of metaphors, including *round the horn*. To sailors this meant a long and tempestuous voyage around one of the Capes; to gangsters it was a description of the process whereby the police could detain a suspect indefinitely and prevent his release on a writ of habeas corpus by taking him from station to station.

In the underworld the names of beasts of the field acquired human meanings. A *badger* was a decoy; *bull* meant a police officer in uniform; *gorilla* was the term for a strong-arm henchman; *roach* was a common prostitute; *snake* was one of several words for a pickpocket; and a *zebra* was a criminal who had done time and worn stripes. Fowls of the air were not above contempt. The names of birds and their attributes afforded terms for betrayal and for drug addiction. A *jungle buzzard* was a criminal who stole from his own kind. A *canary* was an informer, as were *pigeon* and *stool pigeon*. Hence to *squawk* meant to complain to the authorities and to *sing* meant to confess. *Bluebird* and *snowbird* were, respectively, addicts of heroin and cocaine.

Insect vocabulary conveyed danger and menace. Thus to *buzz* meant both to interview and to extort money, while to *put the bee on* meant to question. To *put the wasp on*, which implied stinging, also meant to extort. To *slap the mosquito on*, with its suggestion of sucking blood, meant to rob or to blackmail. And to *sting* was to take money from someone by some nefarious scheme.

Of course hoodlum vocabulary preceded prohibition. For instance, in the late nineteenth century the term *gangster* meant a member of an American political party. Any association he might have with the underworld could, at that time, be construed as part of the conventional political process. But after 1896 the word came increasingly to signify a member of a criminal gang. However, in the twenties everything changed. Immigration had declined to a trickle of its previous flow. In the absence of continuous immigration true assimilation became more likely and organized crime really did make society more homogeneous in the cities. Prohibition was the novel event that induced large numbers of the public to break the law, consort with criminals, and, necessarily, learn their lingo. It bound together rich and poor, respectable and disreputable.

Two expressions are indissolubly associated with prohibition. The first, *to take for a ride*, meaning to entice or kidnap someone by car, kill him en route, and abandon the body by the roadside, actually antedated prohibition by four years. The first victim was Giuseppe Nazarro, alias Joe Chuck, whose body was found on the railroad tracks in Yonkers, New York. By the end of the 1930s the passive *to be taken for a ride* was used simply to denote the enticing and fleecing of a victim. The second expression, *Chicago piano*, was a simile for a Thompson submachine gun. It originated in Chicago. The machine gun did not become an indispensable part of a gangster's armory in New York until after the murder of Frankie Yale in 1928. Other similes were *chopper, grind organ*, and *typewriter*.

Much of the slang was part and parcel of bootlegging activities. In the topsy-turvy terms of pig Latin *Erbay* was beer. *Alky* was alcohol other than beer. Hard liquor was *hardware* and uncut liquor the *real McCoy*. It was provided by the *bootlegger* and served in the *speakeasy* and *blind pig* or the *honky tonk* (a dive with entertainment) at the *mahogany* (bar counter) by an *apron* (bartender). The regular customers were *barflies;* confirmed alcoholics were *lushers.*

Some expressions originated in Chicago and were particularly associated with the windy city: *grand* (thousand dollars); *hitch* (jail term); *office* (signal); *stir* (penitentiary); *spring* (to set free); and *smoke* (shoot).

The underworld had a deserved reputation for mordant wit. There was a good deal of sexul innuendo in words for guns—*hot-rod* (pistol), *long cut short* (sawed-off shotgun)—in keeping with the license of the age. Gallows humor included: *put in the swing* (execute by hanging); *dance hall* (execution block in prison); *necktie* (noose); *flame chair* and *hot seat* (electric chair); and *burn* and *electric cure* (death in the electric chair).

For some criminals such morbid humor was part of their private as well as their professional lives. John T. Nolan (or Noland) of Philadelphia, better known as Jack ("Legs") Diamond on account of his liking for cards and jewels and his fleet escapes, was once bodyguard to Arnold Rothstein. His wife, Alice, accepted his womanizing and remained faithful to him through thick and thin. But in their house at Acra in the Catskills she provided Legs with a reminder that his life hung by a thread. She had a chair wired for electricity. When visitors sat down in it she would turn on the current and give them a shock. Alice told Legs he might as well get used to the chair "because you may have to sit in one yourself sometime." In fact, this was not how he was killed. He was murdered in Albany on December 18, 1931, and Alice was the only mourner at his funeral.

To illustrate how sophisticated hoodlum language was becoming, Hostetter and Beesley invented a telephone monologue. Abridged and adapted, it goes like this:

> A squad o' dicks in monkey clothes wuz riffin de wops' joint on a squawk from some clunk who'd been took for a couple o' fins dere wit' some tops. While they wuz casin' it a runner drove up to de family entrance wit' a load o' merchandise and the apron had a tough job slippin' im de office not to unload. He wuz afraid the flatties would want a split and the damper didn't have enough grease for a nix crack.
>
> Then the Cuter's men had the cops mug the heavy guy for a show up in de Bureau. They sneezed 'im but he didn't turn on the phonograph. Real Prince o' Wales, yet he didn't even sing when they used the goldfish on his mush. So they knocked him off on a bum rap. Now he's on a ten grand front, see. But his lip thinks he won't go to college. He don't have to lam—he can cop a plea.

124

And here is a translation:

> A detail of plainclothes detectives was searching the Italians' saloon without a warrant after a complaint from some fool who'd been cheated of ten dollars there with some loaded dice. While they were searching the premises a smuggler drove up to the secret entrance with a load of alcohol and the bartender had a tough job giving him the signal not to unload. He was afraid the plainclothesmen would expect a share and there wasn't enough cash in the drawer to buy their silence.
>
> Then the state attorney's men had the police pick up the boss for an identity parade at headquarters. They questioned him using intense methods but he didn't break down and reveal anything. Real elegant criminal, yet he didn't even confess when they beat his face with a rubber hose. So they arrested him on an unjust charge. Now he's out on a bond of ten thousand dollars, see. But his lawyer thinks he won't go to prison. He doesn't have to jump bail—he can plead guilty to a lesser crime to evade a heavy sentence.

With the arrival of talking pictures in the late 1920s, particularly the genre of gangster movies, gangsters' slang became even more widely disseminated. New crime writers such as Dashiell Hammett, James M. Cain, and Raymond Chandler gained from, and contributed to, the popularity of the new vocabulary, which then acquired a still wider currency. Several expressions have survived the age of prohibition with their original meanings intact: *big shot, big time, bump off, crack, frame, get a load of, haywire, lay off, muscle in, pinch, run around,* and others. These legacies of 1920s gangsters' slang suggest that some of the cynicism, casuistry, and casual attitudes of criminals during prohibition have since been adopted as conventional wisdom by many city dwellers.

—SIX—

VICE, VIRTUE, AND VANITY

THE ARCHETYPE OF AMERICAN SOCIETY in the twenties was the flapper. The archetype of American fiction was the impotent hero: the soldier, returned from the world war, shattered physically and emotionally beyond repair. A series of war novels by Thomas Boyd, E. E. Cummings, William March, and Charles Yale Harrison, and even Willa Cather, William Faulkner, and Edith Wharton, described the experiences and analyzed the anxieties of their impotent heroes. They blamed a society that had first injured and then abandoned them. But it was Ernest Hemingway in his novel of postwar disillusion among expatriates, *The Sun Also Rises* (1926), who took the metaphor of the impotent hero to its literal and physical conclusion by making Jake Barnes sexually impotent.

John Dos Passos saw the relevance of this metaphor for postwar society in the United States. In compiling his biographies of people who had taken part in the struggle for or against American intervention for *U.S.A.* (his trilogy of novels published between 1930 and 1936), he made sure that the central biography was of Woodrow Wilson. To Dos Passos, Wilson was the supreme impotent hero of the period, a man at the summit of international prestige during the

Paris Peace Conference of 1919 but incapable of securing a peace to justify the war. In the last resort his prestige was of no more avail than that of the Unknown Soldier, honored but dead and buried. The war that began as a test of manhood had ended by destroying Jake Barnes's manhood. The war in which Wilson had intervened as a test of his own statesmanship ended by destroying his statecraft. After a paralytic stroke of October 2, 1919, Wilson could never be sure of his faculties. Moreover, he was incapable of securing Senate ratification of the Treaty of Versailles and the League of Nations.

He was equally impotent to prevent the imposition of national prohibition. "These miserable hypocrites in the House and Senate— voting to override my veto of the bill, many with their cellars stocked with liquors and not believing in prohibition at all—jumping at the whip of the lobbyists." Such was Woodrow Wilson's alleged response to the overriding of his veto of prohibition as revealed by Dr. Hugh Johnson of Johns Hopkins Hospital of Baltimore ten years later, on January 16, 1929. Wilson apparently continued with, "The bill is utterly unnecessary. It was passed during the war for the purpose of saving grain. The need has gone by. The country would be better off with light wines and beers." And Wilson also put this to Senator Carter Glass of Virginia. He wanted the Democratic platform of 1920 to incorporate an alteration to the Volstead Act making light wines and beers legal. Glass opposed Wilson's suggestion lest it submerge the crucial issue of American membership of the League of Nations beneath the divisive issue of prohibition.

Wilson certainly recognized that full performance of government activities under the Volstead Act would tax the resources of the government to their uttermost: the task was too diverse and the federal government too ill equipped to deal with it. He also believed that the states had a duty to prevent illegal sales of alcohol within their boundaries. But Wilson was a shadow of himself, ekeing out a broken old age until 1924. Theodore Roosevelt had already died in 1919 and William Jennings Bryan was confined to the periphery of politics. As Mark Sullivan puts it, "The Titans had gone." But the fore of federal politics was occupied by prohibition. The Anti-Saloon League had ensured that.

The most prominent member of the Anti-Saloon League was the general counsel, a diminutive man with a dynamic personality, Wayne B. Wheeler. The league boasted of the power of "Wheeler and his wheel." During the campaign for national prohibition Wheeler had the caption "Wayne B. Wheeler, the Fighter, the Man

Whom the Brewers Fear" printed beneath his picture on campaign posters. And by the end of the First World War he had prosecuted two thousand cases against saloons. Wheeler furthermore claimed that the time-limit for ratification of the Eighteenth Amendment was the result of a private agreement between himself and Harding. And although in the wake of public resentment against the Volstead Act the Anti-Saloon League tried to shrug off ownership, Wheeler's pride in his power led to an indiscreet admission that he had, in fact, framed it.

In the short run Wheeler's claims and those of the league strengthened their case and promoted their cause, but in the long run they discredited them. They stimulated panic in the public. When the tissue of falsehoods was exposed in the late twenties the league was damaged irreparably. And as soon as rival wet organizations seemed equally strong the league was overcome.

In the 1920s Wheeler identified the cause of the Anti-Saloon League wholly with himself. From 1921 he retained the services of Edward B. Dunford, former attorney to the prohibition commissioner of Virginia, as assistant. He turned over more and more of the boring legal work to Dunford, who did not like the limelight anyway. Wheeler concentrated on his pursuit of personal power over Congress and publicity in the press. He was prepared to fight a war on two fronts and actually did so throughout the twenties. In addition to his fight to retain control of Congress Wheeler had to fight to retain control of the Anti-Saloon League riven by a series of power struggles. His national prestige was resented by other prohibitionists. The Democrats in the Anti-Saloon League thought he was too Republican, the Republicans thought he was too dictatorial.

The first struggle concerned the national superintendency. Purley A. Baker, the incumbent during the early twenties, was seriously ill with diabetes. Acrimonious debate devolved on the choice of his successor. The thirtieth annual convention of the Anti-Saloon League began in Washington on January 12, 1924. Baker was absent and died shortly afterward. His logical successor as national superintendent would have been Ernest H. Cherrington, then in charge of league publications. Thus Cherrington and Wheeler, who coveted Baker's post, were rivals. Underlying their personal antagonism was a profound difference in attitude to policy and strategy. As Wheeler's biographer, Justin Stewart, explains, "Wheeler's idea was law enforcement and his policy was opportunism. Cherrington's idea was law observance and his policy education." Wheeler anticipated

Baker's withdrawal from office and, to prevent Cherrington's election, arranged for his own supporters to invent a story of Baker's imminent recovery. He even ensured that Baker's personal assistant, Reverend E. J. Moore, was brought round to his side. When Baker did submit his resignation on March 12, 1924, Wheeler was ready. He arranged for his own nomination along with those of Cherrington and Dr. Francis Scott McBride, superintendent of the Illinois Anti-Saloon League. He did not think he could win but he wanted to draw votes away from Cherrington, divide the electorate, and thus ensure McBride's succession. This he achieved. And with McBride's election Wheeler became the dominant force in the league—which would not have happened if Cherrington had won.

However, the power struggle was not over. It entered a final phase. Now Wheeler competed for control with Bishop James A. Cannon, Jr. Cannon, a bishop of the Southern Methodist Church, was a former superintendent of the Virginia Anti-Saloon League and a present member of the national executive committee. He had served the Anti-Saloon League as one of its own ambassadors to the Paris Peace Conference with Dr. H. B. Carré and L. B. Musgrove. Partly at their instigation a provision was inserted into Article 22 of the Covenant of the League of Nations. It made it incumbent upon powers holding colonies as mandates to the League to prohibit "such abuses as the slave trade, the arms traffic, and the liquor traffic." Largely at their instigation a clause was inserted into Article 23 whereby a new committee for protection of children would examine the social problems caused by alcohol. The competition between Cannon and Wheeler was jealous and bitter. The specific quarrel was over spheres of influence. Cannon considered the Democrats his area of activity and resented the interference of Wheeler. He thought his rival should work only within the Republican party, even though Wheeler was a close friend of William Jennings Bryan's.

From all their contests Wheeler emerged the victor—for a time. For a salary of eight thousand dollars he was prepared to work himself to death, acquiring a fatal heart condition.

———————◄•►————————

The story of Al Capone and the Chicago underworld lies within the tradition of the tragedy of revenge. The contemporaneous story of Wayne B. Wheeler falls within another dramatic tradition, the morality plays of the Middle Ages and their rejection of vanity.

PROHIBITION

Alcohol, accessible to all and sundry through the liquor trade, had, in the view of prohibitionists, accelerated and exacerbated social and industrial problems. The cure was prohibition. But if the disease was a vice the remedy was a vanity.

Prohibition was an invention. Alcoholism was supposed to be abolished by statute and act. Of course, all laws are devices, and many do not redress the problems they are meant to remedy. But those of the twenties illustrate a point illuminated by Daniel Snowman: that novelty of invention, fashion, and entertainment were prized while radical dissent and fundamental criticisms were derided or suppressed. Thus Congress and administrations hit upon attractive but superficial formulas to treat complex and fundamental problems. The Washington Naval Conference of 1921, the Republicans' attempt to do "something just as good as the League," achieved a reduction in the naval tonnage of the great powers simplistically expressed as: 5:5:3:1.75:1.75. But the participants, the United States, Britain, Japan, France, and Italy, forgot about provisions for enforcement. The inventiveness of the system pleased everybody but underlying problems of arms rivalry were ignored. Another example of a device, prized for its novelty, that led to a ridiculous situation was the Dawes plan for reparations and war debts of 1924. The European allies would only repay America their wartime loans after they had collected reparations for damage in the war from Germany. After all, the American tariff hindered their exports to the United States. Germany could not repay; the finances of the Weimar Republic were foundering. Charles Gates Dawes, a Chicago banker, got the powers to agree that Germany would pay only according to its ability calculated on a sliding scale. But American bankers loaned Germany the money. The two-and-a-half thousand million dollars loaned to Germany was equal to the sum Germany paid Britain and France and equal to the sum they repaid the United States. As William E. Leuchtenburg, the historian, said, "It would have made equal sense for the United States to take the money out of one Treasury building and put it into another." Dawes was rewarded by Calvin Coolidge with the vice-presidential nomination in 1924. Yet politicians and financiers did not understand the system they were operating. And so it was with prohibition.

The supposed virtue of prohibition came to embody every aspect and degree of vanity. It left alcohol within sight—in Canada, in the countryside, on the coast—but out of reach, thus titillating and tempting the public as much as liquor itself had done in the old days. The notion that to achieve salvation you have to experience and overcome sin, like princes in the Arabian Nights who descend to the marketplace in order to recognize and resist its temptations, is a concept known to Catholics, Moslems, and some Protestants. It was quite outside Wayne Wheeler's world picture.

In the United States true order and good government proceed from the president and Congress. Their officers bear it through the states. By promulgating the virtue of abstinence with all the virtuosity of a solo violinist Wayne Wheeler devitalized politics, assuming a central role himself. His virtue resulted in as great a vanity as the viciousness of Al Capone. Historians who emphasize the addiction of administrations to big business in the 1920s are fond of the dictum on Andrew Mellon, secretary of the treasury to Harding, Coolidge, and Hoover from 1921 to 1932: "three presidents served under him." It would be equally true to agree with Wayne B. Wheeler's biographer that six successive Congresses served under him from 1917.

He appreciated accusations that he told congressmen how to vote. He relished the title of "boss." And in July 1921 Wheeler received an ovation from Congress. Sitting in the gallery of the House he was criticized by John Philip Hill of Baltimore during a debate on prohibition, defended by his allies, and applauded from the floor. As the *Dispatch* of Columbus, Ohio, put it on July 12, 1921: "Nothing that could have happened would have demonstrated more clearly the hold which this smiling, alert, keen-witted generalissimo of the drys has on Congress."

This was a period when political lobbies exercised great power in Washington. Even if they were without the huge funds of the liquor trade or the American Medical Association their nuisance value was considerable. Pacifist lobbies like the National Council for the Prevention of War, led by Frederick Libby, and the Women's International League for Peace and Freedom, nominally led by Jane Addams but actually directed by Dorothy Detzer, tried to fuse irreconcilable interventionist and isolationist arguments. But they managed, as a result of perfect timing and effective campaigning, to persuade Coolidge's secretary of state, Frank B. Kellogg, into his ridiculous pact with Aristide Briand, the French foreign minister, to outlaw war in 1928—another superficial formula.

Wheeler himself understood the charges that could be made against Washington lobbies. To justify the continuous injection of the Anti-Saloon League in federal politics he spoke on "Pressure Groups" at Columbia University, New York on October 16, 1923.

131

He defended the league's methods by pointing out that it was third parties, splinter groups, and interest lobbies that had advanced the cause of social and political reform in the United States:

> Political parties have no inherent right to conduct the government. Experience indicates that they do afford the best practical method . . . but their continuance in power and usefulness depends upon their responsiveness to popular will.
>
> To pressure groups we owe nearly all important social legislation . . . public school system, commission managerial government of cities, woman's suffrage . . . child labor restrictions, railroad regulation.

But he qualified his justification with a warning against "selfish or illegal groups" attempting "to subvert the purposes of government through illegal methods. It is possible for a pressure group to combine with other factions and by 'deals' obtain desired legislation in return for the delivery of votes on other questions." It was, of course, such faults that its enemies imputed to the League.

Because of prohibition politicians could not even carry out their customary compromises between conflicting interests. As Richard Hofstadter explains, "That some men may live by principle is possible only because others live by compromise. Excess destroyed this nice symbiosis: it converted the politician into a bogus man of principle, a breed of hypocrite who voted one way while he drank the other." Many a congressman became what H. L. Mencken called a wet dry, "a politician who prepares for a speech in favor of Prohibition by taking three or four stiff drinks."

The private drinking of congressmen was implied in newspaper stories even if estimates of the number of speakeasies in Washington differed. The *Washington Post* claimed there were almost a thousand in the capital in 1928; in 1929 the *New York Herald Tribune* said the number was 342. By the end of the twenties the alcoholic exhibitionism of Congress was as notorious as that of Harding's administration earlier. An assistant attorney general, Mrs. Mabel Walker Willebrandt, published an exposure of Congress, *Inside of Prohibition*, in 1929. Congressmen advocated prohibition in speeches but by their acts persistently violated the Volstead Act. They were sometimes drunk in the Senate and House. A waiter once dropped a bottle of whiskey in the Capital restaurant, yet an agent who applied for a warrant to search the building was refused. In 1924 one congressman was sentenced for conspiracy to sell and transport alcohol. Another was tried for possessing wine but found not guilty. Others claimed freedom of the port when they returned from abroad and thus evaded customs inspection.

Washington, the capital city, was not as infamous for murders as Chicago. But it was equally notorious for its violation of prohibition. Will Rogers, the cowboy philosopher, put it succinctly: "I had a friend who wanted a drink awful bad when we were in Washington but he couldn't borrow a uniform from anybody." The National United Committee for Law Enforcement of February 18, 1929, complained that "The Capital City is seething in lawlessness and saturated with poison liquor, dispensed by bootleggers under various aliases, operating openly and sold in hundreds of places as sugar is sold in groceries."

———————◆◆————————

Prohibition achieved four things for politics: it increased the pusillanimity of the presidents, the parsimony of politicians, the particularism of the parties, and the perniciousness of elections.

The election of 1920, which brought Senator Warren A. Harding of Ohio and Governor Calvin Coolidge of Massachusetts to the presidency and vice-presidency in 1921, was fought on the issue of Woodrow Wilson's foreign policy. But prohibition had propelled both candidates to prominence. Harding, editor of the *Marion Star*, a former governor of Ohio and senator for the state, was the nominee and tool of Harry Daugherty, an ambitious businessman and lawyer. Of the Republican party elders, four were to prove more important than any others in the making of the president: Senator Charles W. Curtis of Kansas (later Hoover's vice-president); Senator Frank Brandegee of Connecticut; Senator Henry Cabot Lodge of Massachusetts, chairman of the Senate Foreign Relations Committee and presiding officer of the convention; and George Harvey, a Democratic apostate. It was these Harry Daugherty had had to persuade to take Harding instead of the front runners, General Leonard Wood and Frank O. Lowden, former governor of Illinois, both of whom had failed to capture the necessary majority after four ballots at the 1920 Republican National Convention in Chicago. Harding may have become president because he looked like one: he is a perfect example of the wet politician who proposed dry laws for the sake of peace and quiet from the Anti-Saloon League.

Coolidge almost always abstained from alcohol. He is a perfect

133

example of the privately dry politician whose public ambivalence toward prohibition allowed him to play both ends against the middle. He won his first political contest for mayor of Northampton, Massachusetts, in 1910 as a personal teetotaler who also happened to be a lawyer for a brewery. Despite his business associations the prohibitionists supported him because his Democratic opponent had once spoken for the wets in a church debate. In a town of eighteen thousand people with eighteen churches and eighteen saloons evenly divided into Protestants and Catholics, old colonial stock and new immigrants, he learned to be silent on race and religion, rum and reform. Thus he held together a personal coalition of wet and dry, Catholic and Protestant, support in a series of political campaigns until he captured the office of governor in 1918.

The Boston police strike, which made Coolidge's name known nationally, was a consequence of wartime prohibition. Policemen were so poorly paid in the city that they depended on saloon bribes for their living. But in the period from 1917 to 1919, they closed the saloons and thus lost a source of revenue. Their integrity made them insolvent. Yet the police commissioner refused to allow the police union to become affiliated with the American Federation of Labor (which would have helped policemen get better wages). The police went on strike. After the dispute had been settled by the mayor of Boston, Coolidge sent his famous telegram to the leader of the AFL, Samuel Gompers: "There is no right to strike against the public safety by any body, any time, any where." For this he was congratulated by Woodrow Wilson and rewarded with the nomination as Harding's running mate.

The men from the smoke-filled room of the Blackstone Hotel, Chicago, who eventually sided with Daugherty in promoting Harding, had already agreed that to balance their conservative candidate the best man for vice-president would be Senator Irvine Lenroot of Wisconsin. Lenroot was unwilling. And, in the event, his cooperation was not necessary. No sooner had Lenroot been proposed to the delegates in Chicago than Wallace McCamant, delegate from Oregon, climbed on his chair, and put forward Calvin Coolidge's name. Immediately the stenographer at the convention recorded "an outburst of applause of short duration but of great report." Coolidge's nomination by $674\frac{1}{2}$ votes out of 984 was recorded "with tumultous applause and cheers"—the only spontaneous event in the entire convention. Harding himself had had to await the tenth ballot for victory.

VICE, VIRTUE, AND VANITY

Prohibition was introduced into the 1920 campaign by the Anti-Saloon League. Harding's Democratic opponent, James M. Cox, had opposed state prohibition in Ohio during his term as governor there. Thus he incurred the enmity of Wayne B. Wheeler and William Jennings Bryan, who worked against his nomination at the Democratic National Convention in San Francisco. While refusing to give official support to either Harding or Cox, since both now supported the Eighteenth Amendment and the Volstead Act, the league gave Harding covert confirmation. It could not forgive Cox his nomination by the wets and Tammany Hall and it thought it could manipulate Harding to its own ends more easily. The campaign was vicious: Cox was slandered as an incompetent alcoholic, and to Harding was attributed a touch of the tar brush.

Early in his campaign, on May 14, 1920, Harding had described the needs of America after the war: "not heroics, but healing; not nostrums, but normalcy; not revolution, but restoration; not agitation, but adjustment; not surgery, but serenity; not the dramatic, but the dispassionate; not experiment, but equipoise." But the qualities he sought had never been characteristic of American society. Prohibition ensured they would not be achieved in the 1920s.

Whatever his private appetites when he became president, Harding thought it was his public duty to accept the Eighteenth Amendment because it had been passed by Congress and ratified by the states. He took advice from the professional prohibitionists, especially Wayne B. Wheeler. Wheeler cherished no illusions about Harding's appetites nor his character but he regarded him as an ally. After all, he had always voted correctly from Wheeler's point of view.

Harding was subject to a continuous barrage of letters from Wheeler on the appointment of prohibition agents and federal judges, on election campaigns and control of Congress. He was dissuaded from appointing Senator Shields of Tennessee to the Supreme Court by Wheeler. Wheeler regarded Shields, correctly, as a political opponent and he would brook no rivals. Wheeler even opposed the appointment of Andrew Mellon, the industrial magnate, as secretary of the treasury, because Mellon had had liquor interests. But Mellon as secretary was as dutiful to Wheeler as Harding. On prohibition he towed the party line. Mellon himself did not want to break with the Anti-Saloon League. He needed it. Gifford Pinchot, governor of Pennsylvania, was making effective attacks on the Mellons in their home state.

Before taking the oath of office Warren Harding may have told ministers, "My prime motive in going to the White House is to bring America back to God," but there could be no order if the president was not ordered himself. The mystery of just government and balanced order could only be understood by those who wanted to learn. Harding took with him into office his former associates, the Ohio Gang. His astute and unscrupulous political manager, Daugherty, was rewarded with the post of attorney general and presided over the political and pecuniary profligacy of the period. William J. Burns ran the Department of Justice for him as a private protection racket. The Ohio Gang sold pardons to bootleggers convicted under the Volstead Act. A special agent, Gaston B. Means, later testified that he collected $7 million from bootleggers in a goldfish bowl which he then turned over to the Department of Justice. In addition the Ohio Gang sold bootleg liquor from 1625 K Street, Washington, quite openly. The liquor was taken there by agents of the Department of Justice after it had been confiscated by the Prohibition Unit.

Harding may have been ignorant of his associates' activities, which attracted national publicity after his sudden death in San Francisco on returning from Alaska on August 2, 1923. But his personal attitude to alcohol was hypocritical. His drinking was an open secret. Yet under pressure from Wayne Wheeler he had the gall to announce that he was teetotal in January, 1923. Harding had emphasized his own addiction to drink to Wheeler and suggested that total abstinence would damage his health. Yet he received Wheeler's plans to reform him as an ultimatum. From Wheeler's point of view the artificial choice he offered Harding between drink and dry support was all bluff. But Harding gave in. He put his bottles out of sight in his bedroom in the White House. Unfortunately for Wheeler, Harding's drinking remained an open secret. Alice Longworth, Roosevelt's daughter, described Harding's mode of relaxation from the problems of the presidency in the White House with the Ohio Gang: "No rumor could have exceeded the reality; the study was filled with cronies, Daugherty, Jess Smith, Alec Moore, and others, the air heavy with tobacco smoke, trays with bottles containing every imaginable brand of whiskey stood about, cards and poker chips ready at hand—a general atmosphere of waistcoat unbuttoned, feet on the desk, and the spittoon alongside." Yet Harding had no qualms about urging others to sustain prohibition and abstain from bootleg liquor.

Despite, or perhaps because of, his own profligacy Harding considered the idea of a conference of interested parties to discuss the breakdown of law and order and the increase in the crime rate in 1922. His public exhortations were based on an appeal to the pioneer spirit. Speaking at Denver, Colorado, shortly before his death he said prohibition was a more fundamental issue than a conflict of wets against drys. It was "one involving the great question whether the laws of the country can and will be enforced." And this theme was renewed by his successor, Calvin Coolidge, at the governors' conference the same year. Coolidge declared that in the ability of the United States to enforce its laws "is revealed the life or death of the American ideal of self-government."

The profligate was succeeded by the puritan. Whereas Harding's amiable facade covered carelessness, Coolidge's unlikable manner concealed a casuistry. He was personally honest. But in saying things like "the business of America is business" he purveyed his integrity as a front for organized corruption by political and business associates. He turned a semantic gift for splitting hairs into justification of political equivocation, evasion, and expediency. Perhaps he believed he owed his position not to his political acumen but to public honesty. He owed much to the political philosophy of the first English prime minister, Horace Walpole. There is not much to choose between Walpole's aphorism, "let sleeping dogs lie," and Coolidge's axiom, "Never go out to meet trouble. If you will just sit still, nine cases out of ten someone will intercept it before it reaches you."

Much has been written of Coolidge's taciturnity, which was represented as mordant wit. When a young woman challenged him to speak at a reception by telling him she had bet money she could get more than two words out of him all evening he replied: "You lose." Even more was made of his stillness from Alice Longworth, who said while he was alive that he was "weaned on a pickle" to Dorothy Parker, who asked after his death, "How could they tell?" He was savagely satirized as Nathan ("Shagpoke") Whipple by Nathanael West in *A Cool Million* in 1934, a year after his death. Unlike Harding, Coolidge did not collect protection money from bootleggers but, like him, he was not prepared to pay for prohibition. He preferred private abstinence to proper policies. It was at his suggestion that Congress cut the appropriations for the Prohibition Unit from $8,500,000 in 1923 to $8,250,000 in 1924.

Both Harding and Coolidge believed that it was up to Congress to bear the burden of prohibition enforcement. The legislature had initiated prohibition, therefore it was its responsibility and not that of the administration to carry the experiment through. Electoral malfeasance and congressional corruption ensured this did not happen.

————————◆◆————————

After prohibition was enacted and before it became a scandal the two major parties continued to blur their attitudes to it. Not until 1932 did the election platforms of either Republicans or Democrats go beyond lip service to law enforcement. However, H. L. Mencken thought prohibition had made a significant impact on party politics, especially among the Democrats. It would not brook burial by their bosses. Drink brought out differences among delegates to Republican and Democratic conventions: "The Republicans commonly carry their liquor better than the Democrats, just as they commonly wear their clothes better. One seldom sees one of them actively sick in the convention hall or dead drunk in a hotel lobby." And this was a metaphor for the place of prohibition in both parties since "Republicans have a natural talent for compromise, but to Democrats it is almost impossible."

Hence the Republican bosses were able to forestall debate on prohibition at all their national conventions in the 1920s. The Democrats were divided by it every time: in 1920, in 1924, and in 1928. Not until 1932, when the South abandoned prohibition for Franklin D. Roosevelt, did the traditional coalition of the northern, industrial, and wet cities with the southern, agrarian, and dry countryside hold fast. It was divided first by William Jennings Bryan in 1920 against the wishes of the dry bosses. Wayne B. Wheeler wanted an election pledge to enforce the Volstead Act, while Bishop James Cannon, Jr., wanted no pledge at all. He argued that since the Republican National Convention at Chicago had not adopted a law enforcement plank "it was better for the prohibition cause" that the Democrats at San Francisco should not do so either. He dreaded public support for the Anti-Saloon League being split along party lines. Cannon's view prevailed. But in postponing the problem the Democratic party was storing up chaos for the future.

As late as January 20, 1924, Woodrow Wilson suggested a tentative platform for the Democratic National Convention of that year, that the government should confine its activities in support of the Eighteenth Amendment and Volstead Act to prevent illegal importation from abroad and the illegal introduction of liquor from one state to another. This would have broken the spirit as well as the letter of the law against liquor. But Wilson's notion was, after his death, forgotten in the debacle of the convention in the old Madison Square Garden, New York.

John W. Davis, a Wall Street lawyer from West Virginia, won the contest for the nomination. It began between the dry William Gibbs McAdoo, Wilson's son-in-law and secretary of the treasury, and the wet Irish-American governor of New York, Alfred E. Smith. Davis was a compromise candidate nominated after 103 ballots cast over seventeen riotous days, beginning on June 24.

It was during his speech nominating Smith that Franklin D. Roosevelt from the chair used the idea of Judge Joseph Proskauer to apply William Wordsworth's phrase "The Happy Warrior" to the governor of New York. Al Smith had throughout a long and distinguished political career in New York been promoted by the boss of Tammany Hall, Charles Francis Murphy. Murphy had placed Smith's name on the list of nominees at the 1920 Democratic National Convention simply to get his candidate known nationally. But Murphy died in April, 1924, and though Smith was relieved to be dissociated from Tammany Hall as far as the general public was concerned, he also lost the advantages of Murphy's considerable political weight and experience.

The number of votes cast at the convention would be 1,098. Under the two thirds rule the winning candidate would have to take not a mere majority but 732. William Gibbs McAdoo reached his greatest strength on the sixty-ninth ballot with 530 votes. This was 19 less than a majority and 202 less than the necessary two thirds. He could only succeed thereafter by acquiring even a few votes on each successive ballot. Smith's bloc denied him these.

To Wheeler the Democrats were dangerous as the party of the wet northern, urban blocs. And thus in the deadlock between Smith and McAdoo Wheeler was, according to Justin Steuart, "the key log in the jam." Al Smith certainly saw things that way, and in a private meeting, he tried to assure Wheeler that, as president, his attitude to prohibition would be accommodating in comparison with his present opposition. Wheeler was not persuaded and remained obdurate. "Governor," he said, "you will never enter the White House." His control of enough dry delegates pledged to McAdoo was proof enough. Wheeler could have accepted McAdoo but preferred Thomas Walsh of Montana. However, it was more important to prevent the nomination of Smith or another wet than secure that of any candidate of his own.

Certain that neither could win, McAdoo and Smith met at the Ritz-Carlton Hotel where McAdoo offered to withdraw if Smith would also do so. But Smith would not accept McAdoo's alternative candidate, E. T. Meredith of Iowa. As late as the hundredth ballot Smith had $351\frac{1}{2}$ votes to McAdoo's 190. By then John Davis had $203\frac{1}{2}$. And by the hundred and third ballot on July 9, Davis had 839 votes to Smith's $12\frac{1}{2}$ and McAdoo's 12.

The convention, broadcast by radio, divided Democrats across the country on a scale unknown since the Civil War and unsurpassed until 1968. Prohibition was not the only divisive issue. Religion—since Smith was a Catholic—and race—since McAdoo was supported by the insurgent Ku Klux Klan at the height of its prestige—also predominated disputes. But they were complementary to prohibition: all three issues were about intolerance. William Jennings Bryan, the elder statesman of the party, was shouted down by the crowd on account of his complacency to the Klan. The nomination of his brother, Governor Charles Jennings Bryan of Nebraska, for vice-president was no consolation. In 1925 he appeared for Tennessee against the schoolteacher John Scopes, who was being defended by Clarence Darrow for teaching Darwin's theory of evolution in violation of the state's insistence on the literal interpretation of the origins of the species in Genesis. Darrow made Bryan's fundamentalism look ridiculous at the trial, and the old man, worn out, died within a month.

Wheeler was not taken by the idea of John W. Davis as president. He remembered that in 1915, when he was solicitor general in Wilson's administration, Davis had not supported the dry cause when two cases about the shipment of liquor from Maryland to West Virginia reached the Supreme Court. Wheeler had contained his resentment. But rather than show outright opposition he prevailed upon Bishop Cannon, who, of course, was a Democrat, to ensure that the Democratic platform included strict adherence to prohibition.

The dry lobbyists concentrated on retaining preeminence in Congress itself, and all five biennial elections of the 1920s returned dry majorities to Senate and House. Wheeler's strategy toward Congress was the same during prohibition as it had been before: to capture a dry majority by all means. He repeated his tactics to individual politicians with the old unerring assurance.

Wheeler recognized that the campaign of 1920 was the first in which prohibitionists in general and the Anti-Saloon League in particular were on the defensive. He also recognized that other league workers did not understand how important it was to ensure the victory of nominally dry politicians. Nor did they see the importance of coming to an understanding with such politicians once elected. The league rank and file believed that the battle was over once the Eighteenth Amendment and Volstead Act went into effect. Wheeler was not so naïve. In about three hundred districts out of 435 one or more candidates announced their opposition to part or whole of the Volstead Act. And in more than a hundred districts these opponents of bone-dry prohibition were competing with congressmen who had supported the Volstead Act in its passage through Congress.

Symbolically the most important contest to the league was that of Andrew Volstead of Minnesota for a seat in the House. That he was able to stand at all was owing to Wheeler's manipulative influence. Even so, the league had to give of its utmost to prevent Volstead's defeat, which was postponed until the next election. In those districts where the league could not win either Republican or Democratic candidates it fielded its own. When the Republican Representative Shreve of Pennsylvania was denied renomination of the Twenty-fifth District (Erie and Crawford counties) by a loose coalition of wet interests from both parties Wheeler secured his nomination as an independent, built up an organization to conduct his campaign, and ensured his victory in the election. Shreve was no longer an independent, of course. He was free only to do Wheeler's bidding.

Wheeler realized that his control of Congress could not last indefinitely. He feared that public resentment of prohibition would be registered in the polls of 1922 and that dry Republicans, elected in 1920 to traditionally wet Democratic seats when people were incensed against Wilson's foreign policy, would not be able to retain them. To forestall this adverse effect he would have liked to spend to the hilt as the league had done in the past, this time to the tune of twenty thousand dollars, a record even for the league. He also provoked the wets into showing their hand. They produced a list of 249 candidates whom they supported. Wheeler asked these candidates if they would or would not support the constitution. When they demurred they were overwhelmed with letters of protest from the electorate at large. Thus they were obliged to deny that they had ever been wet and published statements such as, "I would consider myself a fool to vote wet when my district is dry," and, "I did not speak or ask for the endorsement of the Association Against Prohibition and have publicly repudiated same." As Wheeler repeatedly said of his opponents, "They always snatch defeat from the jaws of victory."

The net result of the midterm elections of 1922 was that the drys increased their number in the House to 296; of 35 senatorial contests they won 25. Almost their only failure was with the hapless Andrew Volstead, who lost his seat in Minnesota. In 1924 the wets published a list of candidates they opposed with worse results than in 1922. Eleven of the thirteen new senators supported prohibition; five out of every six candidates the wets supported in the House were defeated. The three to one majority in both houses had been more than accomplished. The Senate was dry by 72 to 24, the House by 319 to 105, according to Wheeler's own estimation. Wheeler used the league's election program in 1924 to settle old scores. He paid particular attention to the senatorial contest in Kentucky. A. Ousley Stanley, who was fighting to retain his seat there, had dared to attack the league in the Senate itself. Wheeler conducted a successful vendetta against Stanley through his personal assistant, Ira Champion.

However, the league's interference in congressional elections did not always turn out to its advantage. Its involvement in the senatorial contest in Pennsylvania in 1926 is a case in point. Because the Republicans controlled the state the real contest was not in the congressional election but the Republican primary. When the league was divided about whether to support the Mellon family's moderate candidate, Senator George W. Pepper, or the dry governor, Gifford Pinchot, it split the dry vote. And the wet boss of Philadelphia, William Vare, won on a platform calling for legal wine and beer.

In Illinois in the same year the league tried to persuade a dry independent candidate, Hugh S. Magill, not to contest a conventional senatorial contest between Frank L. Smith (Republican) and George E. Brennan (Democrat). He had no chance of winning. The league preferred to retain its dry coalition by supporting Smith despite the fact that he was suspected of corruption. He was chairman of the Public Utilities Commission and had accepted $125,000 in campaign contributions from the public utilities magnate, Samuel Insull. The Democratic opponent, Brennan, was a Chicago boss and a declared wet. The league was so keen to retain power that it would support a corrupt man, Smith, against an honest one, Magill, in order to do so. Wheeler was following an old principle, Rule 14, that it was permissable to favor candidates who were only "partially acceptable" in the cause of saloon suppression. For Wheeler's guiding principle was still political expediency: better to compromise and consolidate than attain nothing at all.

Though prohibition was within the letter of some preceding laws, it was within the spirit of none. The suspicion lingered that it had been accomplished by guile. The guilt of Congress, assuaged in ephemeral palliatives, especially dissipation, was fostered by the disturbances plaguing the opening of the 1920s; strikes, terrorism, frenetic social activity. Congress was already sick and tired of prohibition as a political issue by the time the Eighteenth Amendment was passed.

For the first two years of national prohibition Congress preferred official ignorance of the problems of enforcement to detailed discussion of the difficulties. Congressmen were aided and abetted in this by the dry lobby, within and without, which was unwilling to admit the problems at all and reluctant to ask for additional appropriations for enforcement at a time government was cutting back on expenditures generally. Nor was it willing to concede the inadequacies of the Volstead Act, which had been devised by the august Wayne Wheeler.

However, the Anti-Saloon League was not negligent. When Wilson's attorney general, A. Mitchell Palmer, decided that the Volstead Act placed no limit on the prescription of wine and beer by doctors its command of Congress was as compulsive as ever. The league inveigled Senator Frank B. Willis of Ohio and Representative Philip B. Campbell of Kansas to introduce a bill to close the gate opened by Palmer. This was the Emergency Beer Bill passed as the Willis-Campbell Act in the House on June 27, 1921, by 250 votes to 93 and in the Senate on August 8, 1921, by 39 votes to 20. It drew up a code of practice for physicians. They could not prescribe beer at all. They could not prescribe, nor could druggists sell, wine with more than 24 percent alcohol, nor more than a half pint of alcohol to any one person within any ten-day period. And doctors could only issue a hundred prescriptions for alcohol every ninety days.

Prohibitionists had a choice of alternative responses to a difficult situation: either to recognize that the problems were part and parcel of prohibition and could only be pursued by proper enforcement or to assume the problems were temporary setbacks. In the past prohibition had been partial, and it had been possible to blame difficulties on the wet states. Without wet states, there would be no problem. Once national prohibition was accomplished in name only new social problems surfaced. However, both Congress and the Anti-Saloon League were unwilling to debate enforcement seriously. They clung to the conspiracy theory. Subversion was the work of aliens. Instead of trying to make the law effective Congress passed more legislation. In line with the restriction of immigration of 1921, a bill to deport aliens who violated the law was passed in the House by 222 votes to 73 in April, 1922. And in 1923 Louis C. Crampton of Michigan introduced a resolution calling on the Treasury Department to divulge information on liquor brought into the United States by the staff of foreign embassies. It was passed by 189 votes to 113. But Treasury took the attitude that it could divulge information only if it was compatible with the public interest. And this, clearly, was not.

Congress would not even hear of an investigation into enforcement in 1924. Senator Morris Sheppard of Texas said it would be "a waste of funds and energy and time." He had been a prime mover of the Eighteenth Amendment yet an illicit still was found operating on his farm five miles north of Austin four years earlier. Like others of the dry majority he dreaded the obvious conclusions of an impartial investigation: that enforcement was arbitrary, corrupt, and superficial. With unwitting irony Senator Frank Willis of Ohio could rightly argue against an enquiry: "What could better operate to paralyze the forces of law enforcement than such an inquiry?"

Wheeler described his congressional enemies as the BEER group, the title made up of the initial letters of the names of Senators William Cabell Bruce of Maryland, Walter E. Edge of New Jersey, Edward I. Edwards of New Jersey, and James A. Reed of Missouri. The contest between Wheeler and the BEER group was for power and prestige. Their debates were about the validity of pressure groups in politics and the purpose of the Prohibition Unit.

All wet and dry measures in 1925 were, in the Senate, referred to the Judiciary Committee under Senator Albert B. Cummins of Iowa, which included Wheeler's archenemy, James A. Reed of

Missouri. Reed used the committee to expose widespread political corruption—by copper companies in Arizona, by the Ku Klux Klan in Indiana. He had introduced a measure to investigate expenditure in senatorial primaries. As a result of the committee's work Senators William Vare of Pennsylvania and Frank L. Smith of Illinois were unseated. Even a fishing trip was to be subject to scrutiny. And Wheeler foolishly rose to the bait. He issued press statements about wet campaign funds in Pennsylvania. Thus Reed had him subpoenaed to appear at new committee hearings and give his evidence. And there Reed obliged the ailing Wheeler to trace year by year, as closely as he could, league expenditures since its inception in 1893. Wheeler tried to show "that the League was the most democratic organization doing interdenominational temperance work."

Reed's purpose in committee was to turn the publicity Wheeler courted against him and the league. For instance Wayne Wheeler's claim that the league had spent $50 million on the dry cause since 1893 made it appear to the *New York Times* of March 29, 1926, that the league had bought the Eighteenth Amendment and paid Congress in cash. Charges of conspiracy which the drys had once leveled at the liquor trade were now directed at the league. A former propagandist for the League, W. E. ("Pussfoot") Johnson, admitted to *Hearst's International Cosmopolitan* in May 1926, "Did I ever lie to promote prohibition? Decidedly, yes. I have told enough lies for the cause to make Ananias ashamed of himself." Johnson had lost an eye in the dry cause when a stone was thrown at him by a London mob. The drys' chant that "Pussfoot's eye will make England dry" did not come true. His reputation as a martyr ended with his revelations.

Charging that fabulous sums were spent to subvert the natural democratic processes, Reed sent to Westerville, Ohio, to the publishing house of the league, and had the files of the league searched and seized. Although this exercise of senatorial power was unprecedented Wheeler did not dare oppose it: "If we offer any objection, we will be misrepresented as having something to conceal."

Wheeler could hardly credit that some of the dry members of Reed's committee who were deeply indebted to him made no attempt to defend him or the league. Senators Goff of West Virginia and King of Utah in particular owed their political promotions to him. But in 1926 he was of no immediate use to them. Indeed, his friendship was now a liability and, therefore, to be disowned.

Reed, unintentionally, damaged the Association Against the Prohibition Amendment as much as the Anti-Saloon League. He could not prove conclusively that the league had acted corruptly or even unethically. But the league suffered more in loss of public esteem. The myth of its invincibility was shattered beyond repair. In 1927 newspapers published extracts from the league's minutes and photographic facsimiles of letters seized by Reed's orders. The league was deprived of its own records, which its enemies used for their own ends. Wet organizations and their campaign methods were not made subject to similar surveillance.

Arthur Sears Henning in three articles for the *Chicago Tribune* (July 10, 11, 12, 1927) criticized the common aims and alliances, the personnel and politics of dry, pacifist and radical lobbies in Washington. The league was the most powerful, "the mightiest engine of propaganda the world has ever beheld," spending about $2 million a year on publicity and in putting pressure on politicians. Silas Bent in *Strange Bedfellows* (1928) deplored the union of church and state promoted by organizations like the Federal Council of Churches and the Methodist Board of Temperance. Prohibition and public morals had injected themselves into Washington politics. Of the league, which claimed support from 20 million voters, he said, "It is enough to frighten any Congressmen—especially as the League has a card-index on each 'with special attention to misdemeanours.'"

The league's decline in public favor was reflected in a fall in its finances of one fifth from 1920 to 1926, and more than a half from 1927 to 1933.

The debate over the reorganization of the Prohibition Unit into a new bureau was equally as damaging to the league as the examination into political lobbies.

In 1925 Wayne Wheeler conferred with the brewers through their intermediary, Levi Cooke. In exchange for a beer with an alcohol content higher than 0.5 percent they were prepared to put the bootleggers out of business. Unfortunately, although the brewers were agreed about the principle, they could not agree about the practice or the percentage.

In 1925 the wets in Congress proposed local option by a new constitutional amendment, government sale of liquor with an alcoholic content of 2.75 percent, permitting doctors unlimited prescriptive authority, and allowing home brewing. Wheeler himself favored a reorganization of the Prohibition Unit by law.

Though Wheeler wanted to temporize with the administration

and Congress, other league elders would not. At its 1925 convention in Chicago a resolution blaming Coolidge himself for the lapses in enforcement was proposed by, among others, Governor Gifford Pinchot of Pennsylvania, whose eloquent oratory almost turned the tables on Wheeler. At the very least radical reformers in the league wanted the removal of Roy Haynes as prohibition commissioner. Haynes was Wheeler's tool but an incompetent administrator.

Wheeler's control of prohibition enforcement ended in April 1925, when Brigadier General Lincoln C. Andrews was appointed assistant secretary of the treasury with authority over the Customs, the Coast Guard, and the Prohibition Unit. Mellon had engineered the appointment of Andrews because he wanted to be rid of Haynes. Since the league had asked for a coordination of the activities of Customs, Coast Guard, and Prohibition Unit in 1923 Wheeler could not complain. However, what was at issue was not the new structure but the personnel involved, and the personalities promoting them. Haynes was still commissioner in the department but his position was effectively reduced to that of a liaison officer with dry organizations. He had little to do except draw his salary. Wheeler used Haynes as an intermediary between himself and Andrews.

Wheeler discovered Andrews was a moderate drinker. But he did not expose him. Wheeler's canny combination of political expediency and opportunism led him to wait and see. While Andrews was in charge Wheeler decided to allow him full expression of his policies, to make mistakes and get into a muddle. He hoped Andrews would become disillusioned and retire. Wheeler then planned to elevate Haynes or find another of his own nominees.

Andrews set to, scrapping Haynes's machinery of state directors responsible to a central authority. Instead he preferred a system of twenty-two autonomous federal districts comparable with the system of federal judicial districts. As Wheeler predicted at the time with malicious glee, "Andrews will find that he has stuck his head into a wasps' nest." He knew nothing could stand in the way of political patronage. And senators and leading Republicans forced Andrews to fill the remodeled districts with personnel selected to suit their political convenience. Mellon himself insisted that Congress had to be consulted over the appointment of enforcement officers. Whereas Andrews wanted to hire outstanding men from business as administrators and pay them a salary of $10,000, Comptroller General McCarl advised him that $7,500 was the absolute maximum. Moreover Andrews's plan to employ former officers from the armed services was never implemented. They could not join the unit unless they relinquished their pensions.

Andrews indeed did fall victim to dissatisfaction with a law enforcement he was not allowed to reform. Thus he antagonized Congress and the league. None of Andrews's other recommendations—control of industrial alcohol and prescription liquor, authority to search ships just outside territorial waters, Civil Service rules—were accepted by Congress until after he was obliged to resign. In May 1927 Mellon replaced both Andrews and Haynes with, respectively, Lieutenant Governor Seymour Lowman of New York and Dr. James M. Doran, chemist of the Treasury Department.

However, Congress began to respond to the arguments of General Andrews that year. The House approved a reorganization bill separating the Prohibition Unit from the Commission of Internal Revenue. The agents of the new Prohibition Bureau would be placed under Civil Service rules. It increased the appropriations of the bureau by $2,322,445 and also approved an appropriation of $1 million for the building of nine new coast cutters. The Senate assented in time, but after Congress adjourned in 1927 someone realized that no funds had been voted to establish Civil Service regulations. That had to await debate in 1928. The results of the Civil Service examination, which all employees of the new bureau had to take, revealed the low caliber of the rank and file agents. Only two fifths of the agents passed and some of them did so only at a second attempt. It was clear that the serious attempt to reform the bureau had come too late.

During the debate on the reorganization bill in 1927 the wets made much of their opportunity to discredit prohibition, discourage the Anti-Saloon League and damn Wheeler.

William Cabell Bruce of Maryland led a frontal attack on the drys in the Senate. Revising Samuel Johnson's remark about Oliver Goldsmith, that he touched nothing he did not adorn, he said prohibition touched nothing it did not defile. Drys who opposed Civil Service rules really yearned for a return to the spoils system of the Gilded Age before the reform of the Civil Service in 1883. He excoriated the "third-sex," political agitators who were "part preachers and part stump orators, part clergymen and part political intriguers . . . whose political instruments are scurrilous abuse, bulldozing and the lavish use of money in political campaigns." Wheeler himself was censured as a "professional agitator and unofficial interloper."

VICE, VIRTUE, AND VANITY

Senator Edward I. Edwards of New Jersey in the same debate also denounced the Anti-Saloon League for its "un-American, entirely selfish, bigoted and intolerant appeals." Prohibition had nothing in common with temperance. The two were "as contrary and opposed as black and white." The reorganization bill was a "pork barrel for the Wheelers, the McBrides, and the Wilsons." (McBride was Francis Scott McBride, the league's national superintendent; Wilson was Clarence True Wilson, dry author.) For Edwards imputed a hidden motive to Wheeler, "The real purpose is to create some ten or twelve new jobs for Wayne B. Wheeler . . . Wheeler needs this additional patronage to strengthen his fast-weakening hold on 'dry America.'" Wheeler, once applauded by the House, was now repudiated in the Senate in other remarks, all denouncing the Senate as well as him:

"Wayne B. Wheeler had taken snuff, and the Senate, as usual, sneezed."

"Wayne B. Wheeler had cracked his whip, and the Senate, as usual, crouched."

No other fundamentalist was to endure a more adverse turn of fortune. Wheeler may have worked himself into a frazzle. But it was his wife who was fried. In their country retreat at Little Point Sable, Michigan, on August 13, 1927, Mrs. Ella Belle Wheeler caught fire in a gasoline stove explosion. She was burned alive. Her father, Robert Candy, hearing her cries from another room, came to her rescue. But he dropped dead at the sight of his daughter consumed by flames. Overcome with shock, utterly bereft, Wheeler succumbed to his serious heart condition. He died of a heart attack three weeks later on September 5, 1927.

After Wheeler's death the other league elders made sure no other leader would get the chance to capture public imagination on their behalf. They were still committed to the sort of pressure politics advocated by Wheeler. But when Francis Scott McBride was re-elected as national superintendent in 1928 they agreed to place more emphasis on education, which had always been the principle of Ernest Cherrington, their publisher and Wheeler's rival. And this was "the New Policy of the Anti-Saloon League" announced to the public in the *Literary Digest* of January 7, 1928. However the leopard could not change his spots. Prohibition was not being enforced and never could be.

—SEVEN—

WORD
OF MOUTH

ONE OF THE DISTINCTIVE FEATURES of American literature between the First and Second World Wars was the affinity between creative writing and political commentary. In the twenties principal themes included expatriation and the war and, hence, alienation. War was used as a terrible metaphor of society: prohibition was a ridiculous one. The new creative sensibilities and priorities were most poignantly expressed by the "lost generation." This was the school of novelists assessed by Gertrude Stein for their common rejection of small-town America with its provincial, intolerant values. They were so alienated that they often lived abroad. But their driving obsessions were American. Novelists like Ernest Hemingway, F. Scott Fitzgerald, John Dos Passos, Thomas Wolfe, Erskine Caldwell, and Ring Lardner were not alone. They were supported in their view of society as a wasteland by the poets T. S. Eliot, E. E. Cummings, and William Carlos Williams and the critics Dorothy Parker, Edmund Wilson, Harold Stearns, Walter Lippmann, and, most significantly, H. L. Mencken, "the sage of Baltimore" and the most prepossessing pundit of the age.

The suspicions about misleading official propaganda in the war led novelists, historians, and social critics to distrust all official pronouncements. They thought reality had been misrepresented by language and that language had been debased. Thus Ernest Hemingway gives his character, Frederick Henry, in *A Farewell to Arms* (1929) this rejection of noble cant: "I was always embarrassed by the words sacred, glorious, and sacrifice and the expression in vain."

With few significant exceptions—such as Upton Sinclair, Edith Wharton, and Willa Cather—writers and poets excoriated prohibition. But they did so more in regret for the state of mind it implied than the physical pleasures it denied. The critic Ellen Glasgow wrote in *Periscope* for October 1929: "In the South we are substituting murder for a mint julep and calling it progress." In the more imaginative wet interpretations the web of prohibition, made from the tissue of legal deceits, political corruption and religious bigotry, was a symptom and symbol of the decay of postwar American society. A society that could accept prohibition with all its concomitant hypocrisy and sham was fit only for cynics, egoists, and parasites.

◆

Those sections of the community who opposed prohibition at the outset had not been ready, willing or able to transform their opposition into a cohesive strategy in 1919 and 1920. And in comparison with the prohibitionists these people remained unrepresented in the state capitals and Washington except in the unsolicited and counterproductive activities of the liquor lobbies.

Opposition to the Eighteenth Amendment came in the first instance from the liquor trade. In 1917 brewers and distillers had invoked states' rights against national prohibition, and the Distillers' Association of America had tried, unsuccessfully, to organize referenda against prohibition in fourteen states. In March 1920 the United States Brewers' Association had petitioned Woodrow Wilson to veto the Volstead Act. But apart from labor unions no important organizations outside the liquor interests registered hostility. The American Federation of Labor carried its opposition to the Capitol in Washington in a turbulent demonstration of ten thousand union members, which lasted for three hours on June 14, 1919. Samuel Gompers was reported in the *New York Times* (June 15 and July 4, 1919) as having warned the House Judiciary Committee that prohibition was oppressive to the working class and would foster radicalism and Bolshevism in the United States. But the AFL and the Central Federated Union in New York were unable to sustain direct action in the form of a strike against prohibition. For the time being the contest over prohibition remained limited to the liquor trade and the prohibitive lobbies.

Prohibition had been conceived by progressive reformers as a means of anticipating class war. In effect, prohibition actually fomented it. Pierre Du Pont of General Motors was cited by Irving Fisher as having said, "The great mass of our workmen and poor people feel that prohibition does not prohibit but is a scheme to deny them something which their more fortunate brothers with money can have almost at will." If it applied to all in theory in practice it discriminated alike against the working class and the poor. The rich drank openly and well; others drank secretly and badly. Thus the philosophy of the prohibitionists with its emphasis on puritan abstinence and moral improvement was meaningless to men who toiled and sweated in some mechanized industry.

During the twenties union membership declined from 5 million to 3.5 million. The decline was partly on account of prosperity, partly the open shop and welfare capitalism planned by employers, and partly owing to prohibition. If prohibition increased the possibilities of corruption among employers and unions, both of whom developed a bad reputation for racketeering, it therefore made the attainment of legitimate union demands on wages, conditions and hours of work more difficult. The means to the end, strikes, became well nigh impossible. Labor had never given wholehearted consent to prohibition. Now it defected to the wet side.

In 1922 the American Federation of Labor passed a resolution in favor of modifying the Volstead Act and reaffirmed its protest every year prohibition continued. And Labor's National Committee for Modification of the Volstead Act was established in 1931. Labor leaders who felt most strongly integrated their activities with one or another of the wet lobbies.

Once labor turned, so, too, did capital. In 1922 the *Manufacturers' Record* reported that in a poll of manufacturers, financiers, and academics 98.5 percent favored prohibition in some form. But soon manufacturers who had once advocated prohibition to benefit themselves and their workers supported repeal to protect themselves from their workers. Now they thought it was better for workers to imbibe good beer legally than bad booze illegally. The safety regulations of major companies that proscribed drinking by employees on the job had been quite sufficient to prevent accidents at work before national prohibition.

There was much truth in the drys' accusation that capitalists were concerned only with their own financial interests and that they opposed prohibition because it was inconvenient to them rather than out of consideration for the workers. The loss in government revenue from the liquor taxes had been compensated by additional taxes on corporations and wealthy individuals, both of which were resented by upper classes.

The secretary of the National Association of Manufacturers, James A. Emery, was delegated to ask Congress to legalize strong beer as "an indispensable revenue measure" in 1932. The association wanted a sales tax as well as a beer tax as an alternative to excess profit and income taxes. The rich wanted taxes proliferated, although they were not prepared to share the wealth. Jules S. Bache, a banker with interests in Cuba Distilling and U.S. Industrial Alcohol, told Congress that "the poor could escape the tax by refraining from consumption." Stanley Menken, the founder of the National Security League, an association of corporation executives, said one of its purposes was "to see the income tax lessened at the upper end and enlarged at the lower." Prohibitionists argued in reply that the legalization of beer would once again place the heaviest burden of taxation on the working classes since beer accounted for 90 percent of alcoholic consumption before prohibition and 90 percent of beer drinkers were working class.

Union leaders and industrialists were supported by doctors and lawyers, people who could also distinguish between the well-meaning theory of national prohibition and the disastrous results. These people challenged the obtuseness of prohibitionists in ignoring differences in local sentiment and disturbing the checks and balances against centralized authority inherent in the American system.

The medical profession had by its findings inspired the temperance movement. Now doctors went back on their word. The American Medical Association (AMA) reconsidered its resolution of 1917 against alcohol. In 1921 the council refused to confirm it. Then the *Journal of the American Medical Association* of June 3, 1922, announced it had been "unwise to attempt to determine moot scientific questions by resolution or by vote." In a report published in the same issue it recommended Congress to take no action on the therapeutic effect of alcohol. Professor Raymond Pearl of the University of Maine and, later, Johns Hopkins and Dr. Stewart Paton, also of

Johns Hopkins, Professor Osborne of the Yale School of Medicine and Dr. Samuel Harden Church, president of the Carnegie Institute of Technology, Pittsburgh, were all leaders of the American medical profession who opposed the intentions and consequences of prohibition. Dr. Matthias Nicoll, Jr., commissioner of health of New York, told a conference of the Public Health Service at Washington on May 31, 1927, that he attributed increased alcoholic mortality to "the establishment of a vast national and international machinery for the illicit manufacture, importation and distribution of alcoholic beverages, a large proportion of which are unfit for beverage purposes."

The defection of the doctors from the dry side was a decisive blow to the cause. They had sustained the temperance movement with objective evidence and rational proof. Now they withdrew both their support and their evidence. And they were joined by lawyers. During wartime debates lawyers had not bothered themselves with constitutional issues raised by prohibition. In the twenties they saw it as a threat to life, liberty and the pursuit of happiness. Lawyers had two specific objections to prohibition: the Eighteenth Amendment contradicted some of the others; prohibition cases clogged the courts, impeded true justice, and brought the performance of law into disrepute.

To some extent the successful operation of the Eighteenth Amendment violated rights given to the American people by four constitutional amendments of 1791. The Volstead Act ensured these violations. Whereas the Fourth Amendment assured people of their right "to be secure in their persons, houses, papers and effects against unreasonable searches and seizures," the Volstead Act confiscated personal property and allowed official invasion of people's homes. Although the Fifth Amendment declared that no one "shall be compelled . . . to be a witness against himself" and the Sixth gave "the right to a speedy and public trial by an impartial jury," the Volstead Act turned acts of ordinary housekeeping into crimes and refused trial by jury in some cases. Notwithstanding the Tenth Amendment, which said that "powers not delegated to the United States by the Constitution . . . are reserved to the States . . . or to the people," the Volstead Act extended judicial power beyond any American precedent. In the atmosphere of patriotic solidarity and xenophobic hysteria following the war various courts had chosen to ignore these points when test cases on prohibition were submitted to them. Now wet lawyers deplored what they considered a misguided extension of federal authority. The traditional balance between states and federal government, they believed, had been breached as a result of national prohibition.

Furthermore, most people could not equate having a drink with committing a crime. As the editorial of the *Chicago Journal* of January 17, 1922, put it, "No statute can make the average man regard the purchase or sale of a bottle of beer as he regards the forging of a check or the burning of a store." Thus juries were unwilling to convict people for having a drink. U.S. attorney George Hatfield told the *San Francisco Chronicle* of February 26, 1926, "Officers may make arrests, attorneys may prosecute, and judges may try offenders, but if juries do not convict the work of all these public servants comes to naught."

When juries did convict their reasons for doing so were sometimes perverse. In 1925 the *Virginian-Pilot* of Norfolk, Virginia, reported that when the jury in the case of Julia Rose, a black American charged with selling liquor, filed out to the jury room one of them let fall a half-pint bottle of booze. Rather than risk investigation among themselves the jury reported a verdict of guilty on the defendant and the incident was closed. This was not an isolated, absurd instance of the perversion of trial by jury under prohibition. In January 1928 one jury in San Francisco was itself tried because members had drunk the evidence for a case before it.

The upshot was congestion in the courts. In San Francisco federal courts could not handle all the cases brought to them. There were only three federal judges and they could only manage an average of ten cases a day if the defendant pleaded guilty. If the case was heard by a jury and the evidence given in full they could only try one case a day. In 1924 there were more than five thousand cases awaiting trial. Raids on small bootleggers were bringing in fifty cases a day. It would have been impracticable to give heavy jail sentences—there were not enough cells to hold the number of offenders. When the fine for first offenders was raised to six hundred dollars in 1924 hundreds of defendants refused to plead guilty and thereby impeded court schedules for days on end. This pattern was repeated elsewhere. United States Attorney Emory R. Buckner told the Senate Judiciary Committee in 1924 that the Southern District of New York would require seventeen additional courts in order to process the number of prohibition cases expeditiously—provided that trial by jury was abolished. If trial by jury was preserved then eighty-five additional courts would be required.

Once roused, the lawyers mobilized their forces. A group of New York lawyers incorporated themselves as the Voluntary Committee of Lawyers. Their opposition was essentially legal and expressed in their initial press release to the *New York Times* of December 11, 1927, which declared: "The Eighteenth Amendment is inconsistent with the spirit and purpose of the Constitution . . . and in derogation of the liberties of the citizens . . . as guaranteed by the first ten amendments."

Their attitude was echoed in a series of similar announcements by bar associations throughout the country. On February 14, 1928, the New York Bar Association adopted a resolution calling for the repeal of the Eighteenth Amendment and the Volstead Act preferring that "the subject of prohibition should be remitted to the sole regulation of the several states." And between 1927 and 1930 the bar associations of Boston, Detroit, Philadelphia, Portland, St. Louis and San Francisco and New Jersey State all made similar announcements. In 1930 the American Bar Association itself approved a proposal for repeal which had been put to a popular vote of members and passed by 13,779 to 6,340, a majority of two thirds.

———————— ◆ ————————

Beyond the distinctive opposition of labor leaders, industrialists, doctors, and lawyers what the sum total of American public opinion on prohibition amounted to no one really knew. The people had never been consulted by the federal government whether by referendum, recall, or initiative.

However twenty different referenda were held in eleven states during the twenties. Nine were on questions of amending or repealing the Volstead Act or the Eighteenth Amendment. Two were won by the drys—in Ohio (1922) and Colorado (1926). The other seven were won by the wets: in Massachusetts (1920); Illinois (1922); Illinois, again, Nevada, New York and Wisconsin (1926); and Massachusetts, again (1928). In New York the vote was three to one in favor of modifying the Volstead Act. Drys remained unconvinced. They wanted to believe that wets voted and drys demurred. In New York, for instance, fewer votes were cast in the referendum of 1926 than in the election for governor that year. However, Charles Merz estimates that even if all the 543,166 votes missing between referendum and election had been cast solidly against the proposal to modify the Volstead Act the proposal would still have been carried by well over half a million votes.

156

Most vociferous opposition came from cities. At an election on November 7, 1922, Chicago voters were asked if they wanted the law modified to permit alcohol of less than 4 percent proof. The vote was overwhelmingly for a relaxation of prohibition in every ward with 493,333 voting for and 110,597 against. In some wards the majority was as high as sixteen to one.

The many unofficial polls on prohibition during the twenties had the peculiar advantage over state referenda of being taken across state lines. They also offered the public a choice among a series of proposals rather than a simple decision between two alternatives. The choice was retail and not wholesale. The disadvantage was that no one knew if such polls accurately captured a representative cross-section of opinion or merely a biased, interested, and narrow one.

Perhaps the two most important polls were the *Literary Digest* poll of 1922 and the poll of the Newspaper Enterprise Association of 1926. The *Literary Digest* distributed ballots in forty-eight states in 1922. Of the 922,382 returned, 38.6 percent favored the prohibition laws, 40.8 percent favored modification, and 20.6 percent favored repeal. Thus the dissatisfied proportion was 61.4 percent, not quite two-thirds of the whole.

In the poll taken by the Newspaper Enterprise Association in 1926, 326 newspapers in cities, towns, and villages in forty-seven states participated in a poll of 1,747,630 people. Only 18.9 percent favored the existing laws; 49.8 percent favored modification; and 31.3 percent favored repeal. Thus 81.1 percent were dissatisfied with prohibition.

Prohibitionists gave little credence to such polls. The Anti-Saloon League denounced the newspaper poll to the *New York Times* of March 14, 1926, as unreliable and misleading and "whether so intended or not, part of the wet agitation." The president of the Michigan chapter of the Women's Christian Temperance Union dismissed it with the statement: "The newspapers take straw votes and the wets vote early and often." Nevertheless they reflected growing public unease at the effects of prohibition. This unease was to find fuller expression in the wet lobbies organized to revise the reform, if necessary by repealing the Eighteenth Amendment.

———————◆◆———————

There were three principal organizations in the general movement for prohibition reform.

Captain William H. Stayton founded the Association Against

the Prohibition Movement (AAPA) in the summer of 1919. It was formally incorporated in the District of Columbia on December 31, 1920. People were invited to join the association for a fee of a dollar. The AAPA consolidated by absorbing independent state organizations like the Grape Protective Association of California. By 1926 it was able to tell the Reed Committee it had 720,000 members.

While the association claimed its officers had no interest in the liquor trade and worked without a salary it is also true that men with liquor interests supported it. The inner council of the AAPA consisted of Arthur Curtis James, railroad magnate; E. S. Hastings, oil magnate; Charles H. Sabin, president of the Guaranty Trust—a Morgan bank; Grayson M. P. Murphy, banker; three Du Pont brothers of General Motors and their associate J. J. Raskob; and Professor E. R. A. Seligman, economist of the Brewers' Association.

The association was, as its name implies, opposed to the amendment. But its members were, beyond that opposition, divided among themselves. They all wanted prohibition reformed "in such a way as to guarantee against the return of the saloon." But they could not decide whether to support the Constitution and uphold law and order or to subvert it by encouraging violation of a bad law. Thus William Stayton, first president of the AAPA, advised wet politicians to cooperate with dry officers and not to oppose proposals for enforcement, whether financial, administrative, or legal. He thought it would be a mistake to give the drys some excuse to say their law had not had a fair chance. "We will give them, in short, all of the rope they want to take and we will be careful not to let them accuse us of obstructive politics." Yet, later, subversion became the dominant policy. The AAPA's press slogan of 1927 was "Respect the Prohibition Law! Never!" By 1930, it was urging voters to "Vote As You Drink."

The AAPA copied the political strategy of the Anti-Saloon League. It supported wets of either party in elections, kept records of the votes of congressmen on all matters pertaining to prohibition, supported surveys and published propaganda on the failure of prohibition. Unlike the league, which had always concentrated on local affairs—to make its members feel important—the association emphasized the national scandal of prohibition in its various newspapers—to make its members aware of the extent of the problem it diagnosed. Just as the league had opposed measures for outright prohibition before the time was right, the association opposed reform before it judged the time was propitious.

In 1929 another wet organization, the Crusaders, was launched in Cleveland, Ohio, the home state of the Anti-Saloon League itself. It complemented the AAPA by concentrating its efforts on local politics rather than national affairs. Fred G. Clark, an oil executive of Cleveland, was the first commander in chief of the Crusaders. The executive board was composed of fifty prominent men from the northeastern states. The rank and file were composed of young men under thirty. Robert Kenny, the commander of the Los Angeles chapter, told Gilbert Ostrander, the historian of prohibition in California, that they represented "organized thirst." They were derided by the drys for their sources of support as "Cork-Screw Aiders."

The Crusaders promised the very same reforms as the Anti-Saloon League had in 1913: abolition of the saloon; elimination of the corrupt association between the liquor interests and politicians; reduction of drinking and elimination of alcoholism. Thus Crusaders claimed they were "temperance men" who would achieve what the league had failed to do, and restore the balance between the profligacy of unregulated liquor and the excesses of prohibition.

Women were just as sensitive to the scandal of prohibition as men and became equally militant in their opposition to it. Their opposition was decisive. The Nineteenth Amendment had accomplished woman suffrage, not female emancipation. For woman suffrage did not in itself improve the lot of women. A progressive fallacy was exposed. Moreover, a sex that patronized the speakeasy could no longer be shocked or intimidated by what was supposed to happen in bars. Prohibitionists could not resume the theme of alcoholic and sexual license now that women other than prostitutes frequented them.

But women did not have to accept the situation as final. Major Henry H. Curran, president of AAPA in the early thirties, told H. L. Mencken in June 1932 that the campaign for repeal of prohibition, "offered the women their first chance to show that they could think for themselves in politics, and, what is more, the first chance to prove that they had a very real power. The drys had been depicting all women as natural prohibitionists, which was just as offensive to intelligent women as it would have been to intelligent men. So they leapt at the opportunity to give the dry evangelists a beating."

On June 8, 1928, *Outlook* magazine published an article by Pauline Sabin that began, "I was one of the women who favored prohibition when I heard it discussed in the abstract but I am now convinced it has proved a failure. It is true we no longer see the corner saloon: but in many cases has it not merely moved to the back of a store, or up or down one flight under the name of a speakeasy?" Pauline Sabin was the wife of Charles H. Sabin, president of the Guaranty Trust, a Morgan bank, who was treasurer of the AAPA. Hitherto the most outspoken wets had refrained from criticizing dry women. Mrs. Sabin, however, ridiculed and attacked women who voted for a dry politician without bothering to ascertain his views on other crucial matters believing, erroneously, that prohibition protected their children from drink.

On May 28, 1929, after the election of Hoover and incensed by his dry stand, Pauline Sabin launched the Women's Organization for National Prohibition Reform (WONPR) at the Drake Hotel, Chicago. Chicago was chosen instead of New York because its problems of civic disorder were indissoluble from prohibition. In addition the Sabins wanted to give the WONPR a national and not a regional identity. Their avowed aims were true temperance, not the return of the saloon. The pledge card read:

> Because I believe that prohibition has increased crime, lawlessness, hypocrisy and corruption; because I believe that the cause of real temperance has been retarded and that sumptuary laws have no place in the Federal Constitution, I enroll as a member of this organization, which is working for some change in the law to bring about a sane solution of the problem without the return of the saloon.

Soon the WONPR had a million members. Mrs. Sabin made sure that each local chapter was led by someone well placed in high society with an income of her own, time on her hands, and a flair for publicity. Women like Mrs. Pierre S. Du Pont, Mrs. Archibald B. Roosevelt, Mrs. Coffin Van Rennselaer and others could always command press copy. Joining their organization became the fashionable thing to do. A "Sabine woman" could be received anywhere.

In 1932 Dr. D. Leigh Colvin of the National Prohibition Committee described them as "Bacchantian maidens, parching for wine—wet women who, like the drunkards whom their program will produce, would take pennies off the eyes of the dead for the sake of legalizing booze." And Dr. Mary Armor, president of the Georgia WCTU, said in 1930, "As to Mrs. Sabin and her cocktail drinking women, we will out-live them, out-fight them, out-love them, out-talk them, out-pray them, and out-vote them." But the Sabine women were effective lobbyists. They were persistent in pursuit of politicians. The New Testament parable of the unjust judge and the importunate widow was played out in modern society for all it was worth.

Other organizations opposed to prohibition included the National Association Opposed to Prohibition; the Moderation League; the American Veterans' Association for the Repeal of the Eighteenth Amendment; the Women's Committee for Modification of the Volstead Act, which, in 1927, became the Women's Committee for Repeal of the Eighteenth Amendment.

If groups like the AAPA, the WONPR, and the Crusaders had a partisan political objective it was to convert the Republicans to the wet cause rather than place the already wet Democrats in power. However, in 1926 the AAPA, the Moderation League, the American Federation of Labor, and the Constitutional Liberty League of Massachusetts decided to present Congress jointly with evidence that the law was not being, nor ever could be, successfully enforced. This was certainly the inference the Reed Committee wanted to take but the Senate investigations of 1926 were not especially supportive of wet means and methods of protest to the detriment of the drys.

During the early twenties an uneasy truce existed between prohibitionists and their foes. Wayne Wheeler and the Anti-Saloon League were past masters at the art of political propaganda. They were also experts in political strategy. By keeping the cost of enforcement down they kept taxation at the same level and thus anticipated a potential cause of public resentment. By failing to cut off all sources of illicit liquor they anticipated a potential cause of vociferous public hostility.

They were aware of the new form of opposition but, initially, unperturbed. Their security, they believed, lay in the form of legislation they had achieved—constitutional amendment. By the 1920s more than three thousand amendments had been proposed to the Constitution but only nineteen had been adopted. None had been repealed. Andrew Volstead told the national convention of the Anti-Saloon League in 1921 that there was no chance of revoking the Eighteenth Amendment. The evangelist, Billy Sunday, concurred. There was no more chance of repealing the Eighteenth Amendment, he averred, "than there is of repealing the Thirteenth Amendment and restoring slavery."

Despite the assurances from wets as well as drys, the Anti-Saloon League was quite unprepared for the challenge of the wets. For one thing the new form of opposition was most unwelcome to prohibitionists. Not only were doctors and lawyers well educated, articulate and able to make their opposition effective but they were also genuinely disinterested. Brewers and distillers had been easy targets for dry abuse: they were corrupt and predatory and composed of people from those classes hostile to progressive reforms. The drys would have liked to believe that the new opposition was a front for the old opposition, at best composed of the misguided dupes of the liquor interests and at worst of their interested dependents. In fact by the late twenties wet opposition was led by presidents or chairmen of associations that included those blacklisted by the brewers ten years earlier—the Pennsylvania Railroad, General Motors, Western Union Telegraph, and others.

In its fights to punish trangressors and retain the law, the Anti-Saloon League lost its reputation for the sort of progressive, humane qualities that had originally attracted different sorts of people to it. When Wayne Wheeler was reported by the *New York Times* of December 30, 1926, as justifying the poisoning of industrial alcohol to deter people from drinking it and accusing those who did drink it of committing suicide, he did not convince people that the Anti-Saloon League was motivated by humanitarian concern to save life.

In the mid-twenties the league was also discredited on account of the moral laxity of some of its members. In 1924 William H. Anderson, superintendent of the New York league, was convicted of third-degree forgery and imprisoned in Sing Sing, where he served nine months. On the eve of his trial the league executive committee misguidedly adopted a resolution affirming its confidence in his "integrity, ability, and efficiency." After the trial the league looked particularly foolish. Another case that reflected badly on the league was that of S. S. Kresge, owner of a chain of department stores, who was a most generous patron. He continuously affirmed that he believed in prohibition because it was "a righteous law, contributing to the moral and social good of the people." His moral principles were sufficiently stringent to prevent him supporting any church whose minister smoked. And in 1927 he offered the league $500,000 for its educational campaign. But that year his wife obtained a divorce on account of his misconduct with a stenographer, which was proved in a sensational court case in New York. Asked whether the league would return Kresge's gift, Francis Scott McBride, national superintendent, said it would not. In the past the league had been chary of receiving funds from morally tainted sources. At this juncture it did not have a choice in the matter of finance. But its credibility as a movement for moral reform was undermined.

Many prohibitionists underwent a change of heart because they came to understand that the remedy, prohibition, was worse than the disease, the saloon. Henry B. Joy of Detroit, the Packard manufacturer, was one such who transferred his allegiance from the Anti-Saloon League to the Association Against the Prohibition Amendment, becoming treasurer of the Michigan chapter. Others changed sides not out of personal conviction but political opportunism. Joseph Boyer, a Detroit businessman, turned down the league's annual request for funds in 1928 with the remark "I do not mean that you are on the wrong side, but . . . you are on the losing side, and what is the use of playing a losing game knowingly?"

A major loss to the drys occurred with the defection of William Randolph Hearst, the newspaper magnate, in 1927. He pursued his former allies with the vindictiveness he had so far vented on the wets: "The Anti-Saloon League with its dictation to the elected representatives, with its attempted intimidation of the President, with its usurpation of authority, *must be banished from the United States.*" Hearst later claimed, on April 26, 1929, that "Prohibition has instituted unAmerican methods of spying and snooping." If it had done so it had learned its tricks from him.

Hearst's defection was damaging financially but more so symbolically. For the press, which had once cherished the ideal and supported the intentions behind prohibition, abandoned it in the course of the twenties.

Whereas before the First World War more than half the secular press supported the temperance movement, by the late twenties almost no major newspapers did so. Instead they exposed the vicissitudes of prohibition. The predictions of progressive muckrakers about the evils of alcohol at the turn of the century gave way to prophecies on the "Collapse of Prohibition," in *Leslie's* of November 27, 1920, and in 1930 to the persuasion to "Have a Little Drinkie," reprinted in *The Vanity Fair Book: 1930–1931* (1931). Representative Franklin W. Fort of New Jersey, a dry, told Congress in 1930 that "never have our great and powerful newspapers thrown the whole weight of their influence practically unanimously on the same side of a question before."

The President's Research Committee on Social Trends (published in 1934) discovered that in 1905 out of 175 articles on prohibition published in a series of journals not one was hostile. In 1915, in a larger sample, articles approved of prohibition by twenty to one. By 1920 the ratio had changed to less than four dry articles to every three wet. And by 1930 the ratio had turned against the dry point of view. There was not quite one dry piece for every two wet. Of the New York papers the *Times, Herald,* and *World* consistently opposed prohibition. And in Chicago four of the five city papers did so.

After the imposition of national prohibition the AAPA adopted and adapted the prewar and wartime methods of the drys. It distributed free copy that was ostensibly impartial but actually a part of the campaign to repeal the Eighteenth Amendment. It also put financial pressure on editors to support its point of view when it became an important advertiser.

The drys reiterated their former charge against the press. Wet papers had, they believed, been bought outright or were being heavily subsidized by liquor interests. A more responsible and fundamental criticism by prohibitionists was that press copy emphasized the problems of prohibition, the lapses in law enforcement. Francis Scott McBride told the *New York Herald Tribune* of June 10, 1929, that he deplored "the power of the press to magnify every failure, misfortune or mistake in connection with prohibition out of all proportion to its proper relation toward a great national reform."

But the exposure given to prohibition in the press was partly the result of changes in papers themselves. This was the period when newspaper owners consolidated their holdings by mergers. Small newspapers were submerged and also some large ones in the fierce competition for monopoly control of news and readers. The new chains of newspapers each with its own series of syndicated articles competed for increased circulation. The first American tabloid was the *New York Daily News,* which appeared in 1919. Like much of the Northcliffe press in England it was a picture paper emphasizing photographs and minimizing the amount of printed text. It also made the most of the sort of scare captions that had been developed during the war. Press pretense of objectivity was shattered by sensation, sentimentality and salaciousness. Within five years it had the largest circulation of any paper in New York. William Randolph

Hearst was not to be outdone and launched the *New York Daily Mirror*, a copy of the *News*. And Bernarr MacFadden, another magnate, launched the *New York Evening Graphic*, which exceeded either in its excesses. Prohibition had its own part to play in these developments.

Prohibition had introduced novel events and elements into American society: bootlegging and hijacking; smuggling and moonshining; speakeasies and illicit stills; drives and raids by police, customs, and prohibition agents. These were now the staff of life, the stuff of news. Editors and publishers were in business to make money. Adventures with drama, comedy, and tragedy were good copy. They were also responsive to controversy. Thus they printed stories against prohibition *and* stories that were favorable to prohibition not because they were good sports or unbiased themselves but because they were practical men of business. According to Charles Merz the *New York Times* published 16,231 items of news about prohibition between 1920 and 1927. And although the *Times* opposed prohibition Merz estimated that in 1925, for example, it published 169 stories supporting it.

Wets interpreted press hostility as a sign of public dissatisfaction. Drys believed the press was catering to the predilections of its city clientele. The criticism would have been equally accurate of newspapers in small towns. The Board of Temperance, Prohibition and Public Morals of the Methodist Episcopal Church was reported by the *New York Times* of October 14, 1925, as saying, "New York is bombarding the West with anti-prohibition propaganda which in practice proves to be an incitement to violation of the law." For the city papers were becoming the press of all the states. Between 1925 and 1930 rural subscription to city papers doubled. It had been in rural areas that the prohibition movement had tested its strength. But once the city press extended its influence over the countryside it also ended rural isolation. Without that isolation rural prejudice could not survive.

──EIGHT──

SHORT CUT

THE PRINTED WORD HAD EXISTED for hundreds of years. But American society in the 1920s was affected by newer inventions than newspapers. Like the Gilded Age and the period after the Second World War the 1920s enjoyed a revolution in transportation and another in communications. The development of American society in the late nineteenth century was dependent on the railroad; after the Second World War it was changed by the airplane; in the 1920s it was transformed by the automobile. In the wake of the Industrial Revolution came telegraph and telephone to provide people with instantaneous communication; in the 1940s and 1950s television became a mass medium; in the 1920s motion pictures and radio transformed society. Automobile, movie, and radio did not alter Americans' attitude to prohibition by the sort of argument newspapers could provide. But they transformed people's expectations, established new patterns of social behavior, and undermined the sort of established values on which prohibition rested.

These changes broke down the difference between town and country. R. I. Duffus and Harold Stearns could rightly conclude in their *America Now* (1938) that "The town is no longer self-contained. Invention and change have let the inhabitants out, the outer world in." Whereas half the people lived in towns for the first time in 1920, 56 percent did so in 1930. Although a town comprised only 2,500 inhabitants, half the population was within access of cities of more than 100,000 inhabitants. There was no longer any possibility of prohibitionists intimidating country bumpkins with baleful accounts of city life when countryfolk could experience the city for themselves.

In 1900 there were only 8,000 automobiles in the United States. But after Henry Ford's manufacture of the Model T in 1909 the automobile built with a new metal, Vanadium Steel, became available to the masses. By 1916 there were 3 million cars and by 1920, 7,541,000. By 1930 there were 26.5 million—one car for every five Americans. The increase in the previous ten years was sixteen times the growth of the population.

Automobiles were to make society more homogeneous. The values of the city were brought to the country. Suburban life was possible for millions. At the turn of the century dirt tracks were apologies for roads. Transport and communication between town and country was by horse or iron horse, by bicycle or foot. The new mobility, however, depended on easy access. In 1921 the Federal Highways Act was passed to encourage roadbuilding and the road network was developed out of all recognition. Automobiles became a major source of revenue. In 1924 taxes on motor vehicles amounted to one and a half times the maximum ever received from taxes on alcohol. Cars also advanced major industries such as steel, rubber, glass, upholstery, and—on a scale that cut Standard Oil down to size—oil. John B. Rae estimated that by the mid-twenties cars were "consuming annually 90 percent of the country's petroleum . . . 80 percent of the rubber . . . 20 percent of the steel, 75 percent of the plate glass, and 25 percent of the machine tools."

Once upon a time the car had been a competitor with the saloon—something automobile manufacturers recognized. Henry Ford said in 1928 that it was his cars that had closed the bars: "The speed at which we run our motor cars, operate our intricate machinery, and generally live would be impossible with liquor." And the speed of the car was to become more than a substitute for liquor. It offered a greater freedom than the temporary, physical release of alcohol—the liberty of mobility. Better to be drunk with speed than liquor. Accidents caused by drunken drivers could not be tolerated. And in the first ten years of prohibition the number of deaths in automobile accidents was only a third the number of those in England (which did not have prohibition), although the United States had eight times as many cars. Thus at first the new invention supported the novel idea of prohibition.

The most famous automobile manufacturer, Henry Ford, was a true pioneer: one of the very few men of whom it could be said he transformed the society into which he was born. His technical and commercial acumen suited the business philosophy of the age, for he combined scientific expertise in a new field with a paternalism that was supportive of prohibition yet opposed to labor unions and to commercial banking. As far as prohibition went he was as good as his word. In September 1922 a notice was posted on the walls of his automobile factory in Detroit. It warned, "it will cost a man his job . . . to have the odor of beer, wine or liquor on his breath, or to have any of these intoxicants on his person or in his home. The Eighteenth Amendment is a part of the fundamental laws of this country. . . . Politics has interfered with enforcement of this law, but so far as our organization is concerned it is going to be enforced to the letter."

Clinging to his parochial values, Ford refused to budge on the prohibition issue. He told the *Pictorial Review* of September 1929: "If booze ever comes back to the United States, I am thru [sic] with manufacturing. I would not be bothered with the problem of handling over two hundred thousand men and trying to pay them wages which the saloons would take away from them. I would not be interested in putting automobiles in the hands of a generation soggy with drink." To this the *New York Times* retorted tartly that "it would be a great pity to have Detroit's two leading industries destroyed at one blow." Of course Ford was being hypocritical. He sold cars to European and Latin American countries and to Canada where alcohol was freely bought and sold. And his hypocrisy was as ominous a metaphor for the impurity of prohibition as his parsimony.

Cars conveyed more than their passengers. They could carry packages containing alcohol. They certainly carried change—the conventions of the countryside were challenged by those of the city. They provided means and opportunity for sexual freedom impossible in a static society. In the Lynds' study *Middletown* one judge referred to the car as "a house of prostitution on wheels." Because they were used so much by bootleggers and gangsters automobiles were never dissociated from criminal activities in the public mind. "Don't shoot, I'm not a bootlegger" was the caption popular among car owners in Michigan, and prohibited there by the attorney general in 1929. Whereas at the beginning of the decade automobiles represented an alternative to alcohol at its end they symbolized booze and beer running and everything that was subversive of prohibition. In addition they provided an unfortunate comparison with liquor: how a potentially lethal invention could be controlled and made comparatively safe.

In *Responsible Drinking* (1930) Robert Binkley compared the ill effects of alcohol with those of the automobile. He concluded that morals had withstood centuries of drinking but had broken down after two decades of driving. Driving was intoxicating. Cars had facilitated crime. Driving was habit-forming. Millions of people would hardly be able to use their legs again. But the temperance movement had concentrated on the prohibition of alcohol. It had remained unconcerned by the social upheaval caused by the car. Of course cars were part and parcel of contemporary social and economic life. They were controlled by careful drivers and compulsory insurance policies, by legislation and licenses. Could not liquor be regulated in the same way?

―――――◆◆―――――

The new mass society was also shaped by the motion picture and radio. As the English historian, A. J. P. Taylor, has pointed out, radio and movies were, at first, the obverse of one another. One provided words without pictures; the other, pictures without words—at least until the talkies were invented and millions heard Al Jolson speak and sing in *The Jazz Singer* (1927).

Whereas the automobile was invented before 1920, radio was invented and used commercially that year, commencing on November 2 when KDKA broadcast the election results. By 1922 the annual sales of radio equipment had reached $6 million. By 1929 they had reached $842,548,000—an increase of 1,400 percent. A third of homes had receivers: thus the estimated national weekly audience was 95 million people. By 1933 there were 17 million radios in America. And two out of every five people living in villages and one out of every five farmers had a set.

Whatever its limitations radio stimulated intellect and cultural sensibilities, expanding people's knowledge and sharpening their perceptions. Radio brought a new dimension to political discussion. In 1924 the Democratic National Convention was broadcast from

the old Madison Square Garden, New York: in 1928 both parties used radio for debate. The old half truths that reformers had used to
spell out the importance of prohibition now seemed pretentious and
hollow.

Motion pictures were an earlier invention than radio. The first
kinetoscope parlor opened on Broadway in 1894. It showed a film to
one person at a time. In 1896 a nickelodeon projected pictures on a
screen large enough for several people to see the film at one sitting.
And in 1903 a complete feature story of twelve minutes' duration,
The Great Train Robbery, was shown. The first movie theater
opened, in Pittsburgh, Pennsylvania, in 1905. Soon Hollywood films
were seen by millions and hence the values of innovative directors,
D. W. Griffith, Cecil B. De Mille, and Erich von Stroheim, spread to
all levels of society. According to a report in the *New Republic* there
were more than seventeen hundred picture houses in 1926 and these
constituted 97 percent of all theaters in the country.

Movies inculcated people with the myth of the Roaring Twenties—the mixture of sexual license and criminal excess, social indulgence and political corruption. Even the poor and dispossessed
could share vicariously in escapist entertainment that provided novel
stories, emotional situations, and glamorous settings. Movies
titillated audiences with vice rather than showed them how to avoid
it, offering material solace if only for a few hours.

Stars, not screenplays, captured public imagination. The most
potent stars created their own images. They were screen archetypes.
The lesser players filled in the sketches provided by Theda Bara—the
vamp; Mary Pickford—ingenious ingenue; Rudolph Valentino—
Latin lover; Erich von Stroheim—jaded aristocrat; Lillian Gish—
heroine ennobled by experience; Douglas Fairbanks—swashbuckling
hero; Charlie Chaplin—victorious tramp; Buster Keaton—disingenuous clown. All of these stars were subversive of traditional rural
standards, whether of old-fashioned morality, which they cheated,
or law and order, which they subverted. Not only Chaplin but the
others also represented the individual struggling against the forces of
social conformity. These included prohibition.

Whatever the final verdict of history on the experiment of prohibition and the growth of syndicated crime there can be no doubt
that the performing arts owe them an incalculable debt. Without

them the gangster film would never have taken shape in the way known for more than half a century.

In 1932 gangster movies were the most popular of all film genres. Their vogue was greater than that of romances and musicals and far greater than that of westerns. As Dorothy Manners in *Motion Picture Classic* of June 1931 observed, "Gangsters . . . gunmen . . . gamblers . . . hoodlums . . . heist guys . . . hold-ups . . . 'babyfaced killers' . . . bandits . . . bullets . . . murders . . . morgues . . . molls. Hollywood is going at the pace that 'kills' at the box office! Of all the theme picture epidemics none has equaled the intense rush of gangsters to the box office."

Although Paramount had developed the genre other studios— M-G-M, Fox, De Mille Pictures, Columbia, and Universal—followed their example. One studio, Warner Brothers, was to make the genre its specialty. And nearly every major star played in at least one gangster film during the thirties. Some, such as Humphrey Bogart and George Raft, seemed to play in little else.

Gangster thrillers exercised a double fascination for the public. They combined the realism of a social documentary with the emotional power of a dream. They played on fears that American society during prohibition and the economy during the depression were unstable and foundering. Gilbert Seldes in *The Years of the Locust— America, 1929–1932* (1933) said the gangster film was particularly effective at representing aspirations and desires in the depression: "Rude manners, brutality, and action—contempt of authority, the theme of the bowl of cherries and the raspberry; and the desire for work." Gangster protagonists projected an image of energy and self-assurance that lent encouragement to their public.

The genre itself preceded prohibition. *The Musketeers of Pig Alley*, directed by D. W. Griffith in 1912, was the first gangster movie. The Snapper Kid, the first gangster protagonist, lived in New York's Lower East Side. Griffith's skill transformed a series of conventional enough episodes—an armed robbery, a barroom brawl, a shootout between rival gangs, and a police hunt—into archetypes of the gangster thriller. Whatever its limitations *Musketeers* is a more effective and livelier piece of work than Griffith's lugubrious study of prohibition itself in his last film *The Struggle* (1931).

The new genre conceived by D. W. Griffith owed much to the tradition of songs and *verisimo* operas. Pieces like Mascagni's *Cavalleria Rusticana* (1890), Leoncavello's *Pagliacci* (1892), and Puccini's *Il Tabarro* (1918), and others, also dealt with violence in low life. Their mixture of lurid melodrama, blood-and-thunder romance, and conventional lyricism scored an immediate public success, which did not go unnoticed by those working in other performing arts.

Gangsters in early films were city cousins of western outlaws like Billy the Kid and Jesse James, who had supposedly robbed the rich to help the poor. They were presented as good-natured hoodlums conspiring to overthrow corrupt officers. Outlaws stole from banks and railroad companies rather than people, who were the real prey of politicians and public officials. Whereas the western outlaw roamed the countryside—a horizontal world—and the eastern gangster hustled in the cities—a vertical world—both inhabited canyons. The outlaw lived in the natural environment of mountains, cliffs, crevices; the gangster dwelt in the man-made environment of skyscrapers, office blocks, and bonded warehouses. The difference was that the West was beyond civilization. It suggested man at peace with nature but forced to depend on himself. The East, by contrast, did not treat everyone in the same way. All men were not equal. Vertical planes suggested impossible odds, a corrupt civilization curbing freedom, and complemented the protagonist's rise and fall.

In the 1920s bootlegging in real life completed the acculturation of the criminal classes. Bootlegging in the movies made gangsters popular in the cinema and real life. Films such as *The Bootlegger's Daughter* (1922), *Contraband* (1925), *Poison* (1924), *Four Walls* (1928), and *Broadway* (1929) supplied audiences with the cheap thrill of seeing services rendered and the satisfaction of knowing that though one law was flouted, a rough justice would be meted out to the criminals. If, despite so much adverse publicity, gangsters still retained a glamour that the grammar of respectable routine lacked it was because mass society had inculcated conformity in the majority of its citizens. People thought they were romantic because they supposed they were brave. In a mass society courage was not a common commodity.

Underworld (1927), written by Ben Hecht for Paramount, was erroneously hailed as the first gangster film. Critically and commercially, it was certainly the most successful example of the genre to that time. The core of the plot is a triangular love story about bank robber Bull Weed (George Bancroft), his girl, Feathers McCoy (Evelyn Brent), and alcoholic lawyer Rolls Royce (Clive Brook). When the lawyer reforms and falls in love with the girl and she with him the loyalty of all three is tested.

The director, Josef von Sternberg, skillfully evoked the atmosphere of a city at night. Whereas Griffith had defined the archetypal situations Sternberg defined the iconography. The gangsters' world was dark with flashes of light from car headlights, matches, mirrors, and chandeliers. Over the next half century the gangster thriller of all genres was most resistant to color photography. Even when color became commonplace in other films, gangster thrillers remained lugubrious, their very darkness implying a relationship between environment and crime. Gangster films drew from, and perpetuated, cultural myths more by the way the stories were told than what the plots themselves described.

The Racket (1928) was based on a play by Bartlett Cormack, who, like his friend Ben Hecht, had worked as a reporter in Chicago. It was set in Chicago and its leading character, Nick Scarsi (Louis Wolheim in a part created on stage by Edward G. Robinson), was based on Al Capone. The crooked mayor was inspired by Big Bill Thompson. Lewis Milestone, who directed it for producer Howard Hughes, was painstaking in his attempts to create atmosphere and sought the advice of eight Chicago bootleggers lying low in Los Angeles about details of sets and costumes.

Scarsi's racket is bootlegging and he defies the law openly by having liquor transported in broad daylight. When the police catch his gang a crooked politician intercedes on their behalf on the understanding that they will provide him with fraudulent votes in the forthcoming elections. Scarsi, arrested for murdering a patrolman, is trapped by Captain McQuigg (Thomas Meighan), an officer who cannot be bought off. McQuigg kills Scarsi when he tries to escape from detention. It is rough justice, for McQuigg realizes that the courts would set Scarsi free.

The Racket was subversive from the politicians' point of view. Whereas other films like *Tuned Up* (1924) and *City Gone Wild* (1927) alluded to illicit liasions between gangsters and capitalists, *The Racket* was specific. It showed the public how the relationship between law and crime worked. Criminals protected politicians by providing them with votes and funds in exchange for immunity from harassment by prohibition agents and police and from prosecution by the state. The play had been banned in Chicago, and when the film was released there it was heavily censored. Bartlett Cormack, however, did not mince his words when he told Dunham Thorp for *Motion Pictures Classic* of December 1928 that the close relationship between gangsters and politicians was too close to truth for comfort of Big Bill Thompson. In New York the Motion Picture Commission had scenes showing Scarsi bribing police to have a gangster released excised.

During the 1920s movie gangsters were no longer confined to the slums. They were presented as likable, even debonair, in films such as *The Law and the Lady* (1924), *Grit* (1924), *Dressed to Kill* (1928), and *The Racketeer* (1929) and suave enough to enter sophisticated society in *Come Across* (1929) and *Danger Street* (1928). A gangster's arrival in the demimonde was signaled on screen, as in life, by the exchange of overalls and cloth cap for the accoutrements of upper-class living: top hat and evening dress, diamond jewelry, lavish receptions in art deco mansions or nightclubs.

Automobiles also contributed to the iconography of the genre by showing how gangsters were part of the mechanized world. Automobiles were no longer a novelty but, rather, tools extending man's abilities to create his environment and control his place in it. Gangster films, like gangsters' lives, reflected this.

———◆———

The essential visual qualities of gangster films were well established by the late twenties. But sight was only half of the story: sound would make thrillers more realistic and extend their meaning through aural metaphors. Sam Warner, perhaps in desperation at the incipient decline of Warner Brothers, began to produce short films of vaudeville acts with musical accompaniment from 1926 and then released *The Lights of New York* (1928), the first full-length picture with spoken dialogue throughout. Sound was not, at first, all gain. The camera, which had once moved with ease and grace, was restricted to the range of a stationary microphone. Characters huddled together in a barbershop, or around a sofa in the boss's office. The dialogue of *Lights* seemed interminable. It was full of clichés: "You needed me to stick by you through all the tough times." It also had more than its fair share of mixed metaphors of Shakespearean complexity—without any dramatic flair: "You think you can take any chicken you want and throw me back in the deck?" The artists' attempts to render gang slang intelligible were articulate to the point of artifice. However, public response to both *The Lights of New York* and *The Jazz Singer* (1927) with Al Jolson was such that neither Warners nor any other studio could begin to supply the demand.

Gangster movies were the first genre to realize the full possibilities of sound. The clarion twang of a Brooklyn accent uttered by a gangster's moll became as essential to the genre as the bray of a jazz trumpet. To these were added the idioms of everyday speech, a wit hitherto peculiar to the American stage, and, sometimes, musical routines in a nightclub.

It was not until the introduction of sound that criminals exchanged Anglo-Saxon or Celtic-sounding names like the Scarab, Fancy Charlie, Black Mike, the Peacock, and the Hawk once and for all for obviously Italian and, sometimes, Jewish ones lke Bennie Horowitz, Nick Scarsi, Caesar Enrico Bandello, Tony Passa, Tony Beretti, and Tony Camonte. Not only did such names reflect the emergence of Italian and Jewish criminals in the big time of the underworld but they also pointed up the audience's growing awareness of these developments. However, the immigrant milieu was not depicted with a realism to do justice to the seamy squalor of Bandits' Roost, Poverty Gap, Misery Row, and Murderers' Alley. Movie moguls yearned for a lost community. They insisted on picturesque, sentimental details. Mothers wore simple peasant frocks, spoke with thick accents, and prepared food for others to wolf down and beds for others to loll in.

If gangsters' mothers brought comfort their molls brought despair. The real-life gangster's mythic devotion to one woman was transformed in films. Although Al Capone was a notorious womanizer and Lucky Luciano remained a carefree bachelor, other underworld bosses like Jim Colosimo, Johnny Torrio and Dion O'Banion were famous for fidelity to hearth and home. But in films gangsters distrusted girls. They had good reason to. In *Night After Night* (1932) George Raft, as a speakeasy owner who aspires to a social status he cannot attain, asks one of his molls, "What's with you?" She answers back, "Three cocktails." When a married woman tells him she has obtained a divorce he expresses surprise that she was even married. She has the perfect reply: "Joe, you've been watching me too closely."

This was also Mae West's first film. Her immortal answer to the remark of the hatcheck girl who admires her jewelry, "Goodness, what beautiful diamonds," was, "Goodness had nothing to do with it, dearie." The remark defined Mae West's persona beyond a brief film career. Her success was certainly resented by the nominal star. George Raft later recalled that Mae West "stole everything but the cameras." She became a legend in her lifetime for her good-humored parody of the predatory vamp. Of her own plot for *I'm No Angel*

(1933) she said, "It's all about a girl who lost her reputation but never missed it." Of her character, Tira, she remarked, "She's the kind of girl who climbed the ladder of success wrong by wrong." The butt of her satire was the golddigger, the girl who made a career out of being a blonde and whose hard character was best delineated by Joan Blondell and Jean Harlow.

Like gentlemen, gangsters preferred blondes as mistresses but married brunettes. They discarded one woman after another on their rise from rags to riches. As time passed their humiliation of their molls became increasingly savage. In *Public Enemy* (1931) James Cagney inaugurated a tradition of brutishness by squashing half a grapefruit on the face of his discarded mistress, Mae Clark, and later by beating up a girl who seduced him when he was drunk. This tradition was to become increasingly sadistic, reaching a new level of brutality when Lee Marvin in *The Big Heat* (1953) actually disfigured Gloria Grahame by scalding her face with boiling coffee. In sharp contrast the hero's close friendship with one of his male companions varied from incipient homosexuality in *Little Caesar* (1930) to disinterested but scrupulous partnership in *The Ruling Voice* (1931).

Little Caesar and *Public Enemy* offered a summation of what had been achieved hitherto. Neither has stood the test of time as a work of art. The plots lack proper coordination between their different elements, the characterization is crude. Their huge public success owed much to the atmosphere of the time they were released. Al Capone was at the height of his notoriety. And some knowledge of his career is essential for understanding the apparently inexplicable turns and twists of the plots. Contemporary audiences were familiar with the allusions and expected to interpret the inconsistencies of the stories accordingly. In the history of the performing arts some works are more significant for when they occurred than for what they actually offered. Both *Little Caesar* and *Public Enemy* come into this category.

Little Caesar, directed by Mervyn LeRoy from a novel by W. R. Burnett, is not about a bigshot but a small-time crook. *Public Enemy*, directed by William A. Wellman and based on a story, *Beer and Blood*, by John Bright, begins with a series of episodes to show how a boy brought up in the slums turns to crime as a means of escape.

The most positive achievement of these films was the establishment of Edward G. Robinson and James Cagney as major cinematic talents. Defined early in their movie careers they found it difficult to escape type-casting over the next three decades. Only once did they appear together—in *Smart Money* for Warners in 1931. Whereas Robinson imbued his characters with a sense of power and fate Cagney emphasized courageous anger and, sometimes, sadism. Both conveyed tremendous vigor and authority, partly by abrupt speech and partly by energetic, thrusting movement. When Cagney showed warmth to others he did so not by embracing them but by landing them an affectionate punch.

Scarface (1932) was produced by Howard Hughes for Paul Muni from a screenplay by Ben Hecht and W. R. Burnett, among others. The director, Howard Hawks, was instructed to make it the most lavish gangster film of the day. Eugene Rosow declares he was inspired by Hecht and Burnett to compare Al Capone's rise in modern times with the rise of the Borgias in the Renaissance and to emphasize Italianate scheming and incestuous passion. The rise of Tony Camonte, known, like Capone, as "Snorky" to his friends, follows the career of Capone closely. He begins as a bodyguard for Johnny Lovo (Osgood Perkins) and helps Lovo eliminate Big Louie Costello and take over the South Side liquor trade. They bludgeon North Side speakeasy proprietors to buy their beer and institute open warfare with the North Side concessionaires. Thereafter the story departs from that of Torrio and Capone and begins to encompass that of Torrio and Colosimo. In this version Camonte murders Lovo out of ambition and lust for Lovo's girl Poppy (Karen Morley). He is brought low when his sister Cesca (Ann Dvorak) falls in love with his friend Guido Rinaldo (George Raft) and, while Camonte is in Miami, goes to live with him. To avenge the insult to the family and appease his own jealous rage he returns and murders Guido. When the police arrest his gang and corner him in a hideout he first surrenders and then breaks free to be gunned down in the gutter.

The New York censors demanded the excision of episodes with explicit violence and the addition of a subtitle, "Shame of the Nation," before they would allow it to be released in the state. In the version with the added subtitle Scarface was hanged by the law rather than shot down on the street.

In the development of the gangster genre certain motifs recur. A young man has returned from the World War knowing that the world is not yet ready for democracy. He is forced into bootlegging because no other work is available. The underworld offers wish fulfillment—for a time. After the crash the movie gangster may or may not retain everything he has attained. But in the early years of the

Depression he is made a scapegoat for a society that abnegates its responsibility for the tawdry affluence of the twenties. This is a fair summary of the plot of *The Roaring Twenties* (1939), directed by Raoul Walsh for James Cagney. Mark Hellinger's original story was based on the careers of Larry Fay and Texas Guinan. When Eddie Bartlett, the protagonist, mortally wounded by a rival gang, dies in the arms of Panama Smith on the snow-covered steps of a church she provides his epitaph: "He used to be a bigshot."

————◆▶——————

The continuing popularity of gangster films in the tradition which began in the 1920s suggests public nostalgia for the myths surrounding movie moguls and bootleggers.

Dillinger (1945) was the first explicit gangster biography. Others include: *The Rise and Fall of Legs Diamond* (1960); *King of the Roaring Twenties* (1960), on Arnold Rothstein; *Mad Dog Coll* (1961); *Portrait of a Mobster* (1961), on Dutch Schultz; *Lepke* (1975) on Louis Lepke Buchalter; *Lucky Luciano* (Italian, 1975); *The Virginia Hill Story* (1976), on Bugsy Siegel; and, incidentally, *The Joker Is Wild* (1957), on Joe E. Lewis.

Capone's career was told explicitly in a series of film biographies: *Al Capone* (1959), directed by Richard Wilson for Rod Steiger; *The Scarface Mob* (1962); and *Capone* (1976). Crucial episodes in his rise were dramatized in *The St. Valentine's Day Massacre* (1967) and *The George Raft Story* (1961). His entrapment by income tax agents was told in *Undercover Man* (1947).

Syndicated crime was the subject of *Bullets or Ballots* (1936); *The Black Hand* (1950); *Pay or Die* (1960); *Murder, Inc.* (1960); *The Brotherhood* (1968); *Brotherhood of Evil* (1971); *The Valachi Papers* (1972); *Honor Thy Father* (1973); and, to great public acclaim, both parts of *The Godfather* (1972 and 1974).

The tradition of the American gangster film was founded on paradox in that the genre celebrates freedom of the individual in a nostalgic evocation of the underworld of the twenties and thirties, although the contemporary inception of a national criminal syndicate destroyed that freedom. The irony is that the myth was perpetrated by movie moguls who, within another American tradition, business monopoly, contributed to the growth of an impersonal society dominated by large corporations. Not only were gangsters like robber barons but so, too, were Hollywood tycoons: Pandro S.

Berman at M-G-M; Harry Cohn at Columbia; William Fox at Fox; Samuel Goldwyn at M-G-M; Howard Hughes at RKO; Marcus Loew, Louis B. Mayer, and Irving Thalberg at M-G-M; Albert and Jack Warner at Warner Brothers. Movie moguls fought the same battle for vertical monopolies in the cinema that robber barons had once fought in industry and gang leaders were still fighting in the underworld.

Therefore it is not surprising that although gangster films have offered the public escape of a sort, they have never carried a universal message of freedom triumphing over tyranny with any conviction. An economic system that has enormous problems is not likely to seek their resolution by political means lest the process of solving them prove injurious to interested parties. Nor is it likely to encourage others to seek such a solution. Instead studios offered audiences subtle propaganda in the guise of escapism. While real citizens were hard up in the depression, film characters were well-heeled. The elegance of studio sets and costumes, the inevitable poetic justice of plot and theme answered a genuine enough need. They encouraged audiences to try and attain in their lives the affluence they saw on screen. If that failed people could still share in the luxury of their favorite stars—but at a distance and only once or twice a week. Hollywood's function was to produce escapist entertainment for millions of people and make money for the businessmen who owned and ran it, sometimes from New York. Artistic integrity was not an issue. Crime was not to be seen to pay—except at the box office.

This point was brought home to the public by the sort of comment made in the media following the deaths of Mae West and George Raft within two days of one another in November 1980. Both stars had first shone in gangster movies but whereas he appeared in over ninety films she made only twelve. Yet he died almost a pauper while she was a millionaire. Whatever her screen persona, she had never confused business with pleasure in her private life. He had put his trust in princes and tried to become as indispensable to gangster circles in real life as he was to gangster films; she had put her trust in prices and invested in real estate. Thus, unintentionally, she gave extra significance to the famous double entendre she delivered to her discovery, Cary Grant: "When I'm good I'm very good, but when I'm bad I'm better."

—NINE—

1928-PRIDE
AND
PREJUDICE

IT IS ONLY TOO EASY for outsiders to dismiss the ballyhoo attending an American presidential campaign. The intrusion of vaudeville routines and advertising gimmicks, the general injection of show-business paraphernalia into a serious political contest, seem subversive of proper discussion of fundamental issues. Yet the carnival atmosphere stimulates and releases social and political tensions. And thus it keeps them under control. The rigmarole surrounding a presidential campaign in the second half of the twentieth century is new only in its use of electronic media. It has its origins in the campaigns of the nineteenth century. And it owes some of its special flavor to spectator sports of the 1920s. In that decade spectator sports also provided a means of channeling and containing the conflicting emotions of a diverse society.

During the 1920s the United States, despite its curtailment of mass immigration, was far from being a homogeneous nation. It was deeply divided on matters of race and religion, rum and reform. One inheritance of massive immigration at the turn of the century was a society of perhaps more colors and creeds than any before it. In 1920, 58.5 percent of the population were the children of white native parents; 7.0 percent were of mixed native and foreign parentage; and 15.5 percent were born of foreign parents; 10.5 percent were black Americans; and 13.75 percent first generation immigrants. Not until the depression, when poverty was shared by Jews and Gentiles, Protestants and Catholics, blacks and whites alike, did public opinion become polarized according to class and wealth rather than on race and religion. Until the 1930s the division between town and country cut deeply into America's social fabric.

Society had, however, various devices for maintaining equilibrium between the conflicting interests of disparate groups: the official checks and balances in government; the two thirds rule at Democratic conventions; state laws bypassing federal laws. There were also less formal devices. The games crazes of the 1920s—Mah Jongg in 1922, crossword puzzles in 1924, golf every year—had their part to play in maintaining social equilibrium. More important still were spectator sports.

Team sports were most important as devices to maintain social equilibrium. The player expended his emotional energy in physical competition; the spectator sublimated his in adulation of a favorite star. In football Harold E. ("Red") Grange of Illinois enjoyed a meteoric but ephemeral career. According to the *New York Times* of October 19, 1924, sixty-seven thousand people watched him and the University of Illinois side beat Michigan in the Illinois Memorial Stadium. Of all the games baseball was the most celebrated. Of all the sports' stars the most idolized was George Herman ("Babe") Ruth, first of the Boston Sox and, after 1920, of the New York Yankees. In 1920 a man died of excitement when he saw Babe Ruth hit a ball into the bleachers. In the season of 1921 Ruth hit fifty-nine home runs and he maintained his superiority over other players throughout the decade.

The financial incentive for stars, promoters, and managers as well as newspaper reporters and radio commentators was unprecedented. The public's capacity for vicarious satisfaction reached a peak in attendance at the two boxing matches between Jack Dempsey and Gene Tunney in Philadelphia in 1926 and Chicago in 1927. For the first match 130,000 people paid almost $2 million; for the second 145,000 paid $2.6 million. The Chicago amphitheater was so enormous that two thirds of the audience did not know who had won. Almost 40 million people listening by radio did. And ten of them died of excitement during the bout.

Similarities between spectator sports and presidential contests were noticed even in the twenties. Mark Sullivan was only one of many contemporary journalists to compare political promoters with baseball players and presidential nominees with the actual ball. But whereas according to an old English tradition what matters most in sport is how you play the game, in the United States playing to win is the whole point of the exercise. This is especially true of presidential elections.

Since the first centennial of the Republic only two losing candidates have been better remembered than their winning opponents. Both were Democrats: William Jennings Bryan, who made something of a career in losing the presidency by scoring a hat trick of failures in the elections of 1896, 1900, and 1908; and the Catholic Alfred E. Smith, who lost the election of 1928 to the Quaker Herbert Hoover. Perhaps in Smith's case this is because the winner, Hoover, turned out to be a loser in office. But it is more likely that Smith is remembered because his very candidacy colored the whole campaign. Moreover, Smith's unsuccessful bid for the presidency was a turning point in the fortunes of the two major parties. Hitherto the majority party was the Republican party. Henceforth it would be the Democratic party. Thus Samuel Lubell in his *The Future of American Politics* (1952) maintains that the line Smith drew across the map of American politics has never been erased.

The election of 1928 represented the climax of half a century of political debate about prohibition. Wets said of the congressional debates on the subjects before the 1920s what drys were to say of those after the decade: that the public had never had a full and proper opportunity to discuss first the imposition and then the repeal of prohibition. Of course the subject was being debated all the time. Yet debate on prohibition was never reasoned. Nativist pride, religious prejudice, legal pedantry, and political bigotry were the determining factors. By 1928 the emotive arguments had reached such intensity that they could no longer be kept out of the presidential campaign.

The campaign also represented the conflict between rural America, with its allegiance to proven values, and urban America, with its masses of people committed to social and political experiments. It was a conflict between two civilizations, nothing less. The political commentator, Walter Lippmann, saw it all in advance. In his *Men of Destiny* (1927) he concluded that

> The evil which the old-fashioned preachers ascribe to the Pope, to Babylon, to atheists, and to the devil, is simply the new urban civilization, with its irresistible scientific and economic and mass

power. The Pope, the devil, jazz, and bootleggers, are a mythology which express symbolically the impact of a vast and dreaded social change. The change is real enough. . . . The defense of the Eighteenth Amendment has, therefore, become much more than a mere question of regulating the liquor traffic. It involves a test of strength between social orders, and if, as seems probable, the Amendment breaks down, the fall will bring with it the dominion of the older civilization. The Eighteenth Amendment is the rock on which the evangelical church militant is founded, and with it are involved a whole way of life and an ancient tradition. The overcoming of the Eighteenth Amendment would mean the emergence of the cities as the dominant force in America, dominant politically and socially as they are already dominant economically.

Lippmann's assessment deliberately avoided precise analysis of the specific importance of the different issues he raises—religion, immigration, states' rights, law enforcement, and prohibition. For separation of these issues was impossible. Nevertheless it was prohibition that linked the others. The historian Edmund A. Moore takes this view and, writing after the event, in *A Catholic Runs for President* (1956) relates it to Smith's candidacy: "the very thought of the wet cause led by a New York Catholic magnified Smith's religion, and the cultural complex of which it was a part, into a large menace. Those who had an ingrained conviction that Catholicism could not be other than an abiding challenge to American institutions were often the same men and women who were staunch advocates of Prohibition."

As far as intolerant fundamentalists were concerned Smith's opposition to prohibition made his Catholicism more odious and his Catholicism made his wetness quite obnoxious. The upshot was, as the Protestant theologian Reinhold Niebuhr explained, that the real issues of the campaign were hidden under a decent veil of loyalty to a moral idea—prohibition. This does not mean people voted according to their social behavior. Will Rogers, the cowboy philosopher, pointed out, "If you think this country ain't dry, you just watch 'em vote; and if you think this country ain't wet, you just watch 'em drink. You see, when they vote, it's counted; but when they drink, it ain't."

———◆———

Only two men, Grover Cleveland and Woodrow Wilson, had won the presidency for the Democrats since 1856. They had been able to do so in part because the Republicans had been divided. From the progressive era onward a popular state governor had a better chance of securing the presidential nomination in his party than a senator in Congress. And after the death of William Jennings Bryan, and with a decline in popularity for William Gibbs McAdoo, Governor Alfred E. Smith of New York became preeminent among Democrats. Republicans recognized the threat from Smith quite early. The unofficial Republican slogan in 1926 when Smith ran again for governor of New York against Ogden L. Mills was "Beat Smith now and you won't have to beat him in 1928."

Alfred E. Smith was the son of poor Irish Catholics in New York. His father, a truckdriver, died when he was twelve and he then went to work in Fulton Street Fish Market, of which he later claimed he was an alumnus. His reliability commended him to the Democratic machine at Tammany Hall and he served the party in a variety of elected posts each more important than its predecessor. Although he was a loyal Tammany man he also had a reputation as a progressive reformer as a result of preventative measures he advocated after the 1911 Triangle fire in New York. From 1919 to 1929 he served four terms as governor of New York losing only the 1920 election when Democrats everywhere suffered in the rout of Wilson's foreign policy. Until 1928 this was his only defeat in a political career stretching over a quarter of a century. As governor he brought about better highways and housing and accomplished a variety of social and administrative reforms.

Smith's career before the campaign of 1928 was an illustration of "Americanism," the philosophy that people with different beliefs and from diverse backgrounds could accommodate one another and work toward common objectives. Smith represented those people whose place in society was neither fixed nor assured—people moving from the old world to the new, from the country to the city, or from one class to another. They could not take their social place for granted but they knew that they would be defined by economic success or failure. Thus opportunity for all was a prerequisite, and this Smith seemed to offer, most of all in the example of his own career. In *America Comes of Age* (1927) André Siegfried said of him: "Al Smith . . . has attained national prestige, partly by his honesty and his ability as an administrator but mainly owing to his origin . . . in the slum quarters of East Side New York. . . . The enormous mass of immigrants rightly look upon him as their mouthpiece, for he is Catholic, though not the tool of the Church . . . and above all, he proclaims a new Americanism in which the Nordic Protestant tradition counts for nothing."

1928—PRIDE AND PREJUDICE

After the schismatic convention of 1924 both wet and dry, north and south, elements in the Democratic party had begun to recognize the fact that they could never hope to capture Congress and the presidency without mutual cooperation. The Solid South and the northeastern cities were reluctantly ready to accommodate one another no matter how loose the ensuing coalition would be. In particular the Democratic South recognized that it required the wholehearted support of the party in the crucial northern states of New York, New Jersey, and Massachusetts. For although a presidential candidate could be elected without a southern vote in the electoral college, he could not win without most of the northern industrial votes. Responsive southern Democrats like Senators Cordell Hull of Tennessee, Joseph T. Robinson of Arkansas, and Pat Harrison of Mississippi, and Josephus Daniels of North Carolina believed Smith was the natural choice for the presidential nomination in 1928. But they also realized that his Catholicism and his wetness would be handicaps. Yet they reckoned it would be less embarrassing for the South to accept Smith and risk losing the election than to reject him and risk alienating 4 million Catholics in New York, Illinois, New Jersey, and Massachusetts.

As to his Catholicism, Frank P. Walsh was reported in the *New York Times* of April 6, 1924, before the Madison Square Garden convention of that year, as saying that Smith would "wipe out that unwritten law" that a Catholic could not become a president. In 1926 Catholics accounted for 15.97 percent of the total population. By the time another Catholic, John F. Kennedy, ran successfully for the presidency in 1960 they accounted for 23.2 percent. However, those who were not Catholics—84.03 percent in 1926—were not necessarily Protestant. Only 27.36 percent belonged to Protestant churches. The proportion of Jews was only 3.50 percent. And the majority of Americans—53.17 percent—had no religious affiliation. The statistics, however, belied the incipient religious intolerance of the age.

As to Smith's wetness his first name reduced to Al was coupled alliteratively by his detractors as Al-cohol. Ed Flynn recorded that a cocktail was always available at the governor's executive mansion in Albany. But of course there was nothing illegal about having a drink. Oswald Garrison Villard, editor of the Republican *Nation*, went further in his allegations. In an article of November 30, 1927, he misinformed his readers that Smith drank between four and eight cocktails a day.

Smith's opposition to prohibition was pragmatic. It had not

done away with alcohol, which was available everywhere. Instead it had led to an increase in political corruption and syndicated crime. But he also opposed the Eighteenth Amendment on legal grounds: it had not been ratified by the people; it denied individuals and states their rights; and although it banned intoxicating liquor, it did not define what was intoxicating. And he had ethnic, religious, and political objections. He regarded prohibition as a conspiracy of conservatives against immigrants and Catholics. It was, moreover, subversive of Irish political machines because it led to competition between gangsters and politicians for political control of wards.

With his eye on the main chance Smith began to use his office as governor of New York to advance his presidential ambitions. Therefore in his annual message to the state legislature on January 4, 1928, he emphasized the improvements brought to New York by his administration. He also proposed a modification of the Volstead Act.

Smith also prepared to give himself a different image: he wanted people to know he had the confidence of big business. While maintaining political ties with labor leaders and social reformers he began to cultivate the nouveaux riches of New York: William F. Kenny, James Hoey, and George Getz. Thus in addition to holding his "kitchen cabinet" as governor he also held his "golfing cabinet" as presidential candidate. Kenny, a construction magnate who had known Smith since they were children, maintained a private club in a penthouse on Fourth Avenue and Twenty-third Street. It was called the Tiger Club, a tribute to its decorations and a symbol of Tammany Hall. But it was not just an Irish-American club for tired businessmen. It was a convenient center for political intrigue, what Ed Flynn called a "clearinghouse." It was there Smith met John J. Raskob.

Born in Lockport, New York, Raskob was the son of an Alsatian father and an Irish mother. He was a self-made man. As secretary for Pierre S. Du Pont he was responsible for the Du Ponts' acquiring a controlling interest in William C. Durant's failing car corporation. Together Raskob and Pierre S. Du Pont transformed it into the thriving business of General Motors, of which Raskob became vice-president. The *New York Times* of July 15, 1928, said that Raskob had made millionaires of as many as eighty General Motors executives, some within four years on an initial investment of only twenty-five thousand dollars.

Raskob, stagestruck amateur magician, wanted to build something in New York that would rival the Eiffel tower. Like other manufacturers and financiers, such as the Du Pont brothers, Pierre and Irenee, and Samuel Insull, he wanted to play politics. Unlike them he was not content to work behind the scenes. He coveted a public role. In the description of Frank R. Kent, a political commentator, he was a fat cat, a businessman who is not satisfied with the cream he has got but likes to splash it around. He became the master mind of Smith's campaign strategy.

———————◄◆►———————

The issue of Smith's religion first came to the fore in 1926. Cardinal Bonanzo, papal legate, on his way to attend the Eucharistic Congress in Chicago, stopped in New York where he was received in city hall by Mayor Jimmy Walker and Governor Alfred E. Smith. In deference to his position they kissed his ring. The supposed subversive intent of ring kissing provided a golden opportunity for intolerant Protestants everywhere to attack Smith and his church. Adna W. Leonard, Methodist Bishop of Buffalo and President of the State Anti-Saloon League, told a citizenship conference at Round Lake, New York, in August 1926: "No Governor can kiss the papal ring and get within gunshot of the White House."

In fact, Protestant churches were on the defensive. Protestant churches had committed themselves to support national prohibition before the event. In the ensuing chaos of prohibition they suffered loss of prestige. Ministers were well aware of the false position into which they had put the church. The Federal Council of Churches in its report of 1925 was equivocal about the supposed benefits of prohibition. Moreover, it did not charge that prohibition could not be enforced, only that no adequate attempt to enforce it had yet been made. Pressure from the Anti-Saloon League ensured that a subsequent report by the executive committee endorsed prohibition. However, the Church Temperance Society was so aghast at the perverse influence of the league in politics that it brought its affiliation with it to an end. In future Protestant clergy tried to stay aloof from the controversy. But they could not permit effective competition from the Catholic Church, which in America had consistently adopted a moderate policy on temperance.

What was at stake was not the survival of political beliefs or religious faith. The whole point of the Protestant diatribe against Smith was to have an argument for the sake of it, and achieve emotional satisfaction by giving vent to incipient intolerance and fear.

The most important event in the debate about Smith's religion was the exchange of letters between Charles C. Marshall, an Episcopalian, and Smith himself. In "An Open Letter to the Honorable Alfred E. Smith," published in the *Atlantic Monthly* in April 1927, Marshall questioned the propriety of a Catholic becoming president. He doubted that a true separation of church and state—fundamental to the American political system—could be achieved.

When he knew Smith would answer back, Franklin Roosevelt suggested a humorous tone. Smith could argue that Unitarianism was not Christianity and that former President Taft was, therefore, not even a Christian. In addition he could show that Wilson, Theodore Roosevelt, McKinley, and Cleveland had all been members of different churches and thus secretly obligated to put church before state. When Smith asked Judge Joseph M. Proskauer to refute Marshall on his behalf Proskauer supposedly replied, "Well that would make it perfect. A Protestant lawyer challenges a Catholic candidate on his religion, and the challenge is answered by a Jewish judge." Nevertheless he prepared an entirely serious first draft with the aid of Father Francis P. Duffy.

Smith's answer appeared in the *Atlantic* in May 1927. There would be no question of involving the United States in a foreign war, none of Catholic teaching infiltrating the American public school system nor of subverting law and justice. Smith averred his beliefs in "absolute freedom of conscience" and "equality of all churches, all sects, and all beliefs before the law" and "the absolute separation of Church and State."

Smith was ill advised to have replied at all. Although the Marshall-Smith correspondence elevated the level of the religious debate, it fostered bigotry by feeding controversy. However, the editor, Ellery Sedgwick, was well pleased. The May issue of the *Atlantic* sold seventy-two thousand copies, twice the average amount. But Smith had taken an unnecessary risk—and all for nothing. Sedgwick himself reckoned that 70 percent of *Atlantic* subscribers were Republicans. They would not be voting for Smith in any case.

———— ◆ ————

The contention over Smith's Catholicism made no difference to the outcome of the Democratic National Convention, held, as a concession to the South, in Houston, Texas. And George Olvany, the new Irish Catholic boss of Tammany, made sure that the New York delegation to Houston was led by respectable figures of New York society—George Gordon Battle, Henry Morgenthau, Mrs. Charles Dana Gibson, Franklin D. Roosevelt—and not Tammany hacks with red faces, luminous noses, and pot bellies.

Roosevelt again proposed Smith, stressing his record of reform and "habit of victory." At the end of the first ballot Smith had 724,213 votes—ten short of the necessary two thirds. However, the Ohio delegation had withheld its votes hitherto. Now it gave the entire 45 to Smith. In the customary attempt to balance the ticket Senator Joseph T. Robinson of Arkansas was nominated for the vice-presidency.

To satisfy Bishop James A. Cannon, Jr., and the dry lobbies the platform on prohibition was: "this convention pledges the party and its nominees to an honest effort to enforce the Eighteenth Amendment and all other provisions of the Federal Constitution and all laws enacted pursuant thereto." However, Smith insisted, against advice, on sending a telegram from Albany to the convention in which he made clear he agreed to enforcement of the Volstead Act while it was law but that he would work for its repeal and also that of the Eighteenth Amendment. While affirming his opposition to the return of the saloon Smith suggested that democratic principles of self-government and states' rights be applied to the problems of prohibition.

Bishop James A. Cannon made a pretense of being "stunned" by Smith's telegram with its proposed revision of prohibition. In fact Cannon had said earlier he would neither trust nor support any wet of either party who proposed law enforcement and also that if Smith were the Democratic nominee all such proposals would be devoid of meaning anyway. Yet he described the telegram as "a shameless proposition of political double-dealing." It was an act of "brazen, political effrontery." Smith encountered hostility from another dry. Mrs. Mabel Walker Willebrandt, assistant attorney general, the first official in Coolidge's administration who declared for Hoover, determined to show America how wet New York, Al Smith's city, really was. She arranged for a hundred prohibition agents to raid a score of New York nightclubs on the very night Smith was nominated, June 28.

Over the Democratic plank itself Smith was obdurate. On August 22, 1928, in a speech in New York he advocated an amendment to the Volstead Act giving "scientific definition of the alcoholic content of an intoxicating beverage"; and "an amendment in the Eighteenth Amendment which would give to each individual state itself only after approval by a referendum popular vote of its people, the right wholly within its borders to import, manufacture, or cause to be manufactured and sell alcoholic beverages, the sale to be made only by the state itself and not for consumption in any public place." Thus Smith wanted a temperance system based on the Canadian model whereby sales would be made only by a public agency and only in those states where a majority of the electorate gave its approval in a referendum.

Smith compounded his problems as a confirmed wet and devout Catholic. Whereas his kitchen cabinet and other advisers wanted him to choose Senator Peter Goelet Gerry of Rhode Island as chairman of the Democratic National Committee (the man who would run the actual campaign), Smith deferred to the previously Republican John J. Raskob, who was anxious to do the job. His friends considered this choice a crucial mistake. Gerry came of a well established Dutch Protestant family. Raskob was not only a nouveau riche but also a leading Catholic who had been named a Knight of the Order of St. Gregory the Great after donating more than a million dollars to the church. In addition he was a leading member of the Association Against the Prohibition Amendment. The fact that such a man was Smith's champion, coupled with Smith's own Catholicism and wetness, ensured that the issues of religion and prohibition would be well to the fore of the campaign. In his own speeches Raskob mistakenly emphasized prohibition, his personal hate, instead of issues of local interest.

Franklin D. Roosevelt feared that Raskob's appointment would "permanently drive away a host of people in the south and west and rural east who are not particularly favorable to Smith, but who up to today have been seeping back into the party." However, Smith would not be dissuaded. He told Belle Moskowitz, "It's the only thing Raskob has ever asked of me, and I've got to give it to him." The reason he gave the Democratic National Committee and the party was different. He told them he wanted "to let the businessmen of this country know that one of the great industrial leaders of modern times had confidence in the Democratic Party and its platform." Raskob compounded the suspicions his appointment had raised by setting up the Democratic National Headquarters in offices of the General Motors Building in New York. Tammany Hall veterans were disgruntled at their displacement, Democratic party workers were dismayed by the choice of General Motors' experts to sell Smith to the public like a Chevrolet car.

Moreover the selection of Raskob suggested Smith was becoming conservative at last. Although he had been a progressive reformer, his reforms had been limited to administration, social welfare, and public utilities. He had never been a socialist. His new conservatism was part and parcel of his conviction that he could win the presidency only with the support of big business. It alone could buy enough newspaper copy, radio publicity, and advertising. Matthew and Hannah Josephson in their biography *Al Smith: Hero of the Cities* (1969) believe John J. Raskob hoped to raise $4 million and yet spent at least $5.3 million and possibly as much as $7 million. By comparison the Republicans' financial support of Herbert Hoover was limited to $3,529,000.

In comparison with Smith, Herbert C. Hoover, the Republican candidate, did not arouse much enthusiasm or controversy in his own party. Yet Hoover's rise from rags to riches and his Quakerism were cited as proof of the superior rural values of self-reliance, self-discipline, and thrift.

The son of an Iowa blacksmith, Herbert Hoover was an orphan by the time he was eight. He grew up on a farm in Iowa, was educated in public schools and at Stanford University. As a mining engineer he had helped introduce modern technology in Africa, Australia, China, and Russia. As a result of speculation in various London companies—transactions obscured by the haze of Edwardian summers—he had amassed a fortune of $4 million at the outset of the First World War. In the war he gained his reputation as "The Great Engineer" when he served as chairman of the American Relief Committee, as chairman of the commission for the Relief of Belgium and, later, as United States Food Administrator. By able management he conserved American supplies of grain for humanitarian relief in Europe. At the Chicago Republican National Convention in 1920 he secured enough nominating votes to get noticed by the Ohio Gang and Harding. He was therefore appointed secretary of commerce in 1921, a post he held for eight years under both Harding and Coolidge. His reputation as the Great Engineer was enhanced in the lax administration of both presidents. He was one of the few efficient cabinet secretaries and proudly advertised the fact.

PROHIBITION

Because of pressure from the dry lobbies and Smith's open wetness the Republicans at their convention in Kansas City were obliged to make their stand on prohibition clear. The Republican platform favored law observance and enforcement. Hoover, in his acceptance speech at Palo Alto, California, referred to prohibition as "a great social and economic experiment, noble in motive and far-reaching in purpose." His words were reduced by others to "noble experiment," offensive to wets who did not see anything noble in prohibition and offensive to drys who did not regard it as an experiment. Hoover admitted that "common sense compels us to realize that grave abuses have occurred—abuses which must be remedied." And he declared that, if elected, he would establish a commission to investigate prohibition.

Hoover's proposal undermined any appeal Smith might have had to wet Republicans. Thus they could vote for Hoover with a clear conscience: his candidacy carried the promise of a change in prohibition. Moreover when Hoover said the investigation would be organized and searching of fact and cause this conveyed implicit promise of repeal. The abuses and facts were clear: invasion of personal liberty; the breakdown of law and order by corrupt local authority and misguided federal bureaucracy. If the causes were to be examined, then the assumptions on which prohibition was based and the supposed support of public opinion would be weighed and found wanting.

Prohibition, however, remained Smith's problem, not Hoover's. The Democrats emphasized Smith's theories in the cities and minimized them in the countryside. The Republicans, naturally, emphasized Smith's theories in the countryside and minimized them in the cities. Thus when Senator William E. Borah of Idaho traveled through the smaller cities of the South and West on Hoover's behalf he insisted that prohibition was facing a crisis and that Smith's election would destroy essential American values. Yet, at the same time, Charles Evans Hughes traveled on Hoover's behalf through the larger cities of the North and East, where he minimized the significance of Smith, dismissing the controversy over prohibition as a "sham battle."

The prevailing but ephemeral economic euphoria made it difficult for Smith to carry out a campaign of political censure and economic criticism against the Republicans.

To win Smith had to ride what Hoover called "the three horses of the extreme conservatism in the Solid South, the radical labor and agrarian groups of the North and the corrupt city machines." At the outset Smith underestimated the task. As H. L. Mencken had said in 1927, "The plain fact is that Al, as a good New Yorker, is as provincial as a Kansas farmer. He is not only not interested in the great problems that heave and lather the country: he has never heard of them."

The main strategy of Smith's campaign was a whistlestop tour in a special eleven-car train of those states the Democrats had lost in 1924, beginning in Omaha, Nebraska, on September 19, 1928. Smith would give three different speeches each week and every major one would be broadcast nationally. By comparison Hoover, assured of success, made only seven major speeches. He wisely entrusted his campaign to public relations experts.

To bolster Smith's campaign the composer Irving Berlin wrote "Good Times with Hoover, Better Times with Al." His earlier, "We'll All Go Voting for Al" was revived and was heard everywhere. Eddie Dowling, a Catholic impresario, presented a musical, *The Sidewalks of New York*, with the comedians Smith and Dale and the dancer Ruby Keeler on Broadway in 1928. Dowling wrote the show to further Smith's candidacy and it was a romanticized version of his career. Ironically after his many brushes with Raskob during the run of the show Dowling ended up by detesting Smith.

Although Hoover in his *Memoirs* says that both he and Smith suffered personal abuse in the election and that therefore the slander campaigns canceled one another out, the weight of evidence does not support such a view. No one could take seriously the allegation that Hoover was a naturalized British subject or that he had danced the Charleston in public with a black woman. The charges leveled against Smith were more insidious. If Hoover took no part in them neither did he repudiate the slanders. Senator George H. Moses of New Hampshire, who managed Hoover's campaign in the East, himself organized the mailing of scurrilous literature about Smith to Kentucky.

The problems faced by Smith in the South were exacerbated by the resurgence of the Ku Klux Klan, which made the campaign the most acrimonious since Reconstruction. Inspired by D. W. Griffith's film *The Birth of a Nation*, William J. Simmons, a former Methodist circuit preacher, revived the defunct Ku Klux Klan on Stone Mountain, Georgia, in 1915. The Klan's catchment area was not just the

New South but more particularly the Southwest (especially Texas), Midwest (especially Indiana, Ohio, and Oklahoma), and Far West (especially Oregon and California). The elaborate rituals, secret signs, and severe ceremonies that led men to wear white party frocks made from sheets and white dunces' caps apparently appealed to a provincial populace. It had been bombarded with primitive propaganda about Teutonic barbarism in the war, but cheated of its prey at the end. In 1920 there were not more than fifty thousand members but the Klan provided an outlet for the hysteria of hate that had been generated. New organizers, Edward Y. Clarke and Mrs. Elizabeth Tyler, were astute enough to appreciate the profits that could be made from modern sales techniques and high initiation fees. Within a year the Klan had a hundred thousand members and, by 1925, 5 million.

The Klan represented itself as a defender of white against black, Gentile against Jew, and Protestant against Catholic. Klansmen were trying to perpetuate old-fashioned values. Their hysteria was the result of fear and not just anger that the society around them was changing too fast for their comprehension. The Klan in Kansas released a list of those whom it was fighting in 1926: "every criminal, every gambler, every thug, every libertine, every girl-ruiner, every home-wrecker, every wife-beater, every dope-peddler, every moonshiner, every crooked politician, every pagan papist priest . . . every hyphenated American, every lawless alien . . . ." Thus the Klan profited from the prevalent xenophobia of the 1920s and the concomitant arrogant nativism.

Its means of purification were, however, anything but pure. Along with the Klan came bribery, intimidation, and torture by flogging, mutilation, branding, and acid burning and even murder. In Birmingham, Alabama, a Klansman killed a Catholic priest and was acquitted; in Naperville, Illinois, a Catholic church was burned to the ground. In Louisiana five men were kidnapped, bound with wire, and drowned. A naturalized immigrant was lashed until his back was a pulp of ribboned flesh: he had presumed to marry an American girl. A black American was flogged until he sold his land for a fraction of its true value.

Smith believed in 1924 that the Klan was "so abhorrent to intelligent-thinking Americans of all denominations that it must in time fall to the ground of its own weight. The Catholics of this country can stand it. The Jews can stand it. But the United States of America cannot stand it." But it was only a series of revelations of its corrupt political intrigues and the predatory misappropriations of its funds by its leading Wizards, Dragons, Kleagles, and Goblins that led to a massive fall in membership by the end of the decade. In 1928 it was still a vibrant force. The election slogan of the Ku Klux Klan was "Keep Al Smith in New York." When Smith's train passed through Billings, Montana, passengers were treated to a display of a huge fiery cross outside the town which burned for an hour. The Klan smeared Smith in scurrilous pamphlets with accusations that he had risen from rags to riches on the profits of New York brothels. It made salacious predictions that if he were elected "bootleggers and harlots would dance on the White House lawn."

The Klan's campaign would have gone for little had it not been for the covert support it received from Protestant churches who endorsed its anti-Catholic sentiments. The *Baptist Trumpet* of Killeen, Texas, warned that if Smith were elected "the Romish system will institute persecutions again, and put the cruel, blood-stained heel upon all who refute her authority." Such accusations were widely believed. Frances Perkins, chairman of the Industrial Commission in New York, was told on a campaign trip to the east shore of Maryland that a waterfront estate had already been acquired there for Pope Pius XI, who would soon take up residence, the better to supervise Smith's presidency.

William Allen White, editor of the *Gazette* of Emporia, Kansas, told a political meeting "It is not that Governor Smith is a Catholic and a wet which makes him an offense to the villagers and town dwellers, but because his record shows the kind of President he would make—a Tammany President. . . . Tammany is Tammany, and Smith is its prophet." In an Associated Press dispatch of July 1928 White said Smith "had voted ten times against allowing the people to vote on any sort of a restriction on the sale of liquor; four times against stopping gambling and prostitution in connection with saloons; three times against repealing the law keeping saloons open on Sunday; four times in favor of removing zoning restrictions which would keep open saloons from churches and schools and three times in favor of laws sponsored by organized gambling."

Walter Lippmann remonstrated with White. Smith had opposed bills to regulate prostitution and gambling because he thought them unconstitutional and unenforceable and that their effect would have been to encourage police corruption. Although White later withdrew his charges and the New York papers printed his grudging retractions in August 1928, the damage had been done. Assessing White's work, Elmer Davis said in a letter to the *Times* no one else could have put so much "poison into a libel as he manages to leave in a retraction."

Senator Robert Owens of Oklahoma—a state where the Klan was most influential—announced he would leave the Democratic party on account of Smith's nomination. Smith responded to his challenge in Oklahoma City on September 20, 1928, by addressing himself to Owens's defection and appealing for religious tolerance. Instead of using his prepared address he spoke impromptu. The emotional wave of indignation he felt within him welled up and burst: "In this campaign an effort has been made to distract the attention of the electorate . . . and to fasten it on malicious and un-American propaganda. . . . I know what lies behind all this . . . my religion. Ordinarily that word should never be used in a political campaign." Though he was willing to address himself to the controversy every move he made to defend himself only fanned the flames higher. On September 29, the day after Smith made his speech, the same auditorium was filled to capacity by thirty thousand people who had gone to hear the Reverend Dr. John Roach Straton of the Calvary Baptist Church, New York, denounce "Al Smith and the Forces of Hell."

It required the malevolent genius of Bishop James A. Cannon, Jr., to transform incipient religious prejudice into a malign and durable force. With the death of Wayne Wheeler in 1927 Cannon, already chairman of the Anti-Saloon League's National Legislative Committee, and also chairman of the Temperance and Social Service Commission of the Methodist Episcopal Church, South, had become the dominant force in the League.

Until the spring of 1928 Cannon's attacks on Smith were based on his opposition to prohibition. But on May 14, 1928, at a general conference of the Methodist Episcopal Church in Missouri he shifted his grounds. Thereafter his criticisms were both personal and religious. Cannon quoted an article in the *Osservatore Romano*, the Vatican paper, which described the attempt to enforce prohibition in America as "useless" and advocated its abolition. He sustained the sense of emotional outrage earlier prohibition campaigns had conveyed. Cannon denied over and over that in fighting Smith he was fighting a religious war. But his opinion that the Catholic Church was not even Christian was widely known. He had once described it as the "mother of ignorance, superstition, intolerance and sin." He also ensured that 380,000 copies of his pamphlet *Is Southern Protestantism More Intolerant than Romanism?* were published and distributed.

The southern Protestant Churches were, however, not only composed of self-seeking bigots. Moderate bishops of the Methodist Church, South—Warren A. Candler and Collins Denny—wanted their clergy to take no part in the campaign. But Cannon ensured that they did. It was Cannon alone of southern Protestants who had the stamina for a protracted crusade. He determined to unite all southern Protestants against Smith.

There were more Baptists than Methodists in the South, and Cannon therefore worked closely with a prominent Baptist, Dr. Arthur Barton. Together they summoned a conference of dry southern Democrats at Asheville, North Carolina, on July 18, 1928, to organize a campaign against Smith. Not only Methodists and Baptists but also Presbyterians and Lutherans were involved. Deets Picket, research secretary of *The Voice*, a monthly journal of the Methodist Board of Temperance, Prohibition, and Public Morals, planned another forty Methodist conferences before the election. At each he spoke with Bible-thumping, rabble-rousing oratory, warning delegates not to "pass under the yoke of Tammany" lest they "be only hewers of wood and drawers of water" for machine bosses. The Presbyterians in their *Presbyterian Magazine* and the Lutherans in their various papers were more subtle but no less uncompromising.

In August and again in October Cannon undertook extensive campaign tours, visiting thirteen southern states. He diversified his attack, condemning Smith's championship of immigrants, as well as their liquor. In Cambridge, Maryland, he said: "Governor Smith wants the Italians, the Sicilians, the Poles and the Russian Jews. That kind has given us a stomach ache. We have been unable to assimilate such people in our national life, so we shut the door to them. But Smith says, 'give me that kind of people.' He wants the kind of dirty people that you find today on the sidewalks of New York."

———◆———

Smith's campaign was not a failure everywhere. In Chicago and the East, in Boston, Newark, Philadelphia, and New York, with captive audiences around him, his speeches were inspired, galvanizing supporters. In Milwaukee, a traditional center of the brewing industry, Smith met with great enthusiasm. On September 29 he told sixteen thousand people in the city auditorium what he would do about prohibition: "The cure for the ills of democracy is more democracy. Hand this back to the people. Let them decide it."

One leading Republican, Senator George Norris of Nebraska, declared for Smith and not Hoover: "I'd rather trust an honest wet who is progressive in his make-up and courageous . . . than the politicians who profess to be dry but make prohibition ineffective. And I do not believe Smith would sell out the country's natural power resources to monopolies and trusts as they have been in the past."

However, the *New York Times* of October 3, 1928, summarized the factors inimical to Smith's chances on polling day. The odds were against him: "The primary objection to Smith is his Catholicism. His wet views come second; his Tammany affiliations third. But it is hard to tell where one leaves off and the other begins. The simple truth is that there would be only a negligible amount of bolting among Democrats if Smith were not a Catholic, regardless of his Tammany affiliations and his opposition to prohibition."

In the election itself, Smith won the largest popular vote given to any Democrat to that time, 15,016,443 (40.7 percent) twice as many as John W. Davis had received in 1924. Hoover received 21,392,190 (58 percent). But Smith's numerous near misses in populous states ensured his decisive defeat in the votes apportioned to the electoral college, 87 to Hoover's 444.

Smith had been undermined from the start by the defection of the South. Six southern states went Republican: Florida, Kentucky, North Carolina, Tennessee, Texas, and Virginia. However this defection from the Democrats was unprecedented only in quantity. James B. Cox had failed to carry Tennessee in 1920 and John W. Davis had failed to carry Kentucky in 1924. And, in the future, the splinter parties of J. Strom Thurmond in 1948 and George Wallace in 1968 would benefit from the defection of many traditional Democrats. Because of this development the Democrats would never again count on the Solid South. The new southern divisiveness ensured that Democratic presidential candidates would search out new catchment areas. Thus the electoral significance of the South would diminish at the expense of the industrial cities. There would now be a shift in the traditional alignment of the two major parties.

Drys referred to Hoover's majority of 6 million votes as a mandate for prohibition. It is certainly true that Cannon's successful exercise in personal publicity gave him, briefly, a prominence in national life, hitherto unknown to any clergyman. H. L. Mencken described him as "the most powerful ecclesiastic ever heard of in America."

But whatever the first impression of Cannon and other drys Smith's seemingly insignificant gains presaged the repeal of prohibition. A combination of Irish, Italians, and French-Canadian-Americans carried industrial Massachusetts and Rhode Island for the Democrats for the first time since the Civil War. Though Smith lost Pennsylvania, Illinois, and Wisconsin he had narrowed the difference between the two parties in those states. He gained 122 northern counties from the Republicans, and in 77 of these Catholics were in the majority. He took Boston, Cleveland, New Haven, St. Paul, and St. Louis. Although he lost Chicago, he helped break the complacency of Republicans there.

In the twelve most populous cities (New York, Chicago, Philadelphia, Pittsburgh, Detroit, Cleveland, Baltimore, St. Louis, Boston, Milwaukee, San Francisco, Los Angeles) the Democrats had a total majority over the Republicans of 38,000. This gain, apparently small in comparison with the Republicans' previous majorities of 1,638,000 in 1920 and 1,252,000 in 1924, was by no means insignificant. For as Samuel Lubell explains in his *The Future of American Politics* (1952) the Republican hold on these cities was broken by Smith. He had cut through alignments traditional since the Civil War and cleared the path for Franklin D. Roosevelt in 1932. He inaugurated the trend that was to make the Democrats and not the Republicans the majority party of the nation.

Hoover said in his *Memoirs* (1952): "The issues which defeated the Governor were general prosperity, prohibition, the farm tariffs, Tammany. . . . Had he been a Protestant, he would certainly have lost and might even have had a smaller vote." Ruth C. Silva in *Rum, Religion and Votes* (1962) concludes that if Smith's opposition to prohibition was an electoral strength among wets and an electoral liability among drys there would be a direct correlation between the proportion of votes cast for him and the proportion of wets and drys in individual wards, counties, and districts. Some such relationship did exist comparing Smith's vote with the popular vote on prohibition in the eight states where people voted on the subject in 1926, 1927, and 1928. Yet the general pattern of support from wets and opposition from drys seems insignificant once other factors such as religion are taken into account. However, William F. Ogburn and Nell Snow Talbot in their article "A Measurement of the Factors in the Presidential Election of 1928" for *Social Forces* (December 1929), conclude that attitudes to prohibition are more revelatory of Smith's strengths and weaknesses than any other consideration, including that of religion.

Nothing could compensate Smith for the fact that he had lost and—by the standard of an electoral system favoring first past the post—had lost badly. He was extremely bitter. The day after his defeat, November 7, Smith said in New York: "I certainly do not expect ever to run for public office again. I have had all I can stand of it."

The success of his protégé, Franklin D. Roosevelt, in the contest for governor of New York, did not ease the pain. Franklin D. Roosevelt became the Democratic nominee for governor almost by default. With Smith out of the running and his presidential campaign led by Catholics, immigrants, and nouveaux riches the Democrats needed a gubernatorial candidate who was Protestant, from a long-established family, and, if possible, with an eminent name. Roosevelt, an adult victim of infantile paralysis, was trying in vain to recover partial use of his legs by taking cures at Warm Springs, Georgia. He required much persuasion to run. In the end he did so and won by a freak chance. His Republican opponent, Albert Ottinger, Smith's secretary of state, was a Jew. In a campaign where religious prejudice could harm Smith it could certainly damage Ottinger's chances. And in a fracas in Erie County he was attacked by a Republican boss. Roosevelt was elected governor by the narrow margin of 25,564 votes in a popular poll of 4.2 million. At the time poll analysts estimated that a hundred thousand independent voters who cast their ballots for Hoover as president also did so for Roosevelt as governor. It was also estimated that Roosevelt gained some twenty thousand unexpected Republican votes in Erie County after the attack on Ottinger there. Thus Roosevelt who had campaigned as Smith's chosen candidate survived him and his misfortune.

When the Roosevelts' luggage arrived ahead of them at the executive mansion in Albany Smith christened it with champagne. "Now, Frank," he said as he sprinkled the trunks, "if you want a drink, you will know where to find it."

The impact of the election of 1928 reverberated around Congress itself, where two proposals to improve prohibition enforcement were debated in the early months of 1929. One, the Jones Bill, was concerned with penalties for violation of the Volstead Act; the other was about the appropriations for the Prohibition Bureau. The Jones Bill proposed an increase in the maximum penalties for violations of the Volstead Act to five years' imprisonment or a fine of ten thousand dollars or both. Technically it was an amendment to the Volstead Act itself.

The debate in the Senate produced a vigorous argument against prohibition from the BEER group led by James A. Reed of Missouri. Drys proposed replacing lectures with torture: "We have abandoned the Bible, the prayer book, and the temperance tract for the lash, the prison, the gun, and the bludgeon." Prohibition had filled the jails with 130,000 prisoners in two years. If necessary it would crucify Christ and burn Joan of Arc all over again: "There is no knife so sharp as that held in the hand of the bigot . . . no cruelty so relentless as the cruelty of fanaticism."

The Volstead Act was an idiocy. In comparison with potent farm cider bourbon whiskey was a mild tonic. (When Reed gave the recipe for ensuring cider was as intoxicating as possible—freezing it and extracting the concentrated alcohol from the center—one man hushed another in the public gallery. He wanted to make sure he had got it right.) The saloon had not been abolished: "The bar is condensed into a gripsack. The sales are by the case instead of by the glass. The saloon is still here, and more people are engaged in the business than in pre-Volstead days. You did not exterminate the brewery. You made millions of little breweries and installed them in the homes of the people."

The speech was so forceful that Senator Wesley L. Jones of Washington proposed amending his bill giving courts discretion to distinguish between casual and slight violations by amateurs and major ones by habitual offenders. When the vote was taken in the Senate on February 19, 1929, the wets lost by 65 votes to 18—their most crushing defeat ever. In the House they lost by 90 votes to 284.

Though the Jones Law seemed at the time a dramatic victory for the drys their purposes were undermined by farce. As often in the past the bone of contention between wets and drys was the Prohibition Bureau.

During Coolidge's administration the Prohibition Unit (and Bureau) had not changed substantively. In 1923 it had 3,413 employees and in early 1929 it had 4,129 employees. Its problems, however, had increased well beyond the capacity of its staff. The Department of Justice reported in December 1928 that smuggling from Canada had increased by more than 75 percent since 1925. The production of industrial alcohol had increased from 57 million gallons in 1923 to 92 million gallons in 1928. The quantity of illicit liquor seized by federal agents had increased from 14,346,649 gallons in 1923 to 32,474,233 in 1928—more than twice as much. The wets had a remedy.

During debate on an appropriations bill Senator W. Cabell Bruce of Maryland, also of the BEER group, proposed an amendment to increase the funds of the Prohibition Bureau twenty times over. Dr. James M. Doran, prohibition commissioner, had asked for $300 million. Bruce now agreed with the AAPA that people should see how bad prohibition was. In the future there would be true prohibition. Drys would no longer be able to claim that wets said the law could not be enforced because they ensured it was not. Bruce's amendment for an increase of $256 million dollars to the routine appropriation of $13.5 million for the bureau was passed by wet and dry Senators voting together. Of course Bruce's real purpose was to cause trouble. His proposal was another "wet joker."

The drys outside Congress were divided. Cannon sent a telegram to Andrew Mellon, secretary of the treasury, protesting about his paltry awards for enforcement. But Dr. Clarence True Wilson, secretary of the Northern Methodist Board of Temperance, Prohibition and Public Morals, dreaded the advent of massive enforcement and, with it, renewed public hostility to prohibition, not to mention resentment at the possibility of increased taxes to the tune of a quarter of a billion dollars. In the end, a compromise was reached: an increase of $1,719,654, about 1 percent of the previous amount. Senator Thaddeus H. Caraway of Arkansas observed with some sarcasm that the election had proved most Americans wanted prohibition but whether it was for themselves or their neighbors he could not say.

Since the passage of the Eighteenth Amendment wet strength had become concentrated in the North. The Democrats were split much more according to sectional lines of North and South. The Republicans had, quite simply, become drier. Defeat of a Democratic presidential candidate had been interpreted as a defeat for the wets. As long as the northern wets led the Democrats defeat of a Republican presidential candidate would entail a defeat for the drys. The inevitable realignment of the Solid South with the Democrats would imply its tacit acceptance of a wet platform.

———◆◆———

In the end Smith had his consolation prize. Ignored by Governor Roosevelt, he had his friends to fall back on. On August 30, 1929, Al Smith, president of the Empire State, Inc., announced that the organization would build the world's tallest building. It would be 1,200 feet high, with 102 stories of offices capable of accommodating twenty-five thousand people. The Empire State Building would stand on Fifth Avenue at Thirty-fourth Street and the Waldorf-Astoria Hotel would be demolished to make room for it. The plan had been conceived by Pierre S. Du Pont, John J. Raskob, Louis G. Kaufman, and Elvis P. Earle, other directors of Empire State, Inc. At last Raskob would have his Eiffel Tower. Demolition of the hotel began in September. It was not a month too soon. In October the stock market crashed.

─TEN─

SPEAKS VOLUMES

THE FABRIC OF AMERICAN HISTORY is woven from a skein of contradictions. American immigrants sought refuge from political and religious oppression. But to civilize the New World they were ready to annihilate the indigenous population. The American Revolution was accomplished by radicals in the name of liberty, but the institution of slavery was preserved. Abraham Lincoln won the Civil War to free the slaves; but to preserve the Union he would have freed none. To achieve social reform and good government in the cities progressive reformers imposed the prohibition of alcohol on the whole country. The result was an increase in crime and a breakdown of law and order with the connivance of those in authority. The claim is not exaggerated. And this was how contemporary commentators saw the situation.

War was a common metaphor for the ills of society. Wets such as William Cabell Bruce, Ida Tarbell, and A. Lawrence Lowell and others compared prohibition to civil war. The period of slavery, secession, the Civil War, and Reconstruction was one of social chaos and national crisis. Though prohibition did not surpass the excesses of that period, in the opinion of many wets it ran it a close second.

204

They believed prohibition had led to the disintegration of justice. They dreaded the collapse of an entire social system. For them prohibition held an incipient threat: the subversion of order. They used the Civil War and Reconstruction as metaphors for decay and dissolution in their diatribes against the drys. During the Senate investigations of 1926 William Cabell Bruce of Maryland had compared people's violations of the Volstead Act with violations of the Fugitive Slave Law by Free Soilers before the Civil War.

The progressive journalist, Ida M. Tarbell, still found plenty of muck to rake at the end of the 1920s. In an article for *Liberty* of July 6, 1929, she asked, "Is Prohibition Forcing Civil War?" and compared the period of prohibition to the 1850s and the controversy over slavery and secession. She wondered, "Did North or South in the turmoil before the Civil War show more outrageous outbreaks of violence than we have had in the name of law enforcement?"

"There have been weeks in recent months when the outline of a day's news read like a war communiqué." The authorities had been unable to coerce public obedience to their prohibition laws and had simply added harsher and harsher laws to the statute books as if to prove that because severity did not work there was still scope for greater severity. The Michigan Habitual Criminal Act imposed life imprisonment for four convictions under the state prohibition law, which made the possession of liquor a felony. It was under this "life-for-a-pint" law that a mother of ten children (Mrs. Etta Mae Miller) had been sentenced to life imprisonment.

The means of enforcement had proved as violent as any gang rule. Mrs. Lillian de King had been killed on the outskirts of Aurora, Illinois, on March 25, 1929, as she tried to help her husband. He had been knocked senseless by an officer arresting him for selling liquor. The Coast Guard pursuing a boat at night in Biscayne Bay, Miami, had fired two hundred shots at random toward the city, puncturing the walls of buildings and smashing windows. One woman roused from sleep by the commotion was grazed by a stray bullet.

It was in protest against such incidents that Arthur Lippmann wrote *The Patriot's Prayer*, inspired by the children's prayer in the opera *Hansel and Gretel* by Engelbert Humperdinck:

> *Now I lay me down to sleep—*
> *My life and limb may Hoover keep,*
> *And may no Coast Guard cutter shell*
> *This little home I love so well.*

PROHIBITION

May no dry agent, shooting wild,
Molest mine wife and infant child,
Or searching out some secret still,
Bombard my home to maim and kill.
When dawn succeeds the gleaming stars,
May we, devoid of wounds and scars,
Give thanks we didn't fall before
The shots in Prohibition's War.

Another writer to use civil war as a metaphor for prohibition and develop the theme of "Reconstruction and Prohibition" was A. Lawrence Lowell in an article for the *Atlantic Monthly* of February 1929.

The claims of Bruce, Tarbell, and Lowell are, of course, partisan. But they are not too extravagant. Proof lies in the files and reports of the Wickersham Commission.

———◆◆———

Between his election and taking office Herbert Hoover expanded the plan for an investigation into prohibition. In his inaugural address of March 4, 1929, he proposed "a national commission for a searching investigation of the whole structure of our federal system of jurisprudence, to include the method of enforcement of the Eighteenth Amendment and the causes of abuse under it." The commission would make "such recommendations for reorganization of the administration of federal laws and court procedure as may be found desirable." Hoover would certainly not countenance changes in the law that were unacceptable to the drys who had helped his election campaign. Thus he implied that the ratification of the Eighteenth Amendment had settled the question of whether there should be prohibition once and for all. The commission's brief was to consider the method of law enforcement, nothing more.

On May 20, 1929, Hoover announced the names of the eleven members of the Commission on Law Enforcement and Observance. They would meet under the chairmanship of George W. Wickersham, who had served Taft as attorney general. The others were: Wilson's secretary of war, Newton D. Baker; a former state justice, Kenneth Mackintosh of Washington State; three judges, William I. Grubb, Paul J. McCormick and William S. Kenyon; three practicing lawyers, Henry W. Anderson of Virginia, Monte M. Lemann of New Orleans, and Frank Loesch of the Chicago Crime Commission; the dean of the Harvard Law School, Roscoe Pound; and the president of Radcliffe, Ada L. Comstock. They were all conservative but responsive to the demands of the time as well as responsible to its needs. On May 28 they met for the first time in Washington where Wickersham himself confirmed the worst fears of both wets and drys by telling the press, "This commission is not to be the arbiter between the wets and drys, and I want to emphasize that it was not appointed to decide that question." Despite this claim the commission was, as Charles Merz says, "drawn in the direction of prohibition as irresistibly as . . . steel filings in the presence of magnet."

Despite his press release George Wickersham wrote to Governor Franklin D. Roosevelt of New York on July 15, 1929, suggesting that the states should share enforcement with the federal government. Roosevelt read the letter at the governors' conference, then meeting at Groton, Connecticut. Wickersham was asking for increased cooperation from the states in exchange for allowing them to choose what sort of prohibition they would have.

Wets considered Wickersham's proposal sagacious. Drys deplored it. By July 18 the furor roused by Wickersham's letter was such that the governors dismissed his suggestion, which is precisely what Roosevelt had wanted them to do. A consummate political opportunist, he was not yet ready to show his hand.

Although the United States system of government with its celebrated checks and balances between the executive, legislative and judicial branches survived the corruscating effect of prohibition, it was in peril when the period of prosperity came to an end. This harsh interpretation is sustained by evidence submitted to the Wickersham Commission by judges, attorneys, and other lawyers from all parts of the country. It is their evidence that is so eloquent against prohibition. It speaks volumes on the underworld of the speakeasies or speaks.

Whatever their personal attitude to temperance, the vast majority of people writing to, and appearing before, the commission told members in no uncertain terms that prohibition was not working and should be repealed. These lawyers began with the premise that people disobeyed this law because they disregarded it and that officers flouted the law for financial gain. They concluded that, as a result, all laws were falling into disrepute and the whole legal system had become a matter of public contempt. Justice was no longer an ideal. It was a trade.

For example, Forrest E. Ely, a lawyer of Batavia, Ohio, told George Wickersham in a letter of October 22, 1929, that crime had increased by 50 percent as a result of prohibition. Like many others he emphasized the fact that people disregarded prohibition because it was an infringement of their personal liberties: "We never have and never will legislate morals. Prohibition of the use of alcoholic beverages is a matter of education and not legislation." But contempt for one law led to a corruption of traditional values: "Our increase in Juvenile Delinquency is the direct result of a disrespect for law bolstered in the homes of these delinquents by the parents in the disrespect for the law of prohibition for liquor and the consequent fear and contempt for the righteous sheriff or policeman."

John Marshall Gest of the Orphans Court, Philadelphia, declared in a letter of November 29, 1929: "I have no hesitation in stating my conviction that the present deplorable conditions existing in this country are in great measure attributable to the Eighteenth Amendment, the Volstead Act and similar enforcement legislation, all of which, in my opinion, have produced greater demoralization in politics, morality and society than any laws that were ever enacted."

On January 13, 1930, the Wickersham Commission submitted its first report, devoted exclusively to the Volstead Act. There were four proposals:

1. Codification of all prohibition laws enacted over the previous forty years.
2. New legislation to give extra force to the padlock provisions of the Volstead Act.
3. Transfer of the Prohibition Bureau from Treasury to the Department of Justice.
4. Trial without jury for "casual or slight violations."

There was next to no controversy over the first three recommendations. As a result of the third recommendation, on May 14, 1930, the Senate passed an administration bill transferring prohibition enforcement from the Department of the Treasury to the Department of Justice.

The proposal for trial without jury was almost certainly the idea of Wickersham himself. It was not deduced on the basis of evidence before the commission. He had made up his mind well in advance. The proposal of January 1930 is almost indistinguishable from one he made in an address at William and Mary on May 7, 1929, two weeks before the names of commissioners were announced and three weeks before the first meeting. According to the report of Attorney

General William D. Mitchell on the fiscal year 1928 to 1929, the number of criminal prosecutions instituted by the federal government was 56,786. Of these 18,690 cases were listed as unfinished business at the close of the year, June 30, 1929. Of those which had been settled fewer than 7 percent had come to trial. The defendants had pleaded guilty. Prohibition was being disposed of in the courts by what the commission called in its report an "unseemly process," bargain day. The commission's proposed alternative, trial without jury, would have given district attorneys considerable power. It would have allowed them to decide how the defendant would be charged and, in effect, encourage them to persuade defendants to forgo their rights.

After nineteen months' research at a cost of half a million dollars the commission issued its final report on January 7, 1931. It showed conclusively that prohibition was not working. Yet individual commissioners offered different remedies. Two were for repeal, four for modification of one sort or another, and five for further trial. George Wickersham admitted of the report: "It is more or less of a compromise of varying opinions."

Although seven members were openly critical of prohibition all but one signed a summary endorsing it. According to its final summary the commission opposed repeal of the Eighteenth Amendment; return of the saloon; government involvement in the liquor trade; legalization of light wines and beer. The various revisions proposed were abolition of limitations on alcohol in doctors' prescriptions; repeal of the clause in the Volstead Act that permitted the manufacture of cider; trial without jury for minor offenses (again); increased supervision of industrial alcohol; strengthening of padlock injunctions (again).

Individual parts of the whole form a more persuasive indictment of prohibition than the final summary might suggest. As an account of what had gone wrong and why, the whole report has not been surpassed. Commissioners distinguished between temperance, which could be attained, and prohibition, which could not.

Despite the shortcomings of the law and enforcement, the commission found "There has been more sustained presence to enforce this law than on the whole has been true of any other federal statute." For "No other federal law has had such elaborate state and federal enforcing machinery put behind it." Yet once prohibition was in effect and ineffective, people questioned whether it was the best and most effective way of dealing with the problem. The only way of enforcing complete prohibition would have been by imposing a police state on American society, thereby completing the subversion of democracy that prohibition had instigated.

The fact that prohibition already had a subversive effect was emphasized by one commissioner, Henry Anderson, in his individual report: "The liquor question is obscuring thought, dominating public discussion, and excluding from consideration other matters of vital concern, to an extent far beyond its actual importance in our social and economic life. It must be solved or the social and political interests of our country must be seriously compromised."

Hoover was embarrassed. What he had wanted was a report with a foregone conclusion, supportive of law and order and his administration, something he could endorse without becoming entangled in debate. He ensured that the summary approved of prohibition. Then he tried to assure press, public, and politicians that prohibition was there to stay. In his message to Congress of January 20, 1931, he said: "The commission, by a large majority, does not favor the repeal of the Eighteenth Amendment as a method of cure for the inherent abuses of the liquor traffic. I am in accord with this view." He ought, of course, to have said that it was a *minority* that wanted to retain the Eighteenth Amendment since seven of the eleven commissioners favored some alteration. Wickersham himself was quoted in the *New York Times* of March 13, 1931, as saying the report favored the wets rather than the drys.

But the public had the last word. Everyone associated with the commission was pilloried without mercy. Franklin P. Adams ridiculed commission and administration with a satirical verse for the *New York World* in February 1931:

> Prohibition is an awful flop.
> > We like it.
> It can't stop what it's meant to stop.
> > We like it.
> It's left a trail of graft and slime,
> It don't prohibit worth a dime,
> It's filled our land with vice and crime,
> > Nevertheless, we're for it

Another parody of the commission in the vein of *The Walrus and the Carpenter* by Lewis Carroll was printed in the national press:

Izzy (Isadore Einstein, left) and Moe (Smith), peerless prohibition agents noted for their unexpected appearances and for the diverse disguises they donned. *(BBC Hulton Picture Library)*

Prohibition agents led by Eliot Ness of the Untouchables, seated behind the wheel. *(U.S. Bureau of Alcohol, Tobacco, and Firearms)*

Customs officers apprehend a smuggler with twelve bottles of liquor carried in the pockets of an outsize vest. *(U.S. Bureau of Customs)*

In order to ensure the legal right to apprehend smugglers on the border between the United Staes and Canada, an American customs officer (left) would work together with a member of the Canadian mounties (right). *(U.S. Bureau of Customs)*

Governor Al Smith of New York (center), 1928 Democratic presidential nominee whose open wetness made him a controversial figure. John Julius Raskob (left), a General Motors executive, was his campaign manager; Senator Joseph T. Robinson of Arkansas (right) was his dry running mate. *(Library of Congress)*

Diamond Jim Colosimo (left) with Attorney Charles Erbstein in 1914. Colosimo was a transitional figure in the Chicago underworld, between the old tradition of protection, prostitution, and gambling and the new focus on bootlegging opportunities. *(Chicago Historical Society, DN #63,234)*

Top, The St. Valentine's Day Massacre of 1929 in a Chicago warehouse, intended by Al Capone as the final solution to his feud with the North Side gang. *(BBC Hulton Picture Library)* Below, Al Capone (center), signing a $50,000 bail bond in Chicago on July 6, 1931, on charges of withholding income tax payments. *(BBC Hulton Picture Library)*

Top, Edward G. Robinson (right) with Douglas Fairbanks, Jr., in *Little Caesar* (1930). Director Mervyn Leroy's emphasis on the life styles of leading gangsters during prohibition led to a vogue for gangster movies that lasted more than half a century. *(First National; Museum of Modern Art/Film Stills Archives)* Below, James Cagney with Edward Woods in *Public Enemy* (1931), the film that made Cagney a star and established Warners as the leading producers of gangster movies. *(Warner Bros.; Museum of Modern Art/Film Stills Archives)*

Paul Muni (center) led the cast of *Scarface* (1932), which also included George Raft (right). Many consider this movie, based on the career of Al Capone, one of the best of the genre. *(Warner Bros.; Museum of Modern Art/Film Stills Archives)*

Bishop James A. Cannon, Jr., of Virginia before the Senate Lobby Committee on June 3, 1930. On Wayne Wheeler's death he was regarded as the preeminent champion of prohibition, but his own transgressions discredited him. *(Underwood & Underwood; Library of Congress)*

Top, Pauline Morton Sabin, describing prohibition as "the greatest piece of class legislation ever enacted in this country," founded the Women's Organization for National Prohibition Reform. *(Underwood & Underwood; Library of Congress)* Below, Those aspiring to joing Mrs. Sabin's organization apparently included members of both sexes, as this photograph of a 1930 Chicago enrollment session shows. *(Library of Congress)*

Unemployed men line up for soup, coffee, and doughnuts outside a Depression soup kitchen opened in Chicago by Al Capone. *(National Archives)*

The pathos of poverty is poignantly captured in this Depression photograph of unemployed men standing in line for food at the junction of 6th Avenue and 42nd Street, New York, in February 1932. *(Franklin D. Roosevelt Library, Hyde Park)*

"If eleven men for twenty months
Write all they see and hear,
Do you suppose," the Abstainer said,
"That they can make it clear?"
"I doubt it," said the Drinking Man,
And wept into his beer.

Walter Lippmann, wet political commentator, in a corruscating article, "The Great Wickersham Mystery," for *Vanity Fair* in April 1931 thought commissioners had faced up to the truth. The administration had made them hide it. Prohibition had failed: "Everything possible was done officially to conceal this truth from the public generally, and from the rural voters in particular. It was cut out of the conclusions. It was suppressed in the official summary. It was ignored by the President. . . . What was done was to evade a direct and explicit official confession that federal prohibition is a hopeless failure." Lippmann observed, further, that Hoover could not enforce the law but he refused to revise it. Implicitly and tacitly he was condoning widespread nullification.

———◆◆———

However, compared with Harding and Coolidge Hoover took enforcement of the Volstead Act very seriously. At his instigation the number of people imprisoned for violations doubled between 1929 and 1932. The increased number of prisoners were accommodated in six new prisons. The number of prisoners serving sentences of more than a year was 5,268 on June 30, 1921, but 14,115 on June 30, 1931. The number of prisoners serving long-term sentences for violation of prohibition laws in five leading federal institutions in 1930 was 4,296 out of a total of 12,332. Hoover told the press that his punitive measures would result in true justice. For "if a law is wrong, its rigid enforcement is the surest guaranty of its repeal. If it is right, its enforcement is the quickest method of compelling respect for it."

Hoover's stand was compromised by the strategy of his own administration. The federal government now refused to take sole responsibility for prohibition enforcement. It wanted the states to do their share. The Prohibition Bureau explained the failure of the states to appropriate enough funds to ensure adequate enforcement hitherto as a conspiracy. This was too simplistic. States were reluctant to devote time, energy, and money to enforcement of a law to which the federal government had so far devoted its own resources. Despite the ratification of the Eighteenth Amendment by forty-six states most of them had never even tried anything as severe as bone-dry prohibition before.

The extent to which the law was now being evaded and defied was revealed most eloquently by statistics released by the government itself.

On October 4, 1930, the Prohibition Bureau estimated that the amount of liquor consumed in the fiscal year ending June 30, 1930, was 876,320,718 gallons or more than 7 gallons for every man, woman, and child. Of this 1,444,800 gallons of beer, 155,900 gallons of wine and 3,557,500 gallons of spirits were smuggled into the country. The most common source of liquor was neither industrial nor smuggled alcohol. It was the illicit still. In 1929 the Prohibition Bureau reported that 35,200 stills and distilleries were seized in 1928 together with 26 million gallons of mash. In 1930, it reported that 27,336 stills had been seized in 1929. In December 1931 the United States Treasury Department published its pamphlet, *Statistics Concerning Intoxicating Liquors*, which showed that in the fiscal year ending June 30, 1931, the value of bootlegging property seized by the authorities was $21,484,730. In addition bootleggers surrendered $3,447,558 in fines during the same period, 63,177 bootleggers were arrested by federal officers and 13,234 by state officers.

The total number of people arrested in 1931 was 76,401. The officers conceded this represented a small fraction of the number engaged in the liquor industry. The low estimation was that there was one arrest of every four which would make the number of people breaking the law as 305,604 bartenders, saloonkeepers, bootleggers, rumrunners, and racketeers. The high estimation was one arrest of every ten people involved, which would make the total 764,010.

An old song of railroad and work gangs, which had long been turned to satirize society's indifference to different criminal activities, was now revised with blithe assurance. Its targets were not only illicit alcohol but also narcotics—"snow" signified cocaine and "snow birds," its addicts:

> *My sister sells snow to the snowbirds,*
> *My father makes bootlegger gin,*
> *My mother sells wine from the grapes on our vine—*
> *My God! How the money rolls in.*

It seemed everyone was in on the act.

Mrs. Mabel Walker Willebrandt resigned as assistant attorney general on May 28, 1929. She said she wanted to spend more time with her adopted daughter, Dorothy. Moreover, eight years of working for prohibition was quite enough. But for Mrs. Willebrandt a rest was not quite as good as a change. A foremost opponent of law violation hitherto, Mrs. Willebrandt now changed sides. She joined two friends of Herbert Hoover, Thomas C. C. Gregory and C. C. Teague, as a representative of Fruit Industries, Inc., a corporation of twenty thousand California grape growers. Fruit Industries accounted for 85 percent of the state's sales of grapes but was concerned by the fact that annual surpluses of several hundred thousand tons were depressing their prices. C. C. Teague was also a member of the Federal Farm Board, a creation of the Agricultural Marketing Board of June 15, 1929, authorized to issue federal loans for farm cooperative associations. Willebrandt, Teague, and Gregory sought and obtained loans of $2,555,330 from the Federal Farm Board for Fruit Industries, Inc. Fruit Industries then developed Vine-Glo. This was the grape concentrate in the form of a jello brick. It contained no alcohol. But if sugar and water were added to it and it was left for two months it would turn into wine containing 12 percent alcohol. It was sold in forty-seven states at prices ranging from ten to thirty dollars.

Al Smith, who had been Willebrandt's victim in 1928, congratulated Fruit Industries on securing her services. Mrs. Willebrandt had persuaded the Department of Justice that wine with an alcoholic content of 12 percent was not intoxicating and then secured them a government grant to make it: "Mabel collected a beautiful fee for making the Volstead Act look like thirty cents."

There was nothing illegal about the process. In 1921 the Internal Revenue Service had announced that heads of families could make up to two hundred gallons of wine a year for home use provided they obtained a permit. In 1930 the new prohibition director, Amos W. W. Woodcock, reaffirmed this as official government policy. Taking full advantage of the letter, if not the spirit, of the law, the company's advertisement was blatant enough:

> Now is the time to order your supply of VINE-GLO. It can be made in your home in sixty days—a fine, true-to-type guaranteed beverage ready for the Holiday Season.
>
> VINE-GLO . . . comes to you in nine varieties, Port, Virginia Dare, Muscatel, Angelica, Tokay, Sauterne, Riesling, Claret and Burgundy. It is entirely legal in your home—but it must not be transported.

Vine-Glo stayed on the market until the end of 1931 when the Department of Justice threatened the manufacturers with prosecution on the grounds that their commercial intent was to produce wine. Competitors to Fruit Industries launched other brands such as Vino Sano. But prohibition agents in New York raided the Fifth Avenue store of Vino Sano Distributors on August 5, 1931. They confiscated the grape blocks and arrested the manager. The raid had been instigated by the New York Anti-Saloon League. The company asked Mrs. Willebrandt, by now an affluent Washington attorney, to act as counsel for the defense. "I'm very sorry," she replied in a telegram, "but I do not take prohibition cases."

─ELEVEN─

HUNGER AND THIRST

WHEREAS THE ANSWER TO THE QUESTION "Why was prohibition passed?" is complex, the answer to the question "Why was prohibition repealed?" is simple. It was on account of the Wall Street Crash of 1929 and the depression of the 1930s. Hunger was a better advocate than thirst. It was far more eloquent against prohibition than any speech or sentence.

The immediate cause of the Wall Street Crash of October 29, 1929, when the bottom fell out of the New York stock market was neither fear nor short selling. It was forced selling. The averages of fifty leading shares published in the *New York Times* fell from a record of 311.90 in September 1929 to 164.43 by November 13, 1929—about half their previous value. The worst period of panic was from October 24, when 12,894,650 shares were sold, to October 29, when at least 16,410,030 shares were sold. That was not the end. In the next three years General Motors shares would fall from 73 points to 8, U.S. Steel from 262 to 22, and Montgomery Ward from 138 to 4.

Black Tuesday, October 29, 1929, was not something like the eclipse of the sun, a financial matter unrelated to the economic affairs of the nation as a whole. As Gilbert Seldes finds in *The Years of the Locust* (1933): "The system broke down because it was not checked, because it carried with it the seeds of destruction. Wall Street was a phenomenon of Pittsburgh, Grand Rapids, New York, High Point, Detroit, Des Moines—of every city in which a factory expanded before it had a market." During the 1920s the American people probably spent about $10 billion, more than they earned. The stock exchange was subsisting on borrowed money—credit—and hence borrowed time. According to Thomas Paine, "Credit is suspicion asleep." Awakening from somnolence was a nightmare.

Fundamental causes of the crash have been defined by John Kenneth Galbraith in *The Great Crash* (1954). The national income was badly distributed; wages and farm prices lagged behind exaggerated industrial profits. Thus people's ability to consume was below the nation's ability to produce. The wealthy put money in the stock market, a financial system both exaggerated and uncontrolled. Its holding companies and investment trusts exploited the system. They insisted on profit beyond production in the mania for speculation. In addition, very few banks were under governmental control and there was no system of pooling resources in a crisis. A failure of one bank led to runs on others. Rich people indulged in lavish spending in Europe, where the dollar had a high value. The high tariffs placed on European imports to the United States delayed and sometimes halted repayment by Europe of American loans. Despite the decline in trade abroad which might have absorbed the overproduction of American industry big business insisted on the maintenance of set prices to inspire confidence in investors.

The people in charge of the system did not know what they were doing, before and after the crash. Men in government and business understood economics only partially and had almost no interpretation of them. Their immediate reaction to the crash was to avoid fundamental problems and seek comfort in traditional remedies. Herbert Hoover had been elected to safeguard prosperity. But the Great Engineer could not make the machine work again. Herbert Feis, then economic adviser for the State Department, in his *1933: Characters in Crisis* (1966) recalls that "Hoover was not an insensitive nor inhumane man. . . . But he could not grasp or would not face the grim realities which called for deviation from principles and practices that he deemed essential to American greatness and freedom." He and the business elite believed that the proper policy for government in depressions was to economize and wait until things regulated themselves. This was what had happened after previous depressions. But it did not happen this time.

Hoover called a special session of Congress to consider farm relief and tariff alterations. In June 1930 the new Hawley-Smoot Tariff became law with increased duties on all imports. Objections were made by American bankers' associations, by manufacturers who needed foreign sales, and over a thousand economists. They believed a high protective tariff would defeat its object. Their protests were of no avail. And by 1932 twenty-five other countries had retaliated with high tariffs of their own. The international system of debts and reparation payments broke down. In March 1931 French banks called in short-term German and Austrian notes. Unable to meet the demands upon it the Kredit Anstalt in Vienna collapsed and this set off a chain reaction. The Weimar Republic again defaulted on reparation payments and President Paul von Hindenburg appealed to Hoover. In June 1931 Hoover proposed a one-year moratorium on payment of international debts and reparations alike.

On December 11, 1930, the Bank of the United States failed. The depression had begun. The depression was not a direct consequence of the crash. But it had long been incipient, given the state of the American economy. Although production had been ahead of consumption, 60 percent of families were incapable of sharing in any consumer society and could not help increase national wealth. They were earning less than two thousand dollars in 1929 and a third of them earned less than a thousand when two thousand was barely enough to keep a family with necessities. Sharing wealth might have meant sharing the capacity to consume. Work, not wealth, had been shared and spread in the twenties by the shortening of the working week and the displacement of 2 million workers in the wake of technological advances. From 1922 to 1929 between 5 and 10 percent of the potential work force was unemployed at any one time. The years of plenty were based on exploitation of the many by the few.

Business confidence was certainly a casualty of the crash. In 1930 American business was still making a profit of $2.5 billion. But by 1932 the profit had become a loss of $3.5 billion, a decline of $6 billion. National income fell by more than half. The production of durable goods fell by 77 percent between August 1929 and March 1933.

With the disappearance of paper profits rich and poor alike were disabused of their former hopes. Disillusion was sudden and shattering for all. But it was the poor who were dispossessed. In 1930

3 million people were unemployed. By February 1931 there were 8 million and in November 10 million. In 1932 12 million people were unemployed. That year a million were out of work in New York City alone and 660,000 were out of work in Chicago. Many who lost their jobs were put out of house and home. Mortgages were foreclosed and evictions became common. Masses of unemployed and destitute folk set up squalid camps on the edge of cities. These grotesque suburbs were a mixture of tents made from old sacking and shacks built with corrugated iron and even cardboard. They were called Hoovervilles. Their inhabitants depended on municipal charity for soup and bread. If that was not forthcoming they combed the streets looking for garbage in the gutters and trash in the cans in order to find something to eat.

The arguments against prohibition were neither more nor less true than before. But the Wall Street crash propelled repeal forward as a panacea for the depression. Whereas drys had once argued that prohibition was the basis for true fullness of life, it was now considered its nemesis. As John D. Hicks explains in *Republican Ascendancy* (1960): "In prosperous times the voters could tolerate the inefficiency of prohibition, make jokes about it, let it ride. But with the advent of depression its every fault was magnified, and the best jokes turned stale. The people were in a mood for change. Zealots who had promised the millenium as a result of prohibition, and had delivered bootleggers and racketeers instead, were in a class with politicians who had promised prosperity and delivered adversity. It was about time to wipe the slate clean and start over."

Contemporary observers said much the same thing. Matthew Woll, vice-president of the AFL, declared in 1931, "Certain great employers supported prohibition so that the workers might be more efficient to produce, to produce, to produce. Well, we have produced and six million are unemployed. And prohibition has produced, too. It has produced the illicit still, the rum-runner, the speak-easy, the racketeer, graft, corruption, disrespect for law, crime." Will Rogers made much the same point that year: "What does prohibition amount to, if your neighbor's children are not eating? It's food, not drink is our problem now. We were so afraid the poor people might drink, now we fixed it so they can't eat. . . . The working classes didn't bring this on, it was the big boys that thought the financial drunk was going to last forever."

Thus the most pressing argument for repeal was financial. The federal government was losing about half a billion dollars a year in liquor taxes that were collected instead from corporations and wealthy individuals. The wealth that at one time had accrued to brewers, vintners, and distillers was now diverted to gangsters and corrupt public officials. With the increased difficulty of raising taxes the old argument that the liquor interests had once paid a quarter of the country's revenue appealed to the affluent, who were too selfish to want to provide for the needy and dreaded higher personal taxation.

Extraordinary claims about taxation after repeal were made by leading wets. For example, Henry Curran, president of the AAPA, declared that with the disappearance of prohibition all federal income tax would disappear also—and overnight. The economic benefits of repeal were suggested by improved state revenue in Michigan. A state law of 1929 had introduced a tax of five cents per pound on malt syrup and extract and a small tax on wort. The tax raised was more than $500,000 in Detroit alone. Mayor Frank Murphy of Detroit estimated that "a reasonable tax on beer alone would bring $700 million a year into the public treasury." The beauty of the scheme was that no one was compelled to drink and pay taxes. Only those who chose to drink would share the burden of taxation.

Economic arguments were extended to take in agriculture. Pierce Blewett of the AAPA told farmers in North Dakota that prohibition had destroyed half their resources and that repeal would set this to rights. He was making the same sort of misleading claims against prohibition that drys had made for it during the war.

Yet farmers had suffered little on account of prohibition. After all, their grain crops were still used in the illicit production of spirits. Of all the grain crops corn contributed the highest amount for the production of alcohol. In the ten years before 1917 the average amount of industrial alcohol manufactured from corn was 72,073 thousand gallons. From 1921 to 1928 the average amount was 155,648 thousand gallons, an increase of more than 100 percent. The average number of bushels used in the production of alcohol for drinking was 28,830 thousand in the ten years to 1917 and 57,158 thousand in the twenties. Thus corn was still king after John Barleycorn had been buried. But though the actual amount of corn used to make alcohol was large in the period before prohibition, the actual proportion of the total crop was small, an average of 1 percent before 1917 and 1.9 percent in the twenties.

The argument for repeal was stronger in the case of rye, which was second to corn in the amount used for distilling before prohibition. In the period from 1908 to 1913 the average amount used was 4,718 thousand of bushels, about 12 percent of the total crop, and from 1921 to 1928 the average was 62 thousands of bushels, about 2 percent of the total crop.

Another argument for repeal was that if breweries, distilleries, and wine presses and liquor stores were reopened people who were unemployed would have work. Of course the argument that prohibition had closed breweries and put people out of work was fraudulent. According to the Treasury Department report there were 1,217 breweries and 507 distilleries in operation in 1917. In 1931, fourteen years later, there were no legal breweries at all and only 6 licensed whiskey distilleries. Yet that year 21,541 distilleries and stills were seized.

Wets also suggested that repeal would put an end to radical splinter groups that had emerged in the depression and were thought subversive of the capitalist system. Such groups were associated with prohibitionists whose earlier links with progressives were neither forgotten nor forgiven by their enemies. The political, financial, and social elite took the challenge from the extreme left seriously. They were concerned lest it spread. Most people were dissatisfied with local government on account of its corruption. That corruption was indissolubly associated with prohibition. One way to anticipate the contagion of communism or anarchism was to cleanse local government by getting rid of prohibition. And labor dreaded a rival. In 1932, during Senate hearings on prohibition, Matthew Woll, vice-president of the AFL, blamed the development of radicalism on the Eighteenth Amendment.

Because all crimes, all corruption, all civil disorders, were attributed to prohibition, wets inculcated the public with the idea that all social problems were the result of prohibition. As Peter H. Odegard observed in *The American Public Mind* (1930): "Every time a crime is committed, they cry prohibition. Every time a girl or boy goes wrong, they shout prohibition. Every time a policeman or politician is accused of corruption, they scream prohibition. As a result, they are gradually building up in the public mind the impression that prohibition is a major cause of the sins of society."

HUNGER AND THIRST

Prohibition died of its own irrelevance. Thus the system instituted by the most determined of the drys, Wayne B. Wheeler, was to be terminated by the most dishonest, Bishop James A. Cannon. Wheeler considered virtue the only good, vice the only evil. To him all things external were things indifferent. In his obsession he turned the concept of national prohibition into an empty conceit, a vanity. Cannon was not indifferent to things external. He loved power and prestige, profit and pleasure. Whatever his appetites he did not hunger and thirst after righteousness. Of the many bizarre stories associated with prohibition, none was more strange than that of his career. It provided a ridiculous but sinister metaphor for the perils of prosperity in the wake of the Wall Street crash. Already distrusted by the general public, the drys were thoroughly discredited by Cannon's conduct of his personal and financial affairs. The opprobrium he earned for himself was transferred to the whole prohibition movement. Opponents of prohibition had long suspected that its advocates were hypocrites, appearing abstemious but actually dissolute. Cannon proved their point. His story has been engagingly told in a biography, *Dry Messiah* (1949), by Virginius Dabeny.

In June 1929 Cannon, a leader of the international temperance movement who spent much of his time abroad, returned from a visit to Palestine. With him was his secretary, Mrs. Helen Hawley McCallum. From June 20 onwards he faced a barrage of abuse from the wet press about his transactions with Kable and Company, a New York "bucketshop" then facing bankruptcy proceedings.

A bucketshop was a firm of stockbrokers that sold stock to speculators on precariously narrow margins and favored some customers more than others. Hence the term "bucketshop" was a pejorative one, coined in Wall Street to describe dishonest stockbrokers. Kable and Company had failed because it had withheld purchase of several million dollars' worth of stock, ordered and paid for in advance by its clients. It had done so on the expectation that their value would go down. If the market had fallen the company would have bought the orders for less than it had already charged its clients. It intended to pocket the difference and realize secret profits. On this occasion Kable and Company had miscalculated. The market rose. The price of stocks was now higher than the sums paid by its clients. It had not enough funds to cover the difference. It could not pay customers the profits they thought they had made.

Cannon was a favored client. He had not lost anything. Not only had he been a patron of the firm for eight months in 1927 and 1928 but also one of its largest customers. For an initial investment of $2,500 Kable and Company had bought him stocks worth $477,000 that were sold later for $486,000.

In public Cannon had been a consistent and outspoken opponent of gambling. In 1908 he had been instrumental in breaking up gambling at the Virginia State Fair. Moreover, the General Conference of the Methodist Church, South, had denounced "all forms of gambling" in a resolution of 1922. The repercussions of such revelations about Cannon were bad enough in the cities: they confirmed wet opinion of him and what he stood for. In the countryside they were devastating to his reputation and to that of the prohibition movement.

Cannon made various statements in self-defense: "I thought I was buying stocks for investment, buying on the partial payment plan, as any man may. I did not know there was any gambling by the company." During the court hearings one partner, Harry L. Goldhurst, supported Cannon. Yet he admitted that he had consummated stock transactions for Cannon in his capacity as a member of another firm, Ebel and Company. It, too, had been attacked as a bucketshop and enjoined from doing business. And another partner, Charles W. Kable, contradicted Cannon's version, saying his account "must have been speculative, in view of the amount and volume of the transactions."

There was worse to come. On July 19, 1929, the *New York World* and the *Chicago Tribune* reported allegations that Cannon had been a flour hoarder during the war. This accusation also hit at the temperance movement, for prohibition had been imposed during the war in part as a measure to conserve grain. Cannon escaped prosecution because he bought the flour before the law took effect. Nevertheless, when the charges were repeated in the press in 1929 it seemed that the prohibitionists' wartime claims on the need for conservation were simply a matter of speculation and accumulation. In other words, they were hypocrites. Cannon fodder was food for thought.

On August 3, 1929, Cannon defended himself in print—a manifesto of eighteen thousand words with the title "Unspotted from the World." He had fifty thousand copies printed. Its purpose was to show that even a bishop had to deal with the world as it is and that he, Cannon, had, in forty years' commerce, remained untainted.

Cannon gave more away in his intended exculpation than he imagined—his character.

Methodist ministers and laymen were sufficiently embarrassed by Cannon's nefarious activities with Goldhurst and Kable and his casuistry to ask the church to do something. Led by Josephus Daniels, Wilson's secretary of the navy, G.T. Fitzhugh, former newspaper publisher, and James P. Woods, former representative of Virginia, they sought to bring him to trial. A conference of ninety church elders and laymen met in the First Methodist Church of Dallas, Texas on May 12, 1930, to determine whether Cannon should be tried for unbecoming conduct. When Cannon supplied them with an apology on May 13, this, and a growing conviction that he was being crucificed in the press for his views on prohibition, were sufficient to persuade several delegates to support him. On May 19 by fifty-four votes to eleven the conference decided that a trial was unnecessary. Cannon then read out his apology: "I now realize the impropriety of such transactions and am sorely grieved that my actions have in any wise brought pain and embarrassment to . . . my beloved church." Public and press were incredulous. By admitting his guilt Cannon made the conference's acquittal of him look ridiculous.

A few weeks later, on June 13, 1930, Cannon's correspondence with Kable and Company was published in full in the press. The evidence was now against him. He had lied about the nature of his transactions in his confession of May. It was perfectly clear that between October 1927 and May 1928 he had speculated on the market both eagerly and greedily. He had even obtained an advance on his salary in order to do so. He had continued to deal closely with Goldhurst despite warnings from his financial advisers about the risks he was running. One Sunday he sent at least five separate sets of instructions to the bucketshop.

On June 25, 1930, the *Christian Century*, hitherto Cannon's champion, abandoned him. He was a "lost leader." The picture of an innocent and indifferent investor had faded from view. He was really a "feverishly anxious speculator haunting the telegraph office, exchanging frequent, sometimes daily, cablegrams from Brazil and elsewhere with his brokers, cautioning them against wiring him at certain addresses where the receipt of such messages might cause 'unpleasant complications,' scrambling for funds with which to cover margins or to act upon market tips, directing by wire the purchase or sale of this or that stock, 'on edge and fearful of flop,' scolding his brokers for their failure to carry out his orders, and clamoring for statements of his account." The bubble reputation had burst even in Cannon's mouth.

Cannon continued to provide the press with good copy. Newspapers now had reasons to think that he was not only a rogue but also a roué. On July 15, 1930, Cannon and his widowed secretary, Mrs. Helen Hawley McCallum, were married in Christ Church, London, by special license of the Archbishop of Canterbury. And on July 22, 1930, the *Philadelphia Record* entertained its readers with a record of their courtship.

He had met her in the summer of 1928 in the lobby of the Hotel McAlpin, New York and had introduced himself to her as a writer, Stephen Trent. He immediately pressed money on her and within a short while was giving her two hundred dollars a month, which allowed her to maintain an apartment at 159 West Eighty-fifth Street. He had seen her regularly on his many visits to New York. Just before and after the death of his first wife, Lura Virginia, following a paralytic stroke on November 25, 1928, he could scarcely keep away.

While they were on their honeymoon in Brazil Cannon and his bride learned that four Methodist ministers led by Forrest Prettyman, chaplain of the Senate, had filed charges against him with the chairman of the College of Bishops, W. N. Ainsworth. The charges were of immorality and lying, flour-hoarding and bucketshop gambling, "gross moral turpitude and disregard for the first principles of Christian ethics." They also specifically accused him of adultery with McCallum. The news was published in the press on September 20, 1930.

The hearing was set for November 12, 1930, but was deferred on account of Cannon's illnesses—chronic arthritis and neuritis. Twelve elders heard the evidence against him and his own defense at Vernon Place Methodist Church in Washington on February 3, 1931. They could not distinguish between the individual accused before them and what he represented. Surely no one who stood for prohibition could be guilty of misconduct? He used his illness to elicit sympathy and never appeared in public without a crutch.

The crucial evidence on the charge of adultery was a statement by the second Mrs. Cannon to the press before her marriage. When two false reports reached her in April 1930 that Cannon had married someone else she reacted with all the classic fury of a woman scorned. On April 12 she told three reporters of the *New York Evening Journal* how she had met Cannon and what had transpired between them. On April 14 she even showed one of them his love letters. Within a week Cannon returned from Europe. He cleared up the misunderstanding with Helen McCallum and persuaded her to sign an affidavit for the *Journal* that he wrote himself. In the new statement she declared that the reporters had intimidated her. They had said they would denounce her as a common prostitute if she did not do as she was told.

According to his biographer, Virginius Dabeny, Cannon and his second wife were "entirely innocent" of adultery. But everywhere old jokes about the actress and the bishop were revived. Sometimes alcoholic drinks were named after leading prohibitionists to ridicule them. A potent concoction of vermouth and gin was now called a Bishop Cannon Cocktail. Helen McCallum Cannon had apparently some very special services to offer.

The campaign against Cannon—especially that launched by the Hearst press—strengthened his cause. Drys protested that Cannon was being pilloried simply to discredit prohibition. William Randolph Hearst had instructed the *Los Angeles Examiner* to disgrace Cannon and, thereby, the movement. In a letter he said, "The most important duty of the Hearst papers all over the country now is the destruction of the group which Bishop Cannon represents and controls. *This can be done by constant, though careful, assaults upon him.*" The twelve Methodist elders were persuaded of the perfidy of the press. They declared no trial of Cannon was necessary.

This was not the end of his troubles. Cannon also faced charges of malpractice for his part in the campaign to defeat Al Smith. While the elders were meeting in Dallas the Senate Lobby Committee was investigating election funds. This committee, headed by Thaddeus H. Caraway of Arkansas, was predominantly dry and also included William E. Borah of Idaho, Thomas J. Walsh of Montana, Arthur R. Robinson of Indiana and one wet, John J. Blaine of Wisconsin. But as a result of charges made by Representative George H. Tinkham of Massachusetts against Cannon it was obliged to examine his activities in 1928. Tinkham believed that Cannon had received $65,3000 in cash from Edwin C. Jameson, a New York insurance executive, out of a total of $172,000 Jameson had donated to Hoover's election campaign. It was Republican money that Cannon, a Democrat, would use to his own private ends. In public Cannon had hitherto excoriated New York business interests. He now said he had received only $17,000. When Jameson appeared before the committee he made no bones of the fact that he had given Cannon a series of small checks of five or ten thousand dollars, each made out to cash. They amounted to a sum total of $65,300. He also admitted that Cannon had persuaded him to falsify declarations of not only the actual amounts but also the names of the recipients. Thus instead of declaring that all the money had gone into Cannon's several bank accounts he had pretended that it had been paid to various organizations opposed to Smith.

After his ordeal in Dallas Cannon appeared before the committee on June 3, 1930. He refused flatly to explain either his sources or his activities: "You'll never see that account," he said of the undeclared missing sum of $48,300. And when he reappeared before the committee on June 4 it was only to announce his withdrawal. Reading from a prepared statement he declared, "I must respectfully state that having answered all questions addressed to me by the committee on which I volunteered to appear as a witness, I shall now withdraw as a voluntary witness. If the committee desires to subpoena me that is its right."

Frank B. Kent reported in the *Baltimore Sun* that Cannon's contempt for the senators "was not only legal, but physical, mental, moral and spiritual." He "did everything except stick his tongue out at the committee." The committee was at a loss. Cannon, far from indulging himself, had cálculated things very nicely indeed. Whereas Walsh wanted to discipline him Borah, Caraway and Robinson would not. They would not do anything to discredit prohibition.

Tinkham continued to make his charges about Cannon to the House of Representatives and to the press. Carter Glass of Virginia was also not to be outdone. He introduced a Senate resolution to make Cannon appear before the Select Committee on Senatorial Campaign Expenditures headed by Gerald P. Nye of North Dakota. Nye held some hearings during May 1931 but failed to secure any evidence from his first witness, Ada L. Burroughs, treasurer of the so-called Anti-Smith Democratic Committee. However, in the fall the Nye Committee heard from various witnesses that Cannon had deposited political contributions in his own bank accounts. Basil Manly, its specialist adviser, showed how Cannon had opened no fewer than six new bank accounts during the campaign and only $22,544 of $68,717 held in them had been used against Smith. Cannon had solicited money from several people during the campaign.

A grand jury began its own independent inquiry on October 8, 1931. Cannon now tried to argue that since the campaign had taken place in Virginia it was a matter for a state and not a federal hearing. But he was outwitted by the state attorney of the District of Columbia, John J. Wilson, and, on October 16, 1931, the jury indicted him and Ada Burroughs on ten charges of conspiring to violate the Federal Corrupt Practices Act. Cannon said the indictment was "religious persecution."

On December 21, 1931, the Nye Committee published its findings. Cannon had committed "numerous apparent violations of the Federal Corrupt Practices Act." The funds handled by Cannon and Burroughs in 1928 amounted to more than $130,000. But "of this total only $58,558.62 was accounted for in statements filed with the Clerk of the House of Representatives." Nye also said that none of the $62,300 contributed by E. C. Jameson prior to January 1, 1929, was accounted for. Throughout Cannon insisted that money had been used by the Virginia Committee of the Anti-Smith Democrats. Yet Nye concluded that no such agency had ever existed.

The Nye Committee had found against Cannon. But it could not convict him. That was a matter for the courts. Cannon had been indicted on October 16, 1931. By a series of subterfuges he delayed the day of reckoning. He instituted a series of appeals that did not reach the Supreme Court until January 9, 1934. The Court sustained Cannon's opposition to eight of the ten indictments against him. It did so because, technically, Ada Burroughs, as treasurer of the campaign against Al Smith, was principal defendant. When the case began in the District of Columbia Supreme Court on April 9, 1934, the task of the prosecution was to prove conspiracy between Cannon and Ada Burroughs. As the judge, Peyton Gordon, instructed the jury, either both were guilty of conspiracy or neither. Burroughs, quite clearly, had not known exactly what Cannon had done with the money. The evidence against her was insufficient for conviction. Thus the case against Cannon fell to pieces. On April 27, 1934, after three hours' adjournment, the jury acquitted both defendants. By this time prohibition was a thing of the past, and Cannon was no longer a curiosity. But the fact that in the early thirties he had had to outwit his adversaries in numerous scandals had damaged his cause irreparably. There were alternatives to alcohol that were just as subversive of morality. Drys had once been progressive, radical, or democratic. Now they were regarded as regressive, reactionary, and autocratic.

By the fall of 1930, drys were sufficiently unnerved by the renewed vigor of the whole attack on prohibition by wets to consider a compromise. Some were ready to agree to the legalization of beer and light wines in exchange for an undertaking that the saloon would remain illegal. After all, the current slogan of the AAPA was "Beer and Light Wines *Now*, but No Saloon *Ever*."

In September 1930 drys held a conference in New York to discuss the issue. Delegates included: Frank Garnett, newspaper publisher; Fred B. Smith, head of the Committee of One Thousand; Willis J. Abbott, editor of the *Christian Science Monitor*; Republican congressman Franklin A. Fort of New Jersey; Francis Scott McBride, national superintendent of the Anti-Saloon League; the Reverend Arthur Barton of the Baptist Church. Fort was prepared to ask Congress to reconsider the Eighteenth Amendment by putting forward a resubmission resolution. He was supported by Deets Pickett and the Reverend Dr. Clarence True Wilson. They were willing to allow beer and light wines provided the saloon would still be banned. But confirmed drys like Barton and McBride would not compromise. They recalled that beer and wine together had accounted for 93 percent of the volume of liquor and almost 60 percent of the alcohol consumed back in 1914. At that time about 59 percent of the money spent on alcohol was spent on beer alone. Thus they argued that prohibition of spirits alone would be no prohibition at all.

The abortive New York conference of 1930 and the scandals associated with Cannon presaged the deterioration of morale among the drys and the disintegration of their forces. Patrick H. Callahan, a businessman of Louisville, Kentucky, who was chairman of the Cooperative Committee for Prohibition Enforcement, told Mencken in 1932 that after the conference "it was every man for himself. The dry outfit was divided and full of dissension. What those fellows lack is the capacity to give and take. They have no sense of humor. . . . You can't do much with Puritans. They are too sure about everything."

Some historians, such as J. C. Burnham in the *Journal of Social History* (fall 1968), argue that modification of the Volstead Act to allow beer and light wines would have saved prohibition. The weight of contemporary political opinion is against such amphibious legislation.

Former President William Howard Taft, a foremost opponent of prohibition before the law took effect who subsequently gave it his tacit support, perhaps out of loyalty to Republican administrations, was obdurate on the matter of beer and light wines: "No such distinction as that between beer and wine on the one hand and spiritous liquor on the other is practicable as a police measure." Henry W.

Anderson, a member of the Wickersham Commission who wanted government sale of alcohol as an alternative to prohibition, extended Taft's argument. In his individual report he said: "If the limit of alcoholic content were placed so low that the beverage sold would not be intoxicating in fact it would not satisfy the demand. If it were placed high enough to be intoxicating in fact, it would to that extent be nullification of the Amendment. Under this plan we would have saloons for the sale of light wine and beer, and bootlegging as to liquors of higher alcoholic content. We would then have the evils of both systems and the benefits of neither."

In addition people no longer had any interest in schemes to revise the Volstead Act to allow liquor that was "nonintoxicating in fact" rather than intoxicating or not according to a particular percentage of alcohol.

Until 1932 repeal was by no means a foregone conclusion. Wets despaired of attaining it. Thus drys were complacent. They believed that since the Eighteenth Amendment was part of the constitution it was inviolate. An Associated Press dispatch from Washington of September 24, 1930, carried Senator Morris Sheppard's premature and foolish claim for its permanence across the country: "There is as much chance of repealing the Eighteenth Amendment," he said, "as there is for a humming-bird to fly to the planet Mars with the Washington Monument tied to its tail."

Congress did not come round to the wet side immediately or at once. The hearings against Cannon demonstrated the reluctance of dry members to concede anything, even in the way of reputation. On March 14, 1932, Representatives James M. Beck of Pennsylvania and John C. Linthicum of Maryland introduced a joint resolution to discharge a bill for repeal of the Eighteenth Amendment from the Committee on the Judiciary so that it could be debated on the floor of the House. Beck argued that prohibition was an experiment rather than a reform. It ought to be, therefore, a subject for continuous discussion. Because "no such general revolt against the enforcement of a law has ever been known in our history" this was especially true. Whereas drys maintained the constitution could not be changed their amendment had altered it by destroying the fundamental American principle of self-government. John J. O'Connor of New York pointed out that only eighty-two members of the present House had served

Congress in the war and thus participated in the original debate on the Eighteenth Amendment. Therefore it was time to think again. However the Beck-Linthicum resolution was defeated by 227 votes to 187—a margin that was too close for dry comfort.

What H. L. Mencken called "the death struggles of Prohibition" took place at the two Chicago conventions of 1932.

The Republican National Convention was held from June 14. Herbert Hoover's difficulty lay not in securing nomination but in deciding what to do about prohibition. Hoover's desire to equivocate was undermined by Senator Hiram Bingham of Connecticut and Dr. Nicholas Murray Butler, who favored outright repudiation of prohibition. The Republican platform was neither wet nor dry but moist; it advocated resubmission of the Eighteenth Amendment to the states and reserved the power of the federal government to protect traditionally dry territory and prevent the return of the saloon. Hoover records in his *Memoirs* that he deplored the compromise on prohibition achieved in the interests of party solidarity. He also averred "nothing could be done about it."

The traditional hypocrisy of drinking politicians defying the law in private while upholding its precepts in public continued during the convention. Delegates made free use of a speakeasy opposite the convention hall. However, a journalist wrote a story about it which embarrassed the municipal authorities. Within the hour prohibition agents raided it. As a matter of common courtesy local police led delegates to other speakeasies nearby.

When the Democrats assembled on June 27 they were especially exuberant. It looked as if they could not lose. The drys were openly derided. A delegate from the Virgin Islands, Judge Lucius J. M. Malmin, walked up to James A. Cannon in a hotel lobby and thrust a bottle of rum into his hands. He had informed the press in advance, and photographers were ready to record the scene. When Cannon rose to address the prohibition subcommittee of the resolutions committee on June 25 Senator Carter Glass left the room as a sign of disapproval. Cannon, amidst booing and cat calls, such as "Your broker wants you," read out a telegram from Arthur Barton that warned that Virginia would vote Republican if the Democrats adopted a wet plank. He reminded delegates how six southern states had voted against Smith in 1928. Pauline Sabin was there, too.

Arguing against her own Republican party's moist platform and emphasizing that she represented 1,010,940 women, she asked Democrats to come out clearly for repeal.

The leading contender for the presidential nomination was Governor Franklin D. Roosevelt of New York. Once assistant secretary of the Navy in Woodrow Wilson's administration, he had run as vice-presidential candidate for the Democrats in 1920. Until then his last name was his passport. In 1921 he became crippled with infantile paralysis. His name thereafter carried him less than his character. He started his political career all over again, serving the Democrats in a variety of ways until he succeeded Al Smith as governor of New York.

Over prohibition Roosevelt made a virtue out of necessity. In his early career as a state senator from upper New York State he was dependent on rural support and therefore obligated to respect rural prejudices. He evaded snares of controversial subjects like woman suffrage and prohibition by advocating local option. But in his youth he voted dry. And in 1913 he reluctantly sponsored a city option bill at the instigation of the Anti-Saloon League. It was aimed against Tammany Hall. Thereafter he equivocated with consummate skill. He dreaded the divisiveness that prohibition could introduce into Democratic politics. But his equivocation recommended him to South and West. He had not, unlike Smith, distinguished himself as their enemy.

As governor of New York Roosevelt, like Smith before him, always had his eye on the main chance. His reforms, agrarian in the north of the state and progressive in the south, were meant to redress rural and urban problems and to advance his presidential candidacy. Roosevelt continued to straddle the issue of prohibition until the summer of 1930. By then the tide of opinion against the Eighteenth Amendment had swelled sufficiently for him to feel confident in taking a stand against it.

On September 9, 1930, Roosevelt sent an open letter to Senator Robert Wagner, who was campaigning for his reelection in New York City. He quoted from a resolution of the American Legion in support of his new, wet stand:

> It is my belief that in the state of New York an overwhelming public opinion is opposed to the Eighteenth Amendment. The crux of the matter is that the Eighteenth Amendment has not furthered the cause of a greater temperance in our population, but on the other it has "fostered excessive drinking of strong intoxicants" and has "led to cor-

ruption and hypocrisy," has brought about "disregard for law and order" and has "flooded the country with untaxed and illicit liquor." I personally share this opinion.

Charles Tuttle, Roosevelt's Republican opponent in the contest for governor in 1930, came out for repeal of the Eighteenth Amendment, a major tactical error. By contrast Roosevelt himself deliberately gave the impression of being drier than his party. He avoided open support of the wet plank adopted at the state convention. Thus dry voters thought he was the last dam against the rising tide of repeal sentiment. Roosevelt retained New York with an increased majority, 725,000 votes, which was twice the majority Al Smith had ever polled.

The only obstacle to Roosevelt's nomination in 1932 was Al Smith, who still coveted the presidency. In public both men maintained a specious pretense of party solidarity. Before the convention Smith had assured Roosevelt's men, Jim Farley and Ed Flynn, sent to sound him out, that "he was completely through with politics and that no one could induce him to enter the political arena again." But he was not only resentful of Roosevelt's success as governor but also embittered by the way Roosevelt struck bargains with his former allies in order to secure the nomination. As H. L. Mencken observed, Smith looked on Roosevelt as a cuckoo who had seized his nest.

Roosevelt had prepared the ground well in advance. When he spoke in the primary campaigns he repeated his formula of the 1930 campaign: repeal of the amendment and return of states' rights on alcohol. Although dry democrats like Cordell Hull of Tennessee and Josephus Daniels, once Roosevelt's superior as secretary of the navy, disliked what Roosevelt was saying, they were reluctant to abandon him over this one issue. The alternative would have been someone like Smith who was also wet and, on other, more urgent matters, as conservative as Hoover. Cordell Hull wrote to Josephus Daniels on February 29, 1932: "I am unable to see what alternative there is except chaos and anarchy." He would work actively for Roosevelt and try and persuade others to do the same. "It is now or never with the Democratic party, and so far I see no feasible or available course open without the serious risk of gravitating in behind the leadership of the DuPont-Raskob-Smith forces."

Smith was so immersed in the world of his nouveaux riches friends that he said prohibition rather than unemployment was the major problem of the depression. Thus on prohibition, depression, and nomination together Roosevelt was able to prove the superiority of his political skill to that of Smith. In March 1931 he treated with dry southerners in the Democratic National Committee in Washington and together they opposed Smith's bloc, which wanted outright repeal of the Eighteenth Amendment. When John J. Raskob tried to persuade southerners on March 5 to accept a resolution preferring states' rights on alcohol to national prohibition he got nowhere. Senator Joseph T. Robinson of Arkansas, Smith's running mate in 1928, was much incensed and retorted, "You cannot write on the banner of the Democratic party . . . the skull and crossbones emblematic of an outlawed trade."

However, at the Chicago convention itself Roosevelt only withdrew his objections to Smith's wet plank about fifteen minutes before Smith spoke. This *volte face* was on account of the overwhelming reception given to an earlier address of Senator Alben W. Barkley of Kentucky calling for repeal. Once repeal was in the platform there was no other reason for nominating Smith, who had lost in 1928.

The Democrats voted for the repeal of prohibition by $934\frac{3}{4}$ votes to $213\frac{1}{4}$. Only delegates from two states, Georgia and Mississippi, voted for its retention. However the South as a whole was split on the issue with 165 votes for repeal and 123 for retention. Ohio, home state of the Anti-Saloon League, voted for repeal by 49 votes to 2. The plank read: "We advocate the repeal of the Eighteenth Amendment. To effect such a repeal we demand that Congress immediately propose a Constitutional Amendment to truly representative conventions of the State called solely for that purpose. We urge the enactment of such measures by the separate states as will actually promote temperance, effectively prevent the saloon, bring the liquor traffic into the open under supervision and control by the State."

The convention held its ballots for the nomination itself on the night of June 30 and July 1. Because of the two thirds rule it seemed that Smith and the old guard could still block Roosevelt's nomination. He gained only $666\frac{1}{4}$ of the 740 votes he needed on the first ballot and by the third had reached only 682. His nomination on the fourth ballot came as a result of the intercession of Joseph P. Kennedy of Boston with William Randolph Hearst. The newspaper magnate effectively controlled the California and Texas delegations, nominally led by William Gibbs McAdoo and John Nance Garner. He was in his mansion at San Simeon, California, and there Kennedy called him by phone. Unless Hearst released the Texas and California votes Roosevelt's nomination would be blocked. It would be the deadlock of 1924 all over again and either Al Smith or Newton D. Baker would claim the prize. Hearst detested Smith for impeding his own political ambitions after the war. He distrusted Baker because he was a champion of the League of Nations, and Hearst was an isolationist.

On July 1 William Gibbs McAdoo, anticipating the withdrawal of Mississippi from Roosevelt's side, announced that California "did not come here to deadlock this convention, or to engage in another desolating contest like that of 1924." He then gave all 44 votes of California to Roosevelt. Thus he was revenged on Smith for being denied the nomination in 1924. Illinois, Indiana, and Maryland came round to Roosevelt. At the end of the fourth ballot he had 945 votes. Only Smith from his hotel remained obdurate and refused to allow his delegates to release their votes to make the nomination unanimous.

As H. L. Mencken explained, the opposition to Roosevelt from Smith helped his cause, for "a majority of the Roosevelt men are really not for Roosevelt at all, but simply against Al Smith. They want to get rid of Al, once and for all time." Moreover, the tension at the convention provoked by Smith over the fight for nomination aided Roosevelt. It assured a lively convention which excited press and public.

Until 1932 it was the custom for nominees to deliver their acceptance speeches weeks later from their homes. This was what Hoover did in Washington on August 11. But Roosevelt broke all precedents. He arranged to fly to Chicago immediately to address the convention that had nominated him. The decision to fly was itself a novelty when commercial flights were infrequent. Roosevelt proved he was good copy across the nation as well as in his state. In his address of July 2 he declared: "I pledge you, I pledge myself, to a new deal for the American people. Let us all here assembled constitute ourselves prophets of a new order of competence and of courage. This is more than a political campaign; it is a call to arms. Give me your help, not to win votes alone, but to win in this crusade to restore America to its own people." The next day a cartoon by Rollin Kirby was reproduced across the country. It showed a farmer looking at an airplane in the sky. The plane bore the inscription "New Deal."

Roosevelt did not repeat Smith's tactical error of 1928 in appointing a parvenu as campaign manager. He replaced John J. Raskob as chairman of the Democratic National Committee with Jim Farley, secretary of the New York Democratic Committee. Farley was an Irish Catholic who had never belonged to Tammany Hall. Unlike Raskob he had the common touch. He neither drank nor smoked. Yet he was a wet and enough of a celebrity in his own right as a salesman of construction materials to advertise Lucky Strike cigarettes for the American Tobacco Company.

Roosevelt's strategy was to concentrate on the West. New York he knew he could hold and the South was not likely to treat him the way it had Al Smith in 1928. In order to entice the farm vote he toured the West and Midwest extensively, securing support from maverick Republicans and old Progressives such as George Norris, Henry A. Wallace, Basil Manly, and Judson King. If the farmers and other people of the West were still dry this would not affect the way they voted. Economic issues had superseded prohibition.

Hoover surprised everyone in his acceptance speech in Washington on August 11, 1932, by turning his back on the "noble experiment." He said that his intentions had been consistent, "clear and need not be misunderstood." But he had actually changed his mind. All the arguments that he had used—in his inaugural address of March 4, 1929 and again to the Wickersham Commission on June 19, 1929—to justify retaining prohibition were now turned upside down. Prohibition had led to "a spread of disrespect not only for this law but for all laws, grave dangers of practical nullification of the Constitution, a degeneration in municipal government and an increase in subsidized crime and violence." At last the president had admitted the breakdown of law and order. Hoover could "not consent to the continuation of this regime." He opposed a return of the "old saloon with its political and social corruption" and proposed resubmission of the question to the states.

Thus both Republican and Democratic platforms gave wets and drys Hobson's choice—no choice at all. As Will Rogers remarked, "Both sides are wet and the poor old dry hasn't got a soul to vote for. He is Roosevelt's 'forgotten man.'" Walter Lippmann thought that any conflict over prohibition in either party amounted to a choice of being misleading or frank. Hoover chose to mislead and was distrusted by both the drys, who suspected he was a deserter, and the wets, who were not sure if he had joined them. Roosevelt told an audience at Sea Girt, New Jersey, on August 27, 1932, that criminals and bootleggers were "in a real sense being supported by the government," which presided over prohibition and its diversion of money into their pockets. The response of the Republican administration had been "words upon words, evasions upon evasions, insincerity upon insincerity, a dense cloud of words." Everyone knew Roosevelt was frank.

The burden of Democratic oratory was that Hoover was responsible for the depression, that he had encouraged speculation and overproduction and then done nothing to alleviate the distress he had caused. At Columbus, Ohio, on August 20 Roosevelt satirized Hoover as the Humpty Dumpty of *Alice Through the Looking Glass.*

> A puzzled, somewhat skeptical Alice asked the Republican leadership some simple questions:
>
> "Will not the printing and selling of more stocks and bonds, the building of new plants and the increase of efficiency produce more goods than we buy?"
>
> "No," shouted Humpty Dumpty. "The more we produce the more we can buy."
>
> "What if we produce a surplus?"
>
> "Oh, we can sell it to foreign consumers."
>
> "How can the foreigners pay for it?"
>
> "Why, we will lend them the money."
>
> "I see," said little Alice, "they will buy our surplus with our money. Of course, these foreigners will pay us back by selling us their goods?"
>
> "Oh, not at all," said Humpty Dumpty. "We set up a high wall called the tariff."
>
> "And," said Alice at last, "how will the foreigners pay off these loans?"
>
> "That is easy," said Humpty Dumpty, "did you ever hear of moratorium?"

Hoover was ideally cast as Humpty Dumpty. He was fat. And when he fell he fell off a wall.

Overtaxed by the chores of administration, Hoover repeated his strategy of 1928—a few major addresses in principal cities in the North and West. Unlike Roosevelt he prepared his own speeches. But they were deadly dull. As H. L. Mencken put it, "If he were to recite the Twenty-third Psalm [he] would make it sound like a search warrant issued under the Volstead Act." His reply to charges of selfishness and incompetence—for instance at St. Paul on November 5—was that the Democrat analysis was a "fantastic fiction." Hoover may or may not have been right. It is a matter of opinion. But he was not believed by those whom he sought to convince. That is a matter of fact.

Prohibition should not have been of paramount importance in the campaign. The fact that it was a major issue illustrates the insidious nature of the fiction that repeal would produce recovery and restore the tawdry affluence of the 1920s. Oddly enough only one of the leading wet organizations entered the campaign in support of Roosevelt, the WONPR. Pauline Sabin's endorsement of Franklin D. Roosevelt on account of his opposition to prohibition led to recriminations from 150 members of the WONPR who resigned. Mrs. Douglas Robinson told the *New York Herald Tribune* of July 17, 1932, that she deplored this fanatical support of the Democrats. Pauline Sabin had replaced the initial slogan, "Patriotism before Party," with a subversive one, "Repeal before Patriotism."

While the country's greatest concern was the deepening depression the Anti-Saloon League mistakenly pursued its single-minded campaign. Faced with the threat of repeal the league had organized a National Board of Strategy in 1931. It began to cooperate with the Prohibition party, the WCTU, and other temperance organizations as if its life depended on it. But it could not sustain the show of unity. The league had always been dependent on the small gifts of people in the lower income groups. Now these folk had nothing to spare.

In the election of November 8 Roosevelt received 22,821,859 votes, 57.4 percent of the total, against Hoover's 15,761,841, 39.7 percent. In the electoral college he had 472 votes to Hoover's 59. He carried all but six states, a larger victory than any Democrat before him.

The election was certainly a defeat for prohibition and a victory for repeal. The Democrats now had majorities of 59 to 37 seats in the Senate and 312 to 123 seats in the House. Henry Joy, the Detroit manufacturer who had changed his mind from dry to wet, told Senator Arthur Vandenberg of Michigan: "Prohibition totally broke the back of the Republican party. If we had had good times my opinion is that the Republican party's attitude on prohibition would have broken its back and thrown it out of office."

After the election wets would settle for nothing less than repeal, by elected state conventions. Before Roosevelt's inauguration Congress set the legislative process in motion. Members of both houses introduced seventy joint resolutions to amend or repeal the Eighteenth Amendment. There were also fifty-six bills to amend or repeal the Volstead Act and thirty-four other bills on liquor and the liquor trade. The general feeling was that prohibition had to be removed before other reforms could be recommended. Wet Republicans supported wet Democrats. Mrs. Florence Kahn, a representative from California, said, "Public questions of great moment, on which the stability of our government depends, are pressing for solution. But around them all we find contained the long tentacles of this Octopus—Prohibition." Repeal was necessarily the first step to raise the depression.

On December 6, 1932, Senator John J. Blaine of Wisconsin introduced S. J. Resolution 211, the repeal of the Eighteenth Amendment. The Committee on the Judiciary reported it back on January 6, 1933, and it was passed on February 16 by 63 votes to 23. On February 20 the House passed it by 289 votes to 121. According to the voting on the Twenty-first amendment the North was overwhelmingly wet; the Midwest was divided between wet cities and dry countryside; the Far West was still predominantly dry, and Kansas was completely (and consistently) so; the South was both dry and wet. But it was in the South that the wets had made their greatest gains: 104 votes in the House and 20 in the Senate favored the Twenty-first amendment compared with only 38 votes in the House and 6 in the Senate against the Eighteenth in 1917.

Moreover, leading wets such as Senators Cope, Edge, Tydings, and Glass no longer opposed the return of the saloon. Representative David I. Walsh of Massachusetts averred that since the speakeasy was worse than the saloon and no prohibitive law had succeeded in eliminating the speakeasy it would be better to legalize saloons than continue to endure illegal bars. The only concession to traditionally dry areas was offered in the second section of the bill: "The transportation or importation into any State, Territory, or possession of the United States for delivery or use therein of intoxicating liquors, in violation of the laws thereof, is prohibited."

States were now invited to hold conventions, specially elected to ratify the Amendment. On April 10, 1933, the first state convention to vote for repeal was held in Michigan at Lansing. Of the one hundred delegates elected to consider ratification of the Twenty-first

Amendment on April 3 only one, Eugene Davenport of Hastings, was a dry. In December Utah became the thirty-sixth state to vote for repeal. Because of a mistaken belief that Maine could beat it in the race to repeal prohibition the Utah convention suppressed all debate. It ordered immediate voting because it wanted to be the state that allowed ratification of the new amendment. The last delegate to cast his vote for ratification was S. R. Thurman of Salt Lake City, who did so on December 5 at 3:32 P.M, Mountain Time. The president of the convention, Ray L. Olsen of Ogden, announced the approval of Utah. The Twenty-first Amendment was law.

However, repeal was not encompassed entirely without fraud. Once electoral malpractices by brewers had been a target of reformers who proposed prohibition. During national prohibition these abuses continued at the behest of gangsters. And some of the old tricks were now used to ensure the election of wet majorities to the state conventions. In Shelby County, part of Memphis, Tennessee, there was a majority of 30,515 votes in favor of repeal at the election to the state convention. Yet only 18,000 people had voted. And not all of them were qualified to do so. In New Jersey ward bosses made sure that in eleven counties there were no dry candidates to oppose wet ones at the election of state delegates. In the election in New York City supervisors declared 482,338 ballots void and said another 367,782 were blank.

It is probably true that President Franklin Roosevelt used his discretion to influence state governors. According to the *Pacific Christian Advocate* of September 14, 1933, the governors of Colorado, Kentucky, and South Dakota were given to understand that their states could expect no relief from federal sources unless they first learned to help themselves by legalizing and taxing beer. The new postmaster general, James A. Farley, toured states urging repeal. He claimed taxes would be raised if repeal failed. The *New York Times* of May 25, 1933, reported his comment that "unless the 18th Amendment is repealed every income tax payer in the country will have to contribute six to ten dollars out of every $100 earned."

It is certainly true that the federal government precipitated repeal by anticipating it. In June 1933 the attorney general, Homer S. Cummings, dismissed thirteen hundred prohibition agents, half the bureau's force. The enforcement appropriation was cut by $5,860,000 from $12,440,000.

On March 13 Roosevelt proposed that Congress modify the Volstead Act to allow the sale of light wines and beer with 3.2 percent of alcohol. Beer became legal under new federal dispensation on April 7, 1933. It was freely consumed on that day in Washington and in nineteen states. It was so scarce in New York that the stock joke was that people longed for prohibition so that they could get a drink.

In Detroit Henry Ford astonished his adversaries and alarmed his allies when he served beer at a lunch to launch his latest model, the V-8.

Roosevelt advised all citizens to buy liquor only from licensed dealers and he asked states to oppose the return of the old saloon. But the campaign for repeal had been predicated on economic recovery. Thus states were more interested in revenue than reform or temperance. Saloons reappeared everywhere, usually under different names such as bars or taverns. The titles were fiction, the function was fact. The National Industrial Recovery Act of June 16, 1933, established a Federal Alcohol Control Administration to regulate the liquor trade. Yet at a time of increased government intervention in industry nothing was done to control or curtail the cupidity of private liquor interests. The whole process of their political infiltration of Congress and state legislatures resumed as if prohibition had never existed. When the New Deal increased income taxes on the rich, the opulent, former opponents of prohibition, transferred their hostility to Roosevelt. Leaders of the now-defunct AAPA formed the American Liberty League in 1934 in a mistaken attempt to encompass his destruction. He was master of the situation, perhaps the only perceptive player in the whole drama of prohibition. The others had been slaves of their pretentions or prejudices, their appetites or avarice; he only of his ambition.

APPENDIXES

APPENDICES

— ONE —

PREY FOR PROGRESS

THERE WERE FOUR SORTS OF ARGUMENTS in favor of prohibition: medical arguments, which appealed to scientists, intellectuals, and humanitarians and which inspired the temperance movement: industrial and economic arguments, which appealed to entrepreneurs, businessmen, and factory owners and which justified prohibition to the nation as a whole; religious arguments, which appealed to evangelists, puritans, and countryfolk; social and political arguments, which appealed to reformers of all sorts.

The first of the statewide prohibition laws was passed by Maine in 1851 at the instigation of Neal Dow. By 1855 twelve more states had adopted prohibition laws: Connecticut, Delaware, Indiana, Iowa, Massachusetts, Michigan, Minnesota, Nebraska, New Hampshire, New York, Rhode Island, Vermont. But then the tide turned. Some laws were found unconstitutional by the courts, some were nullified by subsequent laws, and others were repealed outright. Only Maine adopted statewide prohibition by constitutional statute in 1858 and retained the law.

Three new temperance organizations were the basis of the second prohibition wave: the Prohibition party founded in 1869; the

Women's Christian Temperance Union founded in 1874; and the Anti-Saloon League founded in 1893. Ohio was the center of the second prohibition wave: in the 1880s it had the third largest population of the states.

The nucleus of the Prohibition party was a convention of 500 delegates meeting in Chicago on September 1, 1869, as the Temperance party. It became the Prohibition party on February 22, 1873, at Columbus, Ohio. From the outset the new organization aspired to the status of a third party alongside Republicans and Democrats. It campaigned to get its officers elected to Congress and the state legislatures, even to the presidency, on the basis of a single issue: prohibition. It wanted prohibition adopted by the various states in the form of a constitutional amendment. These prohibitionists were committed to a high ideal. They were not fools and they were not oblivious to the defects of the political system. American government was controlled by party. The dominant party was the one that collected most popular votes. But the public had little control over Congress and the state legislatures once they had been elected.

For a time the Prohibition party was a force to be reckoned with. The total number of votes it collected in the midterm elections of 1886 was 294,863, nearly twice the number its presidential candidate had received in 1884. It was called the Snowball party because it doubled every time it turned over. Such was its influence that in 1886 Congress passed the first distinctive temperance legislation for fifty-two years in a measure by which all federal schools were obliged to teach children the physiological effects of alcohol and narcotics. In 1890 the Prohibition party at last succeeded in getting a candidate elected to Congress, Kittel Halvorsen, an American Scandinavian from Minnesota. He was also a candidate of the Farmers' Alliance there. For the party was sensitive to agrarian issues.

An atmosphere of agrarian discontent against the crass materialism of the Gilded Age that culminated in the Populist movement of the 1890s provided fertile soil for the prohibition movement. The seeds were sown by the Protestant churches. The sort of religion brought to the West and Midwest by Baptist and Methodist, Presbyterian and Congregationalist ministers confirmed doubts and fears. It was based on the Old Testament rather than the New and emphasized toil and tribulation, right and retribution. It complemented a landscape in which soil and stone, downpour and drought were as sharply defined as earth and sky. It did not console.

Willa Cather, the novelist of the Midwest, traced the hold of fundamentalism there back to the bleakness of the landscape itself.

Evangelical revivals in the nineteenth century roused the American Protestant churches to make temperance a major issue. They promoted prohibition, partly because their piety and ascetism emphasized private morality and abstinence from worldly pleasures such as alcohol. But, even more important, evangelical emphasis on personal conversion as the crux of religious experience made the converted intolerant of anything that interfered with the experience.

In the early twentieth century religious revival movements were synonymous with temperance reform. The most famous revivalist was Billy A. Sunday, and he and the others, the Reverend R. A. Torrey and the Reverend J. Wilbur Chapman, W. J. Dawson and Rodney ("Gypsy") Smith, all argued for social reform as well as individual conversion, and this included prohibition. The *Literary Digest* of February 20, 1915, reported how two successive crowds of fifteen thousand heard Billy Sunday's "booze sermon" and promised to vote for prohibition.

After the collapse of the Populist revolt prohibition was also taken up by the country because it was a guarantee of preservation from the contamination of the city. Purley A. Baker of the Anti-Saloon League argued for the countryside this way in *The Anti-Saloon League Yearbook* of 1914: "The vices of the cities have been the undoing of past empires and civilizations. It has been at the point where the urban population outnumbers the rural people that wrecked republics have gone down. There the vices of luxury have centered and eaten out the heart of the patriotism of the people."

Many reformers, however, disapproved of the Prohibition party's pursuit of third-party status. In 1890 representatives of more than a hundred temperance societies convened a National Temperance Congress in New York City. The following year they met at Saratoga Springs and passed a resolution urging their societies to seek unity in an affiliation of local leagues. Three alliances ere formed in 1893: the Christian Temperance Alliance of Pennsylvania on April 4; the Anti-Saloon League of the District of Columbia on June 23; and the Ohio Anti-Saloon League, founded in Oberlin on September 5. The last of these was by far the most influential. But it was the Anti-Saloon League of the District of Columbia that organized a national convention in Washington. On December 17, 1895, 161 delegates from 47 organizations met in the Sunday School of the Calvary Baptist Church. They chose a motto, "The saloon must go," and on December 18 constituted themselves the American Anti-Saloon League. The league's very title was ingenious, inviting to people who detested the saloon and the social evils it maintained but were not prohibitionist. After all, closing the saloon was a very different matter from banning liquor. By 1897 there were 161 affiliated organizations and state leagues in California, Iowa, Michigan, Ohio, Pennsylvania, South Dakota, Tennessee, Virginia, and West Virginia. By 1899 state leagues had been instituted in twenty-one states or territories.

Under one superintendent, the Reverend Purley A. Baker, the league widened the scope of its activities, not only establishing new branches but also going into print. From 1907 the Ohio journal of the league, the *American Issue*, became its national newspaper. In October 1909 the first permanent temperance press of the United States, the American Issue Publishing Company, was established under Ernest H. Cherrington at Westerville, Ohio. By 1912 it was producing about forty tons of literature a month and the *American Issue* was being published in thirty-one different state editions. By 1919 its total circulation was 16 million. With this development Baker increased his staff from three hundred in 1903 to fifteen hundred by 1915.

━━━━━◄◆►━━━━━

The saloon became the focal point of prohibition reform for two reasons. First, it was the common ground of the liquor trade that supplied it and the lower classes who frequented it. Second, it was an obvious center of the community, not an abstract symbol of the trusts but an actual place where corruption festered.

Before 1900 prohibitionists experimented with three devices to stop people getting a drink in saloons: high license fees, the dispensary system, and local option. In each case the specific target was the saloon and not the alcohol it sold. The Anti-Saloon League concentrated on local option and the national Prohibition party on state and national prohibition.

Local option was the method by which individual political divisions such as wards or precincts of towns and cities were empowered to grant or withhold licenses to sell alcohol. When the territory included a whole county the term was "county option." Generally the system of voting varied, either every two or four years after dry local option had been adopted or when a petition requesting an election was signed by a certain proportion of voters. Local or county option laws were first enacted in parts of Illinois (1874 and 1881), Kentucky (1874), Michigan (1877 and 1888), Virginia (1883), Maryland (1884), Georgia (1885), Mississippi (1886), and Missouri (1887).

The Prohibition party eventually recognized that local option did not work if the intention really was to prohibit alcohol. Dry districts never spent money on responsible enforcement and illicit bars flourished. This was called "letting the drys have their law but the wets their liquor." The liquor trade treated it as a threat and concentrated its interests in gaining control of towns and cities where profits were most sure.

But local option did establish prohibition in a number of northern cities. In 1907, 199 saloons were closed in Chicago by the local action of voters in 160 precincts. In 1908 Worcester, Massachusetts, adopted local option prohibition and was followed by seventeen other cities in the state including Haverhill and Lynn, and eight suburbs of Boston, including Brookline and Cambridge. Unlike the Prohibition party the Anti-Saloon League preferred prohibition by local option. By stirring up local debate it educated the public and discredited the saloon. It also trained local officers and enabled them to build up their forces in towns and villages where they would encounter least opposition. By abjuring the Prohibition party's quest for status the leaders of the league were attaining its ultimate aims. They were welding disparate social elements into an effective political machine.

———◆———

For the temperance movement the barrier between successes on the local level and those on the national level was broken by the war of 1898. By mischance imperialism injected prohibition into federal politics.

The sale of liquor in army canteens or post exchanges was authorized by the secretary of war, William C. Endicott, in 1889. By 1898 canteens were notorious among prohibitionists as a cause of crime, drunkenness, and disease. In the Spanish-American War only a few soldiers were killed in battle; many died in the camps. When fever carried off men in Cuba it was believed that the first to go were heavy drinkers. Because of public indignation, effectively channeled by prohibition organizations, Congress passed an anti-canteen law. But the brewers were not to be cheated of their army profits. Louis Schade, editor of a Washington liquor paper, the *Sentinel*, found a way round the law. The act forbade soldiers to sell liquor; it did not forbid the army from hiring nonmilitary personnel to sell liquor to soldiers. Both the secretary of war, Russell A. Alger, and the attorney general, John W. Griggs, accepted this sophistry. Civilian bartenders were hired and the law was openly flouted.

Prohibitionists also deplored the fact that the Spanish-American War of 1898 led to a rapid overseas development of the liquor trade. When George Dewey took possession of Manila in the Philippines on August 13, 1898, there were only three saloons there. Within a few months there were three hundred. Whereas the exportation of alcohol to the Philippines was worth $337 in 1898, by 1900 it was worth $467,198. Before the war export of liquor to Cuba was worth $30,000; by 1899 it was worth $629,855. The social consequences of distributing alcohol on an unprecedented scale to these lands disturbed even the United States government. The president of the first Philippine commission agreed with prohibitionist sentiment in his admission that "it was unfortunate that we introduced and established the saloon there to corrupt the natives and to exhibit the vices of our race."

In 1899 the Anti-Saloon League opened its first "legislative," or lobby, office in Washington and appointed the Reverend Edwin C. Dinwiddie national superintendent. One of his first objectives was to reverse the miscarriage of justice in respect of army canteens. The league was strengthening its political pull by exercise. In 1901 Congress passed the second anti-canteen law, this time prohibiting the sale of alcohol on army premises. In 1902 it passed a bill forbidding the sale of alcohol, opium, and firearms to natives on some Pacific islands and in 1903 it forbade the sale of alcohol at immigration stations and in or around the Capitol building.

In the past reform movements had had an impact on local politics, even flourished for a time, but then collapsed. Between state and federal politics was a chasm most could not cross. But the energy generated by progressivism in local politics proved its sustaining power. When Robert M. La Follette of Wisconsin campaigned for the direct primary and took the governorship from the Republican machine he created his own progressive machine. Under his initiative the monopolies to which rank and file progressives objected most—railroads and public utilities—were regulated. Reforms that were successful in one state were tried elsewhere. Albert Baird Cummins in Iowa, James K. Bardaman of Mississippi, Hazen Pingree of Michigan, Charles A. Culberson of Texas, Joseph W. Folk of Missouri, W. R. Stubbs of Kansas, Jeff Davis of Arkansas, Hiram Johnson of California, and "Alfalfa Bill" Murray of Oklahoma were all reform governors on the same lines as La Follette.

The progressive movement became more radical as time went on. The presidency of Theodore Roosevelt from 1901 to 1909 created a social appetite for reform and a political climate in which it could be accomplished. The importance of Roosevelt was the same as that of John Kennedy sixty years later, not so much in what he did as what he made possible. The seminal act was his successful prosecution of one trust, the Northern Securities Company, between 1902 and 1904. Three articles by Ida Tarbell, Lincoln Steffens, and Ray Stannard Baker in a single issue of *McClure's Magazine* in 1903 exposed the malpractices of monopolies. They caused a sensation and led to a journalists' movement described as "muckraking" by Theodore Roosevelt in 1906. In this context the relationship between alcohol and society was an inevitable subject. The seminal muckraking article in a whole series on the ill effects of that relationship was by Dr. Henry Smith Williams in *McClure's Magazine* for October 1908.

The impact of prohibition thinking on progressive reforms was becoming clearer. Even the Pure Food and Drug Act of 1906 was a temperance measure. It required all patent medicines shipped in interstate commerce to bear labels with accurate descriptions of the alcohol, morphine, and other drugs they contained. It also required whiskey bottles to be marked to show whether they contained straight whiskey (distilled from a mash of grain and matured in charred oak barrels), rectified whiskey (neutral spirits distilled from a mash of grain and artificially flavored and colored), or blended whiskey (a mixture of straight and rectified whiskey). In 1908 Congress prohibited the shipment of liquor by mail. In 1909 it prohibited the shipment of liquor in interstate commerce by COD and to fictitious recipients, and required all packages of liquor to be clearly marked as to contents, quantity and addressee.

Was the prohibition movement, therefore, part and parcel of the progressive movement? James H. Timberlake in *Prohibition and the Progressive Movement 1900–1920* (1963) and Andrew Sinclair in *Prohibition, the Era of Excess* (1962), among others, indicate that it was. Their arguments that prohibition was one form of progressive reform aimed at efficiency and good health in the name of humanitarianism and social welfare are unassailable. But if the connection between prohibitionists and progressives is considered closely it seems tenuous rather than true. It is insufficient to argue that some progressives were prohibitionists and some were not, or that prohibition was a divisive issue among the progressives in the same way that American intervention in the First World War was to become. The crux of the matter is that the prohibition movement did not declare its national aim officially until 1913. Various temperance measures had widespread support among progressives while the central aim was the abolition of corrupt saloons. With that many would concur. For what aroused hostility from all sorts of people who would otherwise have been uninterested in temperance reform was the liquor industry's arrogance and ruthlessness, its gross corruption in pursuit of political control.

It is not possible to draw up a historical equation with Populist, progressive, medical, social, industrial, and religious arguments on one side combining together to make national prohibition on the other. Prohibition was not accomplished by an accumulation of grievances. There was plenty of division among the ranks of people opposed to monopolies and interested in social reform. Certain elements were more important than others. Though medical and social reasons suggest industrial and economic reasons for prohibition, they did not prove their case to all businessmen nor to most union leaders. Many businessmen opposed prohibition. They argued that it would destroy the liquor industry and hence cause massive unemployment, and that it would set a precedent for government regulation of the economy and interference and thus constraint on their own political power.

Sobriety was as important to the artisan at work as to his boss, and for the same reasons. A sober work force was also one free of the city machine. But while it was in their interests to promote temperance, and big unions like the American Federation of Labor and its officials, Samuel Gompers, John B. Lennon, John Mitchell, and James Duram knew it, they kept prohibition out of official discussion until 1919. Prohibition was divisive. Workers needed relief and relaxation quite as much as other people. Saloons provided it. Morever, certain liquors were part of the cultural tradition of some ethnic groups. And the liquor industry employed thousands. Not surprisingly, in its convention at Atlantic City 81 percent of AFL delegates opposed prohibition on June 11, 1919.

— TWO —

PROHIBITION, THE PROOF

Prohibition was the most avidly discussed issue in American society during the twenties, a subject of far more interest than foreign affairs or party politics and indissoluble from fashion, entertainment, and crime. What, when, why, and how people drank were questions affording limitless speculation.

Speculation about the effects of prohibition was nothing in itself, but doubts and misgivings led to inquiries and inquiries led to proof. Both wets and drys turned to statistical evidence as proof of the truth of their different tales. The evidence itself was confused and contradictory and was used to suit the teller. Mark Twain supposedly observed that there were three sorts of lies—lies, damned lies, and statistics. And this was certainly true of statistics about American prohibition. At best, thought was inductive. For, as the historian, Herbert Asbury, puts it, "The drys lied to make prohibition look good; the wets lied to make it look bad; the government officials lied to make themselves look good and to frighten Congress into giving them more money to spend; and the politicians lied through force of habit."

PROHIBITION

All statistical arguments involved comparisons of the situation before and after national prohibition took effect. But the period just before prohibition was the period of American intervention in the war. Thus statistics for the period from summer 1917 to fall 1919, some of which are superficially favorable to the prohibition movement, have no fundamental significance. Many people were in the armed forces or directly involved in the war effort apart from the civilian and working population. Because of its great patriotic fervor the public supported increased government restriction of alcohol and tolerated some form of prohibition. There was considerable wartime prosperity. These three factors affected the production and consumption of alcohol, the rates of mortality, and the social and industrial welfare of the nation in the period of American intervention. In addition many of the states—twenty-six—had already adopted some form of prohibition. Thus the period of the war cannot be truly considered one before prohibition. The years before 1910 when only eight states had adopted prohibition set the standard of America before national prohibition. However, any study of this period has to take account of the overwhelming impact of mass immigration at the turn of the century upon a situation of increasing statewide prohibition, a situation that differed from year to year. In other words, although comparisons can be made between the different figures available before and after 1920, they must be made without the benefit of a standard or norm.

Claims and counterclaims about good and ill consequences of the Eighteenth Amendment and Volstead Act depended on assumptions about their prohibitive effects. Was alcohol prohibited? Few wets agreed with dry evidence that the amount of liquor people drank decreased substantially in the period 1911 to 1914 the amount was 1.69 gallons per head; in the period of wartime restrictions, 1918 to 1919, the amount decreased to .97. At the onset of national prohibition, 1921 to 1922, there was a further decrease to .73 of a gallon. Only in the later years, from 1927 to 1930, did the amount rise again to 1.14 gallons. These are the figures of Clark Warburton writing for volume twelve of the *Encyclopaedia of Social Sciences* and, if anything, they are probably generous estimates.

However, in 1926 the Association Against the Prohibition Amendment published its own *Criticism of National Prohibition*. It estimated that there had been a significant increase in alcoholic consumption since prohibition:

PROHIBITION, THE PROOF

WHAT AMERICANS DRANK, 1910–1917

	GALLONS AVERAGE PER YEAR	PRICE PER GALLON	ESTIMATED RETAIL COST
Spirits	142,121,000	$5	$710,605,000
Wines	56,316,000	$4	$226,064,000
Beers, Ale, (etc.)	1,924,552,000	$1	$1,924,552,000
Total	2,122,989,000		$2,861,221,000

A GUESS AT WHAT AMERICANS DRINK NOW, 1926

	GALLONS PER YEAR	PRICE PER GALLON	RETAIL COST
Spirits: From industrial alcohol	105,000,000	$20	$2,100,000,000
Smuggled whiskey	1,660,000	$24	$40,000,000
Moonshine	178,540,000	$4	$714,160,000
	285,206,000		$2,854,160,000
Homemade wine	75,000,000	$4	$300,000,000

This assessment is the one that has taken hold of public imagination ever since. It is, however, possible that law enforcement was more effective initially and that generalizations about the whole period of prohibition have been made on the available statistics of the last years (1926–1933) when alcohol was more readily obtainable.

But how much alcohol and what sort people were drinking were less controversial subjects than who was drinking and where. Chester Powell, a member of the Anti-Saloon League and editor of a Californian paper, confidently reaffirmed the dry argument that alcohol impeded the assimilation of immigrants and that prohibition would reduce ethnic tensions.

As Charles Merz has shown, the truth was rather different from the half truth concealing it. The notion that the rural West and South, composed of Americans with families going back many generations, had agreed about prohibition in some sort of collective spirit was myth. For the West and the South had always shown some doubt, distrust, and dislike of it. For instance, in the eleven states of the West and South that had adopted prohibition by popular referendum during the First World War but before American intervention 44 percent of the poll opposed prohibition.

Lawson Purdy, chief executive of the New York Charity Organization, examined the report of the International Revenue Service for the fiscal year ending 1924 and discovered there was less difference across the United States as a whole or between town and country as far as law observance was concerned than might have been supposed. He examined New York, New Jersey, and Pennsylvania (which had never adopted statewide prohibition) and Georgia (which had done so in 1907) and South Carolina (which had done so in 1915). These five states contained almost a quarter of the total population, the three northeastern states with 22,250,000 (about 21 percent of the whole) and the two southern states with 4,570,000 (about 5 percent of the whole).

It might be assumed that the amount of property such as stills used to violate the Volstead Act and seized in the northern states would be greater than those in the South. This was the reverse of the truth, as the table of seized property indicates:

	NORTHERN STATES	SOUTHERN STATES
Distilleries	439	2,248
Stills	794	2,612
Still-worms	665	1,097
Fermenters	1,146	29,868

It was only the value of property seized in the North that was greater, $3,356,000 as opposed to $853,000 in the South. And it is this statistic that shows that North and South were truly comparable, for the value of property seized in the North was 80 percent of the total for these five states as against 83 percent of their total population. And the value of property seized in the South was 20 percent of the total as against 17 percent of the population. The number of people arrested was in the same proportions—13,602 for the northern states and 3,496 for the Southern states.

What happened in the Northwest confirms nullification of prohibition in the rural areas. The Seventeenth Prohibition District comprised Alaska, Idaho, Montana, Oregon, and Washington State with a population of 3,173,000, about one seventh of the population of New York, New Jersey, and Pennsylvania. In these predominantly rural states 216 distilleries were seized, compared with 439 in the northeastern states and 685 stills, almost as many as 794 for the northeastern states, which had a population seven times larger. Moreover, 548 stillworms and 2,552 fermenters were seized in the Seventeenth Prohibition District, twice as many as in New York, New Jersey, and Pennsylvania.

Whether states had previously been wet or dry, deaths from alcoholism increased after the adoption of national prohibition—the highest increase in the death rate occurred in Wyoming, which had in the past consistently voted dry. Between 1922 and 1926 the death rate there from alcoholism and cirrhosis of the liver had risen by 200 percent to 8.9 for every 100,000 people. In the United States as a whole deaths from alcoholism declined between 1914 and January 1920 until the rate was 1 per 100,000. By 1926 there were 3.9 deaths per 100,000, almost four times as many. In 1920 the rate of deaths from cirrhosis of the liver was 6.2 per 100,000; by 1926 it was 7.3.

However, if the general pattern was an increase in the alcoholic death rate, in cities the specific pattern was a decrease. It could be argued that prohibition at the outset dried up the cities more than might have been thought possible and that this contributed to increased expectation of life. In nineteen cities with a population of 300,000 or more the reported deaths from alcoholism fell from 1,954 in 1916 to 321 in 1920, a decrease of 83 percent. In New York City deaths from alcoholism fell from 687 in 1916 to 98 in 1920. The Metropolitan Life Insurance Company recorded that deaths from alcoholism fell from an average of 4.9 per 100,000 policyholders in the years from 1911 to 1916 to .6 in 1920. But in the course of the twenties the death rate rose once again. Dr. Charles Norris, chief medical examiner of New York City, reported to the mayor in 1927 that deaths from alcoholism increased there from 621 in 1910 to 741 in 1926.

But under prohibition alcohol was responsible for more deaths than those of alcoholics. The Metropolitan Life Insurance Company reported in its bulletin of March 1927 that the number of deaths caused by alcoholic poisoning was understated. The increase in the general death rate was not on account of increased consumption of hard liquor since prohibition but the greater toxicity of the alcohol being drunk.

Statistics on the general death rate vary. But they agree that there was a pronounced decline in the second and third decades of the century. The fall was, according to the widest divergences, from either 13.84 or 14.6 per thousand people in the years from 1912 to 1916 to either 12.12 or 12.7 from 1920 to 1924. Although Wayne B. Wheeler told the *New York Times* of November 27, 1924, that "the saving of human life since prohibition reduced the death rate is equivalent to a million lives," this decrease was almost certainly attributable to other factors: improved standards of hygiene and hospital care; increased vigilance by schools and insurance companies; the new vaccines and serums used in medicine. Opponents of prohibition pointed out that the death rate had also fallen in European countries, which had not adopted prohibition.

The evidence on crime and its relation to liquor and prohibition is extensive. But like evidence on the actual consumption of alcohol it is contradictory. When Andrew Volstead spoke at the International Anti-Alcohol Congress in Copenhagen in August 22, 1923, he said national prohibition in the United States had brought about a 20 percent reduction in the rate of crime. Yet the Committee of Eleven, an organization of civic and religious bodies concerned with social problems in Detroit, criticized a survey by the Methodist Episcopal Church attributing supposed social improvements to prohibition. A group of businessmen led by Robert Croul, a former police commissioner, argued further that crimes of violence associated with drinking had not decreased but, rather, increased under prohibition.

The Bureau of the Census showed in 1929 that the number of prisoners in federal and state prisons and reformatories had risen quite out of proportion to the increases in population and was continuing to rise. In 1910 it was 32.3 per 100,000; by 1923 it was 34.6; and by 1926 it was 41.8. Prohibitionists argued that the rise was on account of social dislocation following the war—as had happened elsewhere—while opponents of the law said prohibition had dispersed criminal activities. In addition citizens were categorized as criminals for making, distributing, and selling alcohol.

Although it was a preventive measure, prohibition had not been conceived as a punitive one by progressive reformers but a means of liberating people and making them more productive. Drys favored prohibition for the positive achievements it would provide as well as the negative effects of alcohol it would prevent.

Obsession with efficiency was at its height in the war. Less obviously, after the war was over the obsession was applied only to alcohol. In 1919 Professor Irving Fisher of Yale said that by enforcing prohibition the United States could increase its productivity by another 10 or even 20 percent and add $7.5 or even $15 billion worth of manufactured goods each year. There was a brief recession after the war from 1919 to 1921, but between 1922 and 1929 there was uninterrupted and increasing economic progress. Industrial production rose by about a half and wages by a third. Corporate profits rose by 76 percent and dividends by 108 percent. Between 1920 and 1930 building and loan assets increased by $6 billion, twenty-one times as fast as the population. The money invested in life insurance policies rose from $35 billon to $78 billion dollars, eight times as fast as the population.

Dr. Leigh Colvin, historian of the Prohibition party, explained all this in 1926 as a direct result of prohibition. However, a report of the Federal Council of the Churches of Christ in America of September 1925 was not so simplistic: "The virtual stoppage of beer drinking alone on the part of millions of workingmen might be assumed, even without any considerable evidence, to have had profound effect on the economic status of their families. At the same time the appeal to specific economic data—increased business activity, growing bank deposits, etc.—to prove the effects of prohibition must be made very guardedly. All attempts to measure this increase in quantitative terms are fraught with danger because of the great increase in prosperity since 1921, due to other causes."

And deposits reported by the American Bankers' Association support this view. They show a continuous progress from 1918, before national prohibition. Moreover, from 1920 wages began to rise. Wage earners were urged to save by thrift campaigns promoted by banks. In the brief recession of 1919 to 1921 people were reluctant to buy securities on a falling market. They preferred to put money in banks, and the release of savings when the Library Loan campaigns ended and the increase in the money supply allowed them to do so.

But the new wealth was not spread evenly throughout society. America was not poor as a nation. But many of its citizens were poor and some were dispossessed. The war had accelerated social and economic ferment under a surface of political unity. The top 1 percent gained about 15 percent of all earned incomes in 1920 and in 1929 the top 5 percent enjoyed a third of all personal incomes. Robert and Helen Lynd discovered in their study of Muncie, Indiana, published as *Middletown* (1929), that although the industrial artisan could usually find work, there were still slumps in the business cycle and then times were hard. Of 165 working-class families the Lynds studied in 1924, 38 percent were always in work, 19 percent lost less than a month's work, and pay, and 43 percent lost more than a month. One of the causes of the Wall Street crash of 1929 was that production exceeded consumption. Thus if people put their savings in banks their money was useless in the economy as a whole. If they invested it in stocks and shares they contributed to another cause of the crash, accelerating speculation, and actually harmed the economy. It was improvident of prohibitionists to claim their reform had produced economic growth: after 1929 they would certainly be blamed for their concomitant part in the crash. If prohibition really had produced the boom of the 1920s and, thence, the crash, then the opprobrium meted out to the drys was deserved.

─TIRREE─

CANADA DRY

WHILE THE UNITED STATES DISCUSSED and enacted national prohibition the Dominion of Canada established its different system of prohibition throughout its nine provinces.

Before 1864 there were no liquor laws in Canada except for those about revenue. In that year the Dunkin Act, passed in the United Province of Canada (later Ontario and Quebec), enabled any county or municipality to prohibit the retail sale of liquor by majority vote. In 1878 this law was superseded by the Canada Temperance Act, or Scott Act, of the Dominion Government (established in 1867). This provided for local option by popular vote in any city or county on presentation of a petition by 25 percent of the electors. As a result local option was adopted throughout the Maritime Provinces. Prince Edward Island was completely dry, and Nova Scotia almost so by the early twentieth century.

In the other provinces, especially Ontario and Quebec, the Scott Act was unpopular more because they were trying to assert their provincial independence from the central government than because they opposed prohibition in itself. Thus local option was developed in a series of provincial statutes. Between 1893 and 1914 local option was adopted in so many country districts and small towns that in the rural areas of Ontario and Quebec and the west licensed hotels (Canada did not have saloons) almost disappeared. The retail sale of liquor was restricted to the cities and larger towns. The New Brunswick provincial assembly adopted a resolution in favor of national prohibition and a nationwide plebiscite was held in 1898 with 278,380 for, and 264,693 against. Although the majority was in some places 78 percent and never less than 63 in others, the government thought the vote was not decisive enough to warrant statutory prohibition. The plebiscite was only advisory and the provincial governments were fully aware of the difficulties of local enforcement when only the Dominion could control the manufacture of alcohol and its commerce between the provinces.

During the First World War, while national prohibition in the United States was being widely debated, approved, and enacted, Canada experimented with prohibition in every province except Quebec, where spirits only were prohibited. As was the case in the United States patriotism was able to achieve what prohibitionists had failed to do. Prince Edward Island had already adopted prohibition. In 1916 and 1917 seven of the nine provinces prohibited the sale of alcoholic beverages. In 1919 Quebec, which had shown the most staunch opposition to prohibition in the plebiscite of 1898, prohibited spirits. And in 1919 the Dominion government agreed to prohibit the importation of liquor into provinces that had prohibited its sale provided the provincial assembly voted in favor.

During the period of national prohibition in the United States eight of the nine Canadian provinces experimented with government control and sale under various commissions and boards. The progress to provincial prohibition had been proposed on the understanding that after the war there would be another popular vote. In fact no proposal was made for a return to the system of licensed hotels but plebiscites were taken to determine the actual form of prohibition. In 1920 and 1921 Quebec and British Columbia adopted government sale and control and the other seven provinces voted to sustain prohibition. However, in the course of the twenties they modified it and inaugurated a system of government sale and control. Manitoba did so in 1923, Alberta and Saskatchewan in 1924, Ontario in 1927, New Brunswick in 1927 and Nova Scotia in 1930. Only Prince Edward Island sustained prohibition.

These provinces established control boards or commissions of from one to five members of which only the chairman worked full time. They were responsible to different branches of government in the different provinces. In Saskatchewan and British Columbia they were responsible to the legislature, in Quebec to the provincial treasurer, and in the other five provinces to the executive, specifically the attorney general.

The innovative intention behind the control system was the replacement of government regulation for competitive, commercial distribution, on the supposition that the government was not out to make a profit but to eliminate abuse. The commission established stores that did not display their goods or advertise them. Legal and discretionary limits were placed on the amount of alcohol customers could buy. Prohibitionists thus insisted there was no inducement on people to buy.

Gross sales of alcohol were only $37 million in 1922 (when only Quebec and British Columbia had adopted the system). They were as high as $150,969,000 in 1929 (when five other provinces had adopted the system). By 1931 they had fallen to $130,802,000 on account of the depression (with eight provinces using the system). Thus legal sales of alcohol amounted to about fifteen dollars per head in 1929 and about thirteen dollars in 1931. The revenue obtained by the provincial governments on sales, permit, and license fees and taxes on beer was respectively $6 million and $33 million in 1929. The revenue obtained by the Dominion government from excise and customs duties and taxes was $10 million in 1919 and $59,595,000 in the fiscal year ending March 31, 1929, a seventh of its total revenue.

In 1922, 2,040,514 gallons of spirits were consumed, and this amount rose steadily after 1925 to 3,130,119 gallons in 1929. The lowest per capita consumption was 0.203 gallon in 1923 and the highest 0.425 gallon in 1928, an increase of 108 percent. In 1922 the consumption of malt liquors was 35,422,481 gallons, which rose to 61,868,349 gallons in 1929. The lowest per capita consumption was 4.048 gallons in 1921 and the highest 6.07 gallons in 1938, an increase of 50 percent. The consumption of wine rose from 803,027 gallons in 1922 to 5,450,642 gallons in 1929. The per capita consumption was lowest in 1919 with 0.152 gallon and highest in 1928 with 0.679 gallon, an increase of 346 percent.

The number of deaths from alcoholism rose from 0.12 percent of the population in 1921 to 0.32 percent of the population of all the provinces in 1928 except Quebec, which had a different system and allowed beer and wine.

PROHIBITION

Statistics in Canada indicate that an increase in immoderate drinking, following the spread of control, was partly responsible for an increase in serious crimes. In 1922 there were 15,720 convictions for indictable offences and in 1928 21,720 convictions, an increase of 38 percent and more than three times the increase in the population. The authorities tried to ascertain the amount of liquor drunk by criminals and did so for about half of the prisoners in jail. In the period from 1922 to 1928 the number of criminals who were moderate drinkers increased at the same rate as the total number of convictions. But the number of criminals who were immoderate drinkers increased by 64 percent, or nearly twice as fast.

Convictions for drunken driving rose from 202 in 1922 to 1,322 in 1928. This was an increase of 554 percent in six years during which the number of cars on the roads only doubled.

SOURCES

THE STORY OF PROHIBITION has been essayed by many authors in different ways. The accounts that have held their own over the years are the contemporary ones. Charles Merz, *The Dry Decade* (1931), was the first to probe the factors governing the introduction of prohibition and those leading to its disruption by analyzing available statistics on Congress, statewide prohibition, electoral apportionment, and the Prohibition Unit and Bureau. On these subjects the book is definitive. D. Leigh Colvin, *Prohibition in the United States* (1926), a partisan history of the Prohibition party, contains much useful information not available elsewhere. It is especially valuable for its analysis of the relationship between politics and the liquor interests in the Gilded Age, prohibition and imperialism at the turn of the century, and the antipathy between the Anti-Saloon League and the Prohibition party.

Andrew Sinclair's *Prohibition: The Era of Excess* (1962) was the most comprehensive history of prohibition to the date of its publication. Its distinctive contributions to knowledge were a literary investigation of the sort of culture that could inspire the prohibition movement and an examination of the motives of leading politicians who sustained it. Over a third of the text is devoted to the period before 1920. Much less was known about the world of organized crime when Andrew Sinclair prepared his text and consequently there is comparatively little on that subject. But the masterly notes make the book an indispensable reference point for all students of the period.

James H. Timberlake's *Prohibition and the Progressive Movement 1900-1920* (1963) is a closely argued account of the place of prohibition in the movement for social and political reform which began in the nineteenth century and culminated in the administrations of Theodore Roosevelt and Woodrow Wilson. The relationship between prohibition and the progressive movement is illustrated in a series of literary conceits—surveys of the various medical, political, economic, and social arguments for temperance reform. The revisionist school of thought that insists prohibition was a reform rather than an experiment is exemplified by J. C. Burnham in "New Perspectives on the Prohibition 'Experiment' of the 1920's," *Journal of Social History* (Fall, 1968). Although many of the individual points made by Professor Burnham are beyond reproach I do not share his belief in the beneficence of prohibition and he attributes to Andrew Sinclair an opinion on the legalization of beer and light wines which may surprise readers of *Prohibition: The Era of Excess.*

The most diverting of contemporary writers among the wets are H. L. Mencken, Clarence Darrow, Robert Binkley, Walter Lippmann, and Will Rogers and, for reasons which they might not appreciate, among the drys, Irving Fisher and Mabel Walker Willebrandt. Although the partisan interpretations of the effects of prohibition published by the Association Against the Prohibition Amendment and the Anti-Saloon League contain much useful information, readers seeking a more objective approach are advised to consult a whole series of articles of the *Annals of the American Academy of Political and Social Science*, especially the issue of September 1932, which is devoted to the subject.

The final report of the Wickersham Commission—the National Commission on Law Observance and Enforcement—published in five volumes with a summary in 1931 is not to be disparaged. It and the evidence presented to the commission still constitute the most comprehensive collection of material on prohibition. The files of the Wickersham Commission are held in the Washington National Records Center, Suitland, Maryland, and extend to some 110 feet in length. Surprisingly after the passage of half a century, they are still checked by staff before being cleared for students' research. The opinions of lawyers and judges writing to the commission are especially interesting, and, for the most part, telling against the argument that prohibition constituted a beneficent reform. The various congressional subcommittees on different aspects of prohibition are reported in *Congressional Record.* They reveal more about politicians and their motives than the topics under review and, for this, extend our knowledge of the whole subject.

Of the many accounts of prohibition and individual states the most successful are those that relate the experience of one state to the issues confronting the whole country: Gilman Ostrander, *The Prohibition Movement in California, 1848–1933* (1957) and Larry Engelmann, *Intemperance: The Lost War Against Liquor* (1979), about prohibition in Michigan.

Thomas M. Coffey's *The Long Thirst* (1975) is an anecdotal history of prohibition. And the anecdotes are telling—prohibition as experienced by its principal protagonists. Each of the biographies of the principal prohibitionists, Justin Steuart, *Wayne Wheeler: Dry Boss* (1928), and Virginius Dabeny, *Dry Messiah: The Life of Bishop Cannon* (1949), is not only revelatory of both interested and impartial motives in its subject but also invaluable for anyone looking for the flesh as well as the bones of the prohibition movement.

Most political memoirs and biographies give scant attention to prohibition, which is seen as a comparatively minor political inconvenience to pursuit of a successful career. However, all the biographies of Al Smith emphasize the subject. Those by Oscar Handlin (1958) and Matthew and Hanna Josephson (1969) are especially revelatory as are two accounts of the campaign of 1928: Edmund A. Moore, *A Catholic Runs for President* (1956), and Ruth C. Silva, *Rum, Religion and Votes* (1962). Of the accounts of Franklin Roosevelt's rise the most thorough on the subject of prohibition is by Frank Freidel in volumes two and three of his excellent biography, *Franklin D. Roosevelt* (1954 and 1956). H. L. Mencken, *Making a President* (1932) is illuminating on the Chicago conventions of 1932. Mencken's mistaken assumption that thirst rather than hunger was the central problem of America in the early thirties is not, of course, a liability in his treatment of the campaign of that year.

The relationship between organized crime and prohibition is less well documented than any other aspect of prohibition. At a time when police records on prohibition are no longer available for cities like New York and New Orleans the archives held by the Chicago Crime Commission are especially valuable. My conclusions about Chicago and prohibition are based almost entirely on research carried out in the Chicago Crime Commission. In support John Kobler's *Capone* (1971) is a thorough and witty biography of a most famous gangster about whom there are dozens of articles. But for the development of syndicated crime students must refer to various articles in the *Annals of the American Academy*, especially pieces by Henry Barrett Chamberlin, John Landesco, and Mark Haller as well as several books on the Mafia: Joseph L. Albini, *The American Mafia* (1972); Fred J. Cook, *The Secret Rulers* (1966); Francis A. J. Ianni with Elizabeth Reuss-Ianni, *A Family Business* (1972); and Gaia Servadio, *Mafioso* (1976). These writers do not agree with one another on each and every point but there is a consensus of opinion that I have tried to reflect. Albini distinguishes between literary and historical myths and hard criminal fact. The Iannis emphasize the sort of social structure that was a prerequisite for syndicated crime and explain why it was not achieved in America until the 1920s. Gaia Servadio synthesises both approaches.

The growth of smuggling is engagingly described in a series of recent books: by Larry Engelmann in his history of prohibition in Michigan; by Alan S. Everest in *Rum Across the Border* (1978); and by Malcolm F. Willoughby in *Rum War at Sea* (1964). Richard Hammer's *Playboy's Illustrated History of Organized Crime* (1975) contains a wealth of photographs of gangsters, alive and dead.

For the student of prohibition and the cinema three books on Hollywood are preeminent: Philip French, *The Movie Moguls* (1966); Gerald Mast, *A Short History of the Movies* (1971), perhaps the most perceptive of all such short histories; and Eugene Rosow's *Born to Lose* (1978), which has many acute observations about the methods, styles, and aspirations of gangster heroes on film and of Hollywood moguls, robber barons, and bootleggers in real life. The collection of production stills and other illustrations is full and varied and superbly presented.

On the topic of repeal most histories of prohibition are brief. Again the best coverage is provided by Charles Merz writing *before* the event but arguing forcefully on the basis of campaigns launched by new wet organizations. Andrew Sinclair treads the same ground but, given his literary predilection, also offers opinions on changes in American culture in the twenties. Not surprisingly the very hostile interpretation of Ernest Gordon in *The Wrecking of the Eighteenth*

Amendment (1943) exposes political chicanery by the wets. Although his bias does not reflect the true state of public opinion, it probably does not distort information about electoral malpractices.

Perhaps no other period in twentieth-century American history can compare with the 1920s for the quality of general histories. To my mind the most distinguished are: Preston William Slosson, *The Great Crusade and After, 1914–1928* (1930), and William E. Leuchtenburg, *The Perils of Prosperity 1914–1932* (1958), for mixing political and social accounts and interspersing both with pithy comments; Mark Sullivan, *Our Times*, volume 6, *The Twenties* (1935), for political analysis of the period 1919 to 1925 and a cultural survey of the whole decade; and Daniel Snowman in his opening chapter of *America since 1920* (1968). He alone is able to provide a structured argument rather than a catalogue of events for the frenetic social and political life of the 1920s. His argument is both artistically pleasing and historically sound. The definitive history of the Wall Street crash is John Kenneth Galbraith, *The Great Crash—1929* (1954).

Without the benefit of others' research and conclusions my task would have been harder. For the period to 1920 I acknowledge a particular debt to James Timberlake's survey of medical and political arguments in favor of prohibition; and to Andrew Sinclair's assessment of prohibition and the West, and the attitudes of Theodore Roosevelt, Bryan, and Wilson to the subject. For discussion of gangster films I have been greatly influenced by Eugene Rosow's interpretation.

BIBLIOGRAPHY

Documents

National Commission on Law Observance and Enforcement, *Enforcement of Prohibition Laws of the United States*, Summary and five volumes, 71st Cong., 3rd Sess. (Washington, 1930)

U.S. Congress, Senate, Subcommittee of the Committee on the Judiciary, "Brewing and Liquor Interests and German and Bolshevik Propaganda," 66th Cong., 1st Sess. (Washington, 1919)

U.S. Congress, Senate, Subcommittee on the Judiciary, "The National Prohibition Law," 69th Cong., 1st Sess. (Washington, 1926)

U.S. Congress, House of Representatives, Committee of the Judiciary, "The Prohibition Amendment," 71st Cong., 2nd Sess. (H.D. 722) (Washington, 1931)

U.S. Congress, Senate Subcommittee of the Committee on the Judiciary, "Modification or Repeal of National Prohibition," 72nd Cong., 1st Sess. (Washington, 1932)

D. C. Nicholson and R. P. Graves, *Selective Bibliography on the Operation of the Eighteenth Amendment* (Bureau of Public Administration, University of California, 1931)

PROHIBITION

Histories of Prohibition

Books

Donald Barr Chidsey, *On and Off the Wagon* (New York, 1969)

Norman Clark, *Deliver Us from Evil: An Interpretation of American Prohibition* (New York, 1976)

Thomas M. Coffey, *The Long Thirst—Prohibition in America 1920–1933* (New York and London, 1975, 1976)

Izzy Einstein, *Prohibition Agent No. 1* (New York, 1932)

J. C. Furnas, *The Life and Times of the Late Demon Rum* (New York, 1965)

John Kobler, *Ardent Spirits: The Rise and Fall of Prohibition* (New York, 1973)

— J. H. Lyle, *The Dry and Lawless Years* (Englewood Cliffs, N.J., and London, 1960)

R. McCarthy (editor), *Drinking and Intoxication* (New Haven, Conn., 1959)

Charles Merz, *The Great American Band Wagon* (Garden City, New York, 1928)

———, *The Dry Decade* (New York, 1931; Seattle, Washington and London, 1969, 1970)

Andrew Sinclair, *Prohibition—the Era of Excess* (London, 1962)

James H. Timberlake, *Prohibition and the Progressive Movement 1900–1920* (Cambridge, Mass., 1963)

Articles

Annals of the American Academy of Political and Social Science, "Prohibition: A National Experiment," issue of September, 1932 (Philadelphia, 1932)

J. C. Burnham, "New Perspectives on the Prohibition 'Experiment' of the 1920s," *Journal of Social History* (Fall, 1968)

D. Gerard, "Intoxication and Addiction," *Quarterly Journal of Studies of Alcohol* (December, 1955)

Paul A. Carter, "Prohibition and Democracy: The Noble Experiment Reassessed," *Wisconsin Magazine of History* (Spring, 1973)

Joseph R. Gusfield, "Prohibition: The Impact of Political Utopianism," in John Braeman, Robert H. Bremner, and David Brody (editors), *Change and Continuity in Twentieth Century America: The 1920s* (Columbus, Ohio, 1968)

Dissertations

Nuala M. Drescher, "The Opposition to Prohibition, 1900–1919: A Social and Institutional Study" (University of Delaware Ph.D. dissertation, 1964)

BIBLIOGRAPHY

Louise P. Duus, "There Ought to Be a Law: A Study of Popular American Attitudes Toward 'The Law' in the 1920s" (University of Minnesota Ph.D. dissertation, 1967)

The Brewers

Stanley Baron, *Brewed in America: A History of Beer and Ale in the United States* (Boston, 1962); Thomas C. Cochran, *The Pabst Brewing Company: The History of an American Business* (New York, 1948); John E. Siebel and Anton Schwarz, *History of the Brewing Industry and Brewing Science in America* (Chicago, 1933)

The Prohibition Movement

Books

Sister J. Bland, *Hibernian Crusade: The Story of the Catholic Total Abstinence Union of America* (Washington, 1951); Joseph R. Gusfield, *Symbolic Crusade: Status Politics and the American Temperance Movement* (Urbana, Ill., 1963); D. Leigh Colvin, *Prohibition in the United States* (New York, 1926); P. Odegard, *Pressure Politics—The Story of the Anti-Saloon League* (New York, 1928)

Memoir and Biographies

James Cannon, Jr., *Bishop Cannon's Own Story*, edited by R. Watson (Durham, North Carolina, 1955); Virginius Dabney, *Dry Messiah—The Life of Bishop Cannon* (New York, 1949); Herbert Asbury, *Carry Nation* (New York, 1929); W. McLoughlin, *Billy Sunday Was His Real Name* (Chicago, 1955); Justin Steuart, *Wayne Wheeler,—Dry Boss* (New York, Chicago, London, and Edinburgh, 1928)

Article

J. Gusfield, "Social Structure and Moral Reform: A Study of the Women's Christian Temperance Union," *American Journal of Sociology* (November, 1955)

Dissertations

Norman H. Dohn, "The History of the Anti-Saloon League" (Ohio State University at Columbus Ph.D. dissertation, 1959)
Samuel Unger, "A History of the Women's Christian Temperance Union" (Ohio State University Ph.D. dissertation, 1933)

271

PROHIBITION

Prohibition and the States

Books

Norman Clark, *The Dry Years: Prohibition and Social Change in Washington* (Seattle, 1950)

Larry Engelmann, *Intemperance—The Lost War Against Liquor* (New York and London, 1979)

Jimmie Lewis Franklin, *Born Sober—Prohibition in Oklahoma, 1907–1959* (Norman, Oklahoma, 1971)

Paul E. Isaac, *Prohibition and Politics: Turbulent Decades in Tennessee, 1885–1920* (Knoxville, Tenn., 1965)

Gilman Ostrander, *The Prohibition Movement in California, 1848–1933* (Berkeley, 1957)

James B. Sellers, *The Prohibition Movement in Alabama, 1702–1943* (Chapel Hill, N.C., 1943)

Daniel J. Whitener, *Prohibition in North Carolina, 1715–1945* (Chapel Hill, N.C., 1945)

Dissertation

William Elliot West, "Dry Crusade: The Prohibition Movement in Colorado, 1858–1933" (University of Colorado Ph.D. dissertation, 1971)

The Great Debate

Books

George Ade, *The Old-Time Saloon* (New York, 1931)

T. S. Arthur, Jr., *Ten Nights Without a Barroom* (Indianapolis, 1930)

Association Against the Prohibition Amendment, Charles S. Wood (editor), *A Criticism of National Prohibition* (Washington, D.C., 1926)

Harry Elmer Barnes, *Prohibition versus Civilization* (New York, 1932)

Robert C. Binkley, *Responsible Drinking–A Discreet Inquiry and a Modest Proposal* (New York, 1930)

Martha Bensley Bruère, *Does Prohibition Work: A Study of the Operation of the Eighteenth Amendment Made by the National Federation of Settlements Assisted by Social Workers in Different Parts of the United States* (New York, 1927)

Celestin Pierre Cambiaire, *The Black Horse of the Apocalypse* (Paris, 1932)

Ernest Hurst Cherrington, *America and the World Liquor Problem* (Westerville, Ohio, 1922)

BIBLIOGRAPHY

—— (editor), *Standard Encyclopaedia of the Alcohol Problem* 6 volumes (Westerville, Ohio, 1924–1928)

Clarence Darrow and Victor S. Yarros, *The Prohibition Mania, A Reply to Professor Irving Fisher and Others* (New York, 1927)

J. Erskine, *Prohibition and Christianity* (Indianapolis, 1927)

H. Feldman, *Prohibition: Its Economic and Industrial Aspects* (New York, 1927)

Irving Fisher, *Prohibition at Its Worst* (revised edition, New York, 1927)

——, assisted by H. Bruce Brougham, *Prohibition Still at Its Worst* (New York, 1928)

Roy Haynes, *Prohibition Inside Out* (New York, 1923)

John Judge, Jr., *Noble Experiments* (New York, 1930)

Will Rogers, *The Cowboy Philosopher on Prohibition* (Stillwater, Oklahoma, 1975)

Mabel Walker Willebrandt, *Inside of Prohibition* (Indianapolis, 1929)

Articles

Willis J. Abbot, "Prohibition in Practice: IV—The Cities of our TransMississippi States," *Collier's* (May 17, 1919)

Jane Addams, "Prohibition and Chicago," *Survey Graphic* (October, 1929)

W. Anderson, "Prohibition—Anderson Answers," *Forum* (July, 1919)

Robert Barry in *New York World* (August 9 to 16, 1926)

F. Brown, "Prohibition and Mental Hygiene," *Annals of the American Academy* (September, 1932)

D. Cassidy, "Moonshine on the Mississippi," *New Republic* (May 15, 1929)

J. Chapman, "Drink, and the Tyranny of Dogma," *Outlook* (January 16, 1924)

J. Clark, Jr., "The Prohibition Cycle," *North American Review* (May, 1933)

F. Cockrell, "Blunders that Outlawed the Liquor Traffic," *Current History* (October, 1930)

J. Cooper, "Prohibition from the Workingman's Standpoint," *North American Review* (September, 1925)

V. and R. Cornell, "It's All Moonshine!" *Collier's* (January 17, 1920)

E. Davis, "Hoover the Medicine Man," *Forum* (October, 1930)

J. Flynn, "Home, Sweet Home-Brew," *Collier's* (September 1, 1928)

L. Graves, "Getting the Stuff in Carolina," *New Republic* (May 26, 1920)

A. Hadley, "Law Making and Law Enforcement," *Harper's* (November, 1925)

Dr. S. Hubbard, "Why Does Not Prohibition Prohibit?" *New York Medical Journal* (July 18, 1923)

M. Le Sueur, 'Beer Town,' *Life in the United States* (New York, 1933)

PROHIBITION

Walter Lippmann, "The Great Wickersham Mystery," *Vanity Fair* (April, 1931); "Our Predicament Under the Eighteenth Amendment," *Harper's* (December, 1926)

"Mild-Mannered Mr. Volstead, the 'Goat' of the Wets," *Literary Digest* (December 27, 1919); "The New Policy of the Anti-Saloon League" (January 7, 1928)

A. Lawrence Lowell, "Reconstruction and Prohibition," *Atlantic Monthly* (February, 1929)

R. Lusk, "The Drinking Habit," *Annals of the American Academy* (September, 1932)

H. Miller, "An Economist Looks At Prohibition," *Town and Gown* (October, 1930)

G. Mills, "Where the Booze Begins," *Collier's* (October 15, 1927)

C. Norris, "Our Essay in Extermination," *North American Review* (December, 1928)

I. Oakley, "The Prohibition Law and the Political Machine," *Annals of the American Academy* (September, 1932)

D. Pickett, "Prohibition and Economic Change," *Annals of the American Academy* (September, 1932)

Henry F. Pringle, "Obscure Mr. Volstead," *World's Work* (July, 1919)

Proprietor, "Running a Speakeasy," *New Freeman* (June 11, 1930)

C. Robinson, *Straw Votes* (Columbia Univ., 1932)

R. Scott, "Prohibition As Seen by a Business Man," *North American Review* (September, 1925)

R. Smith, "Politics and Prohibition Enforcements," *Independent* (October 3, 1925)

S. Strauss, "Things Are in the Saddle," *Atlantic Monthly* (November, 1924)

Ida M. Tarbell, "Is Prohibition Forcing Civil War?" *Liberty* (July 6, 1929)

———, "Ladies at the Bar," *Liberty* (July 26, 1930)

F. Tompkins, "Prohibition," *Annals of the American Academy* (September, 1923)

H. Van Loon, "Heroes All," *Forum* (January, 1925)

T. Walnut, "The Human Element in Prohibition Enforcement," *Annals of the American Academy* (September, 1923)

C. Warburton, "Prohibition and Economic Welfare," *Annals of the American Academy* (September, 1932)

Wayne Wheeler, "Are the Wets Hypocrites in Their Pleas for State Rights?" *Current History* (October, 1926)

G. Whidden, "Our Arid Press," *New Freeman* (September 10, 1930)

O. White, "Workers in the Vineyard," *Collier's* (October 6, 1928)

W. Williams, "Worker's Speakeasy," *Survey Graphic* (February 1, 1931)

C. Wilson, "Call Out the Marines," *Collier's* (July 13, 1929)

F. Vernon Wiley and Guy Locock, "America's Economic Supremacy," *Current History* (January, 1926)

BIBLIOGRAPHY

Politicians: Memoirs and Biographies

W. and M. Bryan, *The Memoirs of William Jennings Bryan* (Philadelphia, 1925); William Allen White, *A Puritan in Babylon* (New York, 1938); H. Warren, *Herbert Hoover and the Great Depression* (New York, 1959); Herbert Hoover, *The Memoirs of Herbert Hoover*, volume 2, *The Cabinet and the Presidency, 1920–1933* (New York and London, 1952); Frank Freidel, *Franklin D. Roosevelt*: volume 2, *The Ordeal*; volume 3, *The Triumph* (Boston, 1954; 1956); H. L. Mencken, *Making a President* (New York, 1932); Arthur Link, *Wilson: the Road to the White House* (Princeton, 1947); *Wilson: The New Freedom* (Princeton, 1956); *Woodrow Wilson and the Progressive Era, 1910–1917* (Princeton, 1954)

Al Smith and the Election of 1928

Books

Oscar Handlin, *Al Smith and his America* (Boston and Toronto, 1958); Matthew and Hanna Josephson, *Al Smith: Hero of the Cities* (Boston, 1969); Richard O'Connor, *The First Hurrah, A Biography of Alfred E. Smith* (New York, 1970); Emily Smith Warner with David Balch, *The Happy Warrior* (New York, 1956); Edmund A. Moore, *A Catholic Runs for President—The Campaign of 1928* (New York, 1956); Ruth C. Silva, *Rum, Religion and Votes—1928 reexamined* (Philadelphia, Penn., 1962)

Article

William F. Ogburn and Nell Snow Talbot, "A Measurement of Factors in the Presidential Election of 1928," *Social Forces* (December, 1929), 175–83

The Underworld

Books

- Herbert Asbury, *The Gangs of New York* (New York, 1927)
——, *Gem of the Prairie: An Informal History of the Chicago Underworld* (New York, 1940)
Ovid Demaris, *Captive City—Chicago in Chains* (third printing; Chicago, 1969)
Neil McCullough Clark, *Mayor Dever and Prohibition* (Westerville, Ohio, 1925; first published in *McClure's* for April, 1925)

PROHIBITION

Denis Tilden Lynch, *Criminals and Politicians* (New York, 1932)

— Virgil W. Peterson, *Barbarians in Our Midst—A History of Chicago Crime and Politics* (Boston, 1952)

— Craig Thomas and Allen Raymond, *Gang Rule in New York* (New York, 1940)

Biographies

John Kobler, *Capone: The Life and World of Al Capone* (New York, 1971); George Wolf with Joseph DiMona, *Frank Costello: Prime Minister of the Underworld* (New York, 1974); Hank Messick, *Lansky* (New York, 1971); Art Cohn, *The Joker Is Wild: The Story of Joe E. Lewis* (New York, 1955); John Boettiger, *Jake Lingle* (New York, 1941); Paul Sann, *Kill the Dutchman: The Story of Dutch Schultz* (New York, 1971); Frank J. Wilson and Beth Day, *Special Agent: A Quarter Century with the Treasury Department and the Secret Service* (New York, 1965)

Articles

"Al Capone's Victory," *New Republic* (September 9, 1931)

"Philadelphia Justice for Chicago's Al Capone," *Literary Digest* (June 15, 1929); "Capone's Amazing Proposal" (March 14, 1931); "Uncle Sam Taking Capone for a Ride" (June 27, 1931); "Gangdom's King Guilty as a Tax Dodger" (October 31, 1931)

Herbert Asbury, "The St. Valentine's Day Massacre," *'47 The Magazine of the Year* (September, 1947)

James O'Donnell Bennett, *Chicago Gangland* (Chicago *Tribune*, 1929)

Ray Brennan, "Al Capone," *True Detective* (August, 1961); "Dion O'Banion," *True Detective* (June, 1961)

Henry Barrett Chamberlin, "Organized Crime in Chicago," *Illinois Crime Survey* (Chicago, 1929)

M. W. Childs, "The Inside Story of the Federal Government's Secret Operations in Convicting Al Capone," *St. Louis Post-Dispatch Sunday Magazine* (September 25, 1932)

Charles De Lacy, "The Inside on Chicago's Notorious St. Valentine's Day Massacre," *True Detective Mysteries* (March–April, 1931)

Jack Dillard, "How the U.S. Govt. Caught Al Capone!" *Master Detective* (February, 1932)

Daniel Fuchs, "Where Al Capone Grew Up," *New Republic* (September 9, 1931)

John Gunther, "The High Cost of Hoodlums," *Harper's* (October, 1929)

Mark H. Haller, "Urban Crime and Criminal Justice: The Chicago Case," *Journal of American History* (December, 1970); "Organized Crime in

BIBLIOGRAPHY

Urban Society: Chicago in the Twentieth Century," *Journal of Social History* (Winter, 1971-72)

Gordon L. Hostetter and Thomas Quinn Beesley, "The Rising Tide of Racketeering," *Political Quarterly* (London, July-September, 1933)

John Landesco, "Prohibition and Crime," *Annals of the American Academy* (September, 1932)

A Lindesmith, "Organized Crime," *Annals of the American Academy* (September, 1941)

William Mangil, "Torrio the 'Immune,'" *True Detective* (September, 1940)

Curtis Rodann, "'Big Daddy' of the Underworld (James Colosimo)," *True Detective* (August, 1960).

Edward Dean Sullivan, "I Know You, Al," *North American Review* (September, 1929)

Frank J. Wilson (as told to Howard Whitman), "How We Caught Al Capone," *Chicago Tribune Sunday Magazine* (June 14, 1959); "How We Trapped Capone," *Collier's* (April 26, 1947); "The Al Capone Story," *Retirement Life* (October, 1954)

Edgar Forest Wolfe, "The Real Truth About Al Capone," *Master Detective* (September, 1930)

Histories of Syndicated Crime

Joseph L. Albini, *The American Mafia—Genesis of a Legend* (New York, 1971)

— Fred J. Cook, *The Secret Rulers: Criminal Syndicates and How they Control the U.S. Underworld* (New York, 1966)

Donald R. Cressey, *Theft of the Nation: The Structure and Operations of Organized Crime in America* (New York, 1969)

Richard Hammer, *Playboy's Illustrated History of Organized Crime* (Chicago, 1975)

Francis A. J. Ianni with Elizabeth Reuss-Ianni, *A Family Business—Kinship and Social Control in Organized Crime* (New York, 1972)

Humbert S. Nelli, *Italians in Chicago, 1880-1930: A Study in Ethnic Mobility* (New York, 1970)

——, *The Business of Crime in the United States* (Oxford, 1976)

Gaia Servadio, *Mafioso—A History of the Mafia from Its Origins to the Present Day* (London, 1976)

Histories of Smuggling

Robert Carse, *Rum Row* (New York and Toronto, 1959)

Albert B. Corey, *Canadian American Relations Along the Detroit River* (Detroit, 1957)

Merrill Donison, *The Barley and the Stream* (Toronto, 1955)

PROHIBITION

Alan S. Everest, *Rum Across the Border* (Syracuse, N.Y., 1978)
Reginald W. Kauffman, *The Real Story of a Bootlegger* (New York, 1923)
Frederic F. Van de Water, *The Real McCoy* (Garden City, 1931)
Malcolm F. Willoughby, *Rum War at Sea* (Washington, 1964)

Gangster Films

Books

John Baxter, *The Gangster Film* (London, 1970)
——, *Hollywood in the Thirties* (London, 1971)
William R. Burnette, *Little Caesar* (New York, 1929)
Philip French, *The Movie Moguls* (London, 1969)
Ezra Goodman, *The Fifty Year Decline and Fall of Hollywood* (New York, 1962)
Ben Hecht, *A Child of the Century* (New York, 1954)
Mae Huettig, *Economic Control of the Motion Picture Industry* (Philadelphia, 1944)
Pauline Kael, *Kiss Kiss, Bang Bang* (New York, 1968)
Colin McArthur, *Underworld USA* (New York and London, 1972)
Gerald Mast, *A Short History of the Movies* (New York, 1971)
Hank Messick, *Beauties and the Beast: The Mob in Show Business* (New York, 1973)
David Robinson, *Hollywood in the Twenties* (London, 1968)
Eugene Rosow, *Born to Lose—The Gangster Film in America* (New York, 1978)
Norman Zierold, *The Hollywood Tycoons* (London, 1969)

Articles

Ralph Cassidy, Jr., "Some Aspects of Motion Picture Production and Marketing," *Journal of Business of the University of Chicago* (April, 1933)
Raymond Durgnat, "The Family Tree of Film Noir," *Cinema* (August, 1970)
Otis Ferguson, "Cops and Robbers," *New Republic* (May 15, 1935)
Charles Grayson, "They've Battled the Depression—That's Why They're Stars," *Motion Picture Magazine* (January, 1933)
Gladys Hall, "Little Caesar Tosses Some Verbal Bombs," *Movie Classic* (November, 1931)
Stuart Kaminsky, "*Little Caesar* and Its Role in the Gangster Film Genre," *Journal of Popular Film* (Summer, 1972)
Lincoln Kirsten, "James Cagney and the American Hero," *Hound and Horn* (April/June, 1932)

BIBLIOGRAPHY

Literary Digest, "Are Gang Films Wholesome?" (March 4, 1933)

Walter B. Pitkin, "Screen Crime vs. Press Crime," *Outlook* (July 29, 1931)

Alan Warner, "Gangster Heroes," *Films and Filming* (November, 1971)

Robert Warshow, "The Gangster as Tragic Hero," *Immediate Experience* (New York, 1962)

Richard Whitehall, "Crime, Inc.: A Three Part Dossier on the American Gangster Film," *Films and Filming* (January, February, March, 1964)

Repeal

Books

F. Dobyns, *The Amazing Story of Repeal* (New York, 1940)

Ernest Gordon, *The Wrecking of the Eighteenth Amendment* (Francestown, N.H., 1943)

Grace Cogswell Root, *Women and Repeal* (New York, 1954)

J. Pollard, *The Road to Repeal* (New York, 1932)

Dissertation

Dayton Heckman, "Prohibition Passes: The Story of the Association Against the Prohibition Amendment" (Ohio State University at Columbus Ph.D. dissertation, 1939)

General

Frederick Lewis Allen, *Only Yesterday* (New York, 1931) and *Since Yesterday—The Nineteen Thirties in America* (New York and London, 1939, 1940); John D. Hicks, *Republican Ascendancy, 1921–1933* (New York, Evanston, and London, 1960); John Kenneth Galbraith, *The Great Crash 1929* (Boston, and London 1954 and 1955); William E. Leuchtenburg, *The Perils of Prosperity, 1914–1932* (Chicago, 1958); R. Miller, *American Protestantism and Social Issues, 1919–1932* (Chapel Hill, N.C., 1958); Gilbert Seldes, *The Years of the Locust: America 1929–1933* (Boston, 1933); Preston William Slosson, *The Great Crusade and After, 1914–1928* (New York, 1930); Daniel Snowman, *U.S.A.: Twenties to Vietnam* (London, 1968; alternative title *America Since 1920*), Chapter 1; Mark Sullivan, *Our Times*, volume 6, *The Twenties* (New York, 1935); Stanley Walker, *The Night Club Era* (New York, 1933)

INDEX

281

INDEX

INDEX

INDEX

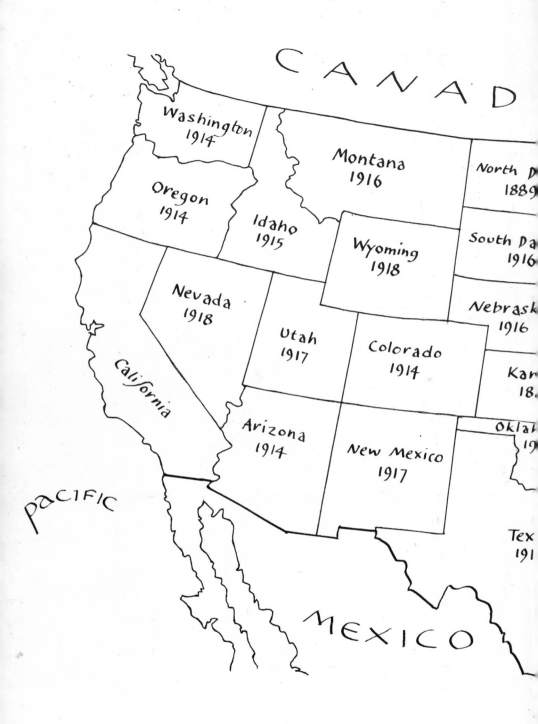

**Years in which the States
Adopted Prohibition**